As I read Mark Morrison-Reed's *The S* [barcode] shedding tears as I relived the events (civil rights activists, anyone alive in those turbulent times, and those yet to be born, will find themselves caught up in these vivid recollections of those critical days. The book includes insights, anecdotes, and personal stories—and it acknowledges for the first time key contributors to the success of the march from Selma to Montgomery. In particular, the section on women and the march elaborates on the under-reported story of women in the struggle for civil rights, and the broader ongoing struggle for women's liberation. Perhaps this book had been waiting for a scholar who identifies as both African American and Unitarian Universalist to do the diligent research required and bring the story of Selma to light.
  —Rev. Orloff Miller, witness to the attack that killed Rev. James
    Reeb in Selma in 1965

Here is the first full, nuanced story of Unitarian Universalist involvement in the Selma voting rights campaign. Mark Morrison Reed gives a detailed recounting of the events of 1965, and much more. He also tells of the preceding issues and faltering forward steps leading to our participation, and the tensions in Unitarian Universalism deriving from hundreds of ministers and lay people being radicalized by their involvement. Both our achievements and our limitations are clearer by the final page.
  —Rev. Gordon Gibson, founding member, Living Legacy Project

Those of us who are concerned about the UUA's future should resolve to integrate Mark Morrison-Reed's impassioned scholarship in recounting our Selma past into our lifetime learning curricula. Young and old alike must read and deeply reflect on the content (including endnotes) of this amazing book.
  —Denise Taft Davidoff, former moderator of the Unitarian
    Universalist Association

Selma changed the United States, and Selma changed Unitarian Universalism. Mark Morrison-Reed tells the story in exquisite detail, tracing the hundred-year history and the interdependent web of relationships that led hundreds of Unitarian Universalists to march for justice in Selma. In a work of scholarly depth and heartfelt passion, Morrison-Reed gives voice to both his admiration for the achievements of Unitarian Universalists and his anguish at our shortcomings, inviting all of us to align our values in practice with our espoused values.
  —Dan McKanan, Ralph Waldo Emerson Unitarian Universalist
    Association Senior Lecturer in Divinity, Harvard Divinity School

Mark Morrison-Reed has produced a magnificent book that provides so much depth, background, tears, and hope. It will have a profound impact on our ministers, congregations, boards, and denominational committees. It is inspiriting and needed!

— Rev. Clark Olsen, witness to the attack that killed Rev. James Reeb in Selma in 1965

The Selma Awakening offers soul-stirring insight into the amalgamation of forces that allowed Unitarian Universalists to be courageously present at a moment when risking everything mattered so much. Personal stories are interwoven with historical details to provide a nuanced and unflinching narrative of who we are. Readers will be left with haunting questions about our current capacity to live our espoused values with the sacrifice and humility required to minister to our world and save the soul of our faith.

— Tamara Payne-Alex, First Unitarian Church of San Jose, California

Mark Morrison-Reed's engaging study of two liberal religious traditions' responses to Selma and the civil rights movement deftly excavates the gap between their espoused religious values and lived-out practices. Along the way, Morrison-Reed uncovers untold stories, eyewitness accounts of James Reeb's murder and its aftermath, sermons, articles, and actions that trace a shift in thinking among Unitarian and Universalist ministers, lay people, and denominational leaders. This is a long-needed and carefully researched contribution to American religious history.

— Rev. Nicole Kirk, Frank and Alice Southworth Schulman Professor of Unitarian Universalist History, Meadville Lombard Theological School

In this book, Morrison-Reed places the iconic moment of Selma in the larger context of Unitarian Universalism. Within this larger frame, he both accentuates the importance of participation in Selma, highlights all that could have happened—and delineates what did not. By showing how UU participation was *not* inevitable, he underscores the significance of that participation while placing it in a proper scale with the other commitments and non-commitments made in the arena of race relations. An essential read for anyone continuing the struggle to embrace the need for continued racial justice work today.

— Rev. Leslie Takahashi-Morris, co-author, *The Arc of the Universe Is Long: Unitarian Universalists, Anti-Racism, and the Journey from Calgary*

THE SELMA AWAKENING

THE SELMA AWAKENING

How the Civil Rights Movement Tested and
Changed Unitarian Universalism

Mark D. Morrison-Reed

Skinner House Books
Boston

www.skinnerhouse.org

Printed in the United States

Cover design by Kathryn Sky-Peck.
Front cover photo by James Karales. Copyright © the Estate of James Karales.
Text design by Suzanne Morgan.

print ISBN: 978-1-55896-733-5
eBook ISBN: 978-1-55896-734-2

6 5 4 3 2 1
17 16 15 14

Library of Congress Cataloging-in-Publication Data
Morrison-Reed, Mark D., 1949-
The Selma awakening : how the Civil Rights movement tested and changed Unitarian Universali sm / Mark D. Morrison-Reed.
    pages cm
  Includes bibliographical references and index.
  ISBN 978-1-55896-733-5 (pbk. : alk. paper)—ISBN 978-1-55896-734-2 (ebook) 1. Unitarian Universalist Association—History. 2. ivil rights movements—Alabama—Selma—History—20th century. 3. Selma to Montgomery Rights March (1965: Selma, Ala.) 4. Selma (Ala.)—Race relations. I. Title.
  BX9833.M67 2014
  289.1'73—dc23

                                                                    2013049326

We gratefully acknowledge permission to reprint photographs taken by Orloff Miller, above the captions that read: "Activist in Selma, 1965," "Jack Kent, Clark Olsen, Clifton Hoffman," "Kenneth Marshall orienting group...," "Cornelius McDougald and Richard Leonard...," and "Martin Luther King Jr....".

We also gratefully acknowledge the assistance and research materials provided by Andover-Harvard Theological Library in Cambridge, Massachusetts.

CONTENTS

INTRODUCTION

In the early hours of Monday, March 8, 1965, Rev. Dr. Martin Luther King Jr. dispatched a telegram that read,

> In the vicious maltreatment of defenseless citizens of Selma, where old women and young children were gassed and clubbed at random, we have witnessed an eruption of the disease of racism which seeks to destroy all of America. No American is without responsibility. All are involved in the sorrow that rises from Selma to contaminate every crevice of our national life. The people of Selma will struggle on for the soul of the nation, but it is fitting that all America help to bear the burden. I call therefore, on clergy of all faiths representative of every part of the country, to join me for a ministers' march to Montgomery on Tuesday morning, March 9th. In this way all America will testify to the fact that the struggle in Selma is for the survival of democracy everywhere in our land.[1]

Along with much of the country, Orloff Miller, director of the Unitarian Universalist Association's Office of College Centers, had watched the attack on civil rights marchers when it exploded across the network news the night before. So he wasn't surprised when Homer Jack, who directed the UUA Social Responsibility Department, called on Monday morning to say the UUA had received a telegram from King. From his sixth-floor office at UUA headquarters in Boston, Miller rushed down to the first floor. After a quick consultation with Jack, and with a copy of the telegram in hand, he began phoning across the country to the college center clergy with whom he worked.

James Reeb was in his office in the Boston neighborhood of Roxbury when the call from the UUA came at around noon. Reeb, a white American, had forsaken parish ministry to work and live in the African-American community. He wanted to go to Selma. After a hectic afternoon, he went home to talk with his wife. Marie Reeb, as the parent responsible for taking care of their four children—including an infant—questioned why he needed to go. They had walked side by side during the March on Washington but, having watched the broadcast the night before, she knew this march was different. She strenuously objected, while he steadfastly insisted, until, reluctantly, she ceded to the urgency of his need.

Miller spent hours on the phone, including a call to his wife, Mary Jane. Mindful that they had two young children, she said, "I don't want you to go, but I know you feel you must." Late that afternoon, when his appointments were done, Miller gathered together a small spiral notebook, a large yellow legal pad, a tiny Minox camera, and a toothbrush. His wife picked him up and he took her out to celebrate her thirty-fourth birthday.

In Berkeley, California, Clark Olsen, minister of the Berkeley Fellowship of Unitarians, was driving his Plymouth Valiant convertible and listening to the noon news when he heard of King's appeal. He wanted to go. What stood in the way wasn't his fragile health—due to a heart damaged long before by two bouts of rheumatic fever—but rather, a lack of money for the airfare. When he arrived home he found a message waiting: A couple from his congregation had offered to pay his way. He immediately had a conversation with his wife and decided to go. Like Reeb and Miller, he had a child—a three-year-old daughter.

On Long Island, Farley Wheelwright, minister of the Nassau County Unitarian Universalist Church, felt reluctant to go. Bargaining with his conscience, he spent the afternoon calling friends whom he knew couldn't make the trip. He would go if they would.

But his conscience was not so easily bought off, and on Monday night he left for Selma.

After Miller's wife dropped him at Logan Airport, he spotted Reeb at the ticket counter. By 11 p.m. Monday night they, along with a dozen others, were on their way to Atlanta. By Tuesday morning Miller and Reeb were in Selma; coming from the West Coast, Olsen arrived that afternoon. Following the march, they ate together in Walker's Café, while down the block fate awaited them.

People converged on Selma: clergy and laity, men and women, blacks and whites, Catholics, Orthodox Christians, Protestants, Jews, Unitarian Universalists, and atheists. They came from across the United States and Canada. The events of March 1965 in that county seat in Alabama's Black Belt represented a pivotal moment in American history. For over three weeks, the unfolding drama held the world's attention. It was a cultural upheaval in which hope confronted intransigence. Protest was met with fury. Violence begot sacrifice and suffering. Blood was spilled, and the slayings of Jimmie Lee Jackson, James Reeb, and Viola Liuzzo triggered a transfiguration. This twentieth-century continuation of the American Revolution was a spiritual battle that brought the country closer to the freedom proclaimed in the Constitution and granted by the Emancipation Proclamation, but reneged upon following the passage of the Fourteenth and Fifteenth Amendments.

For Unitarian Universalism, whose most progressive elements had long been champions of freedom in its broadest sense, Selma was a test. Did freedom merely mean freedom of belief and conscience? Or did it also include the civic, political, and economic freedoms that the educated, middle-class, liberal religious constituency took for granted? Was this not a struggle for a nation's soul? Did commitment mean passing yet another earnest resolution? Or might it include placing one's life at risk, as did the white Unitarian Colonel Robert Gould Shaw, who died leading the all-black Fifty-Fourth Massachusetts Volunteer Infantry Regiment into battle during the Civil War? And what of the UUs who answered King's call? Unitarian Universalists responded, but why they did remains to be analyzed. What was Selma's impact on Unitarian Universalism? In a decade when voting rights have re-emerged on the U.S. agenda and immigration reform has become our most pressing national human rights issue, we need to answer these questions and draw lessons from the experience. That is what this book attempts to do.

Universalism and Unitarianism both have roots in the American Revolution. Among the signers of the Declaration of Independence, John Adams, Benjamin Rush, and Thomas Jefferson championed not only political freedom but also liberal religious heresies that defended freedom of belief. Universalists organized congregations in the 1790s and Unitarians founded the American Unitarian Association in 1825. But in March 1965 the Unitarian Universalist Association, the successor to these traditions, was not yet four years old. Newly consolidated, it was still redefining and discovering itself as the civil rights movement rose to a crescendo.

Was the rush to Selma a natural and obvious development for the new UUA, or did it represent a break with the past? When reviewing UUA history starting in 1963—with the establishment of the UUA Commission on Religion and Race, the presence of sixteen hundred UUs at the March on Washington for Jobs and Freedom, and the denomination's response to the bombing of the Sixteenth Street Baptist Church in Birmingham—going to Selma seems the most natural thing in the world. But on the contrary, given Unitarian and Universalist attitudes about race during the half century preceding the Second World War, what transpired in the 1960s was *not* inevitable.

The route to Selma was long. And the Second World War is the key to understanding the shift in race relations in America generally and among religious liberals in particular. To appreciate the magnitude of Unitarian Universalism's journey, we must begin by surveying the stance of religious liberals regarding race during the latter years of the nineteenth and the first half of the twentieth centuries. When we compare the *espoused values* of Universalism and Unitarianism to their *values in practice*, we find a stark disparity.[2]

WHAT UNITARIAN UNIVERSALISTS SAID

P. T. Barnum—showman, huckster, philanthropist, and perhaps the most well-known Universalist ever—was also a politician and member of the Connecticut legislature when, in May 1865, it ratified the Thirteenth Amendment to the United States Constitution, abolishing slavery. Addressing that assembly a few days later Barnum said,

> Let the educated free negro feel that he is a man; let him be trained in New England churches, schools and workshops; let him support himself, pay his taxes, and cast his vote, like other men, and he will put to everlasting shame the champions of modern democracy, by the overwhelming evidence he will give in his own person of the great Scripture truth, that "God has made of one blood all the nations of men." A human soul, "that God has created and Christ died for," is not to be trifled with. It may tenant the body of a Chinaman, a Turk, an Arab or a Hottentot—it is still an immortal spirit; and amid all assumptions of caste, it will in due time vindicate the great fact that, without regard to color or condition, all men are equally children of the common Father.[3]

Was Barnum exceptional in this belief, as he was in so many other ways? How was race seen in the context of Universalism's theology? What attitudes did belief in a loving God foster among Universalists? And in what ways were Unitarians similar and different? To identify the values espoused by Universalists and

1

Unitarians, we can examine the public documents in which they articulated their self-understandings and aspirations. The best of these are the resolutions passed at annual meetings, the findings of commissions, annual reports, and denominational journals.

The Universalists

In 1889 the Universalist denomination ordained Joseph Jordan, the first African American ever welcomed into its ministry. He was drawn to the faith by reading Thomas Whittemore's *The Plain Guide to Universalism.* It is not known which passages most influenced him; nevertheless, one in particular must have spoken to him:

> As he is Creator, so is he the Parent, of all. See, then, that there is a common bond,—a tie,—uniting the vast family of man. No national boundary can dissolve this tie, no distance,— no circumstances of birth, or of color,—no misfortune, no oppression; neither poverty, nor vice, nor disgrace, nor death, can sunder it. When men can cease to be offspring of God, then they will cease to be a brotherhood. Who, believing and realizing this, can be unkind? . . . Who can be oppressor of his brethren?[4]

This understanding of Universalism was shared by Quillen Shinn, the Universalist missionary who supported Jordan in bringing Universalism to the black community of Norfolk, Virginia. Shinn said, "No man can be a Universalist whose love does not take in all races and colors of men."[5] There should have been no question about the charge that a belief in a loving God lay upon its adherents. Yet in 1897 William H. McGlauflin, while serving as Universalism's southern missionary, advised the annual meeting that no effort be undertaken to admit African Americans to local Sunday schools or Young People's Christian Unions (YPCUs). This recommendation was based on his belief that for whites such an effort would be the same as "a lighted match [in] a powder magazine."[6]

Twenty years later, in 1917, the Universalist General Convention published its "Declaration of Social Principles," the official statement of its values. While it heralds "man's universal brotherhood," it does not mention race. When the convention recast this document in 1943 as the "Affirmation of Social Principles," it was more explicit: "We must recognize that today Americans of Negro, Indian and Oriental descent . . . are suffering from unjust forms of discrimination." The "Declaration of Social Principles" adopted in 1957 went still further: "Three basic beliefs characterize the Universalist fellowship and provide the basis for personal and social values. . . . First, the worth of the person regardless of race, creed, or standing." This was elaborated upon in two clauses:

6. Civil Rights

All citizens should have equal access to educational, vocational, and recreational and residential opportunity. Knowing the blighting effect of segregation, discrimination, and prejudice, we support all responsible defenses of civil rights when these have been denied on the basis of race, creed, national origin, or otherwise. . . .

8. School Integration

We hold the public schools to be a crucial training ground of democracy and therefore support efforts to effect integration in those areas where race or other irrelevant factors have defeated democracy.[7]

While Universalists passed few resolutions regarding race, their conventions were not completely silent. In October 1937 the Universalist General Convention in Chicago passed a resolution on "Racial Antagonisms." In that pre–Second World War era, its focus was on anti-Semitism: "RESOLVED, that we again condemn the spirit of violence and racial antagonisms that prevails so widely in the world today, conspicuously manifesting itself in the persecution of the Jews in Germany."[8] In 1943 at the Universalist General

Assembly in New York City, Universalist general superintendent Rev. Robert Cummins declared the Universalist Church to be a place where "all are welcome: theist and humanist, unitarian and trinitarian, colored and colorless. A circumscribed Universalism is unthinkable."[9] The keynote address at the 1944 Pennsylvania State Convention was delivered by Rev. Dr. John Murray Atwood, dean of St. Lawrence Theological School. In "The Great Task of a Small Church" he said that Universalism's aim was "to win people to the way of life that will save all . . . based on a belief in the supreme worth of every personality."[10]

Proclaiming that Universalists believe in the inherent worth of every person and are concerned with and open to everyone, "colored and colorless," was easier than making it so. When the Universalist General Convention adopted a resolution on ministerial recruitment in May 1947, it mentioned neither women nor African Americans. Likewise, in the Universalist Year Books of 1950, 1951, 1953, 1954, and 1956, little appears about race relations except the annual reports on the longstanding Universalist mission to African Americans in Suffolk, Virginia. The topic didn't appear in the denominational journal the *Universalist Leader* until six months after the U.S. Supreme Court's May 1954 ruling in *Brown vs. Topeka*. However, when a resolution titled "Public Schools and Non-Segregation," which urged "speedy desegregation in public schools," came to the floor of the biennial meeting in August 1955, it seems to have been adopted without rancor.

Within Universalism, unlike Unitarianism, much of the power resided in state conventions. At that level, we find in May 1956 the Illinois State Convention passed one resolution opposing colonialism and another expressing solidarity with the Montgomery bus boycott and inviting Martin Luther King Jr. to become an honorary member of the Illinois Universalist Convention.[11] That October when the Montgomery bus boycott was in its eleventh month, King gave the keynote address at the New York State Universalist Convention's annual meeting. In the address, titled "Non-violent Procedures to Inter-racial Harmony," he said that "in Montgomery, we can walk and never get weary, because we know that there will be a great camp meeting in the promised land of freedom and justice."[12]

The Universalists issued statements about race relations only intermittently. However, year after year from the late 1880s they published articles about the mission schools in Norfolk and Suffolk, Virginia, in the Universalist Year Books and the *Christian Leader* (later the *Universalist Leader*). In 1911 Joseph Fletcher Jordan, the Suffolk school's principal, presented the Universalist leadership with a plan that would expand the school to include a seminary. The enthusiastic support of the board of the Universalist General Convention was announced in the *Leader*, as was the fund-raising tour Jordan was to make across New England. Reports appeared during the ensuing year with titles like "Our Mission to the Colored People," publicizing his itinerary. But the tour never raised sufficient funds to establish a seminary.

When Joseph Fletcher Jordan died in 1929 the *Leader* carried his necrology. The school persisted for another ten years. Then the *Universalist Biennial Reports and Directory, 1939–1940* noted that a change of the Suffolk School to a social work project had been approved. That year's directory also alluded to a fundamental shift. The Universalist leadership in Boston changed the mission's name from the Suffolk Normal Training School to Jordan Neighborhood House and took control of the school away from its longtime director, Jordan's daughter, Annie B. Willis. Nonetheless, Universalists supported the mission in Virginia from 1889 until the denomination's consolidation with Unitarianism in 1961.

Universalism's muted message on race relations is, in part, due to John van Schaick, the editor of the *Christian Leader*. Van Schaick believed in the superiority of the white race. Under his influence, Universalism's theology proclaiming the oneness of the human family was muddled and twisted in its national journal. In 1903, prior to becoming the journal's editor, van Schaick was the one member of a three-member commission who wanted to close the mission school. In 1911 he was the lone member of the Universalist leadership to oppose its expansion. Before his editorship, feature articles about the Suffolk Mission had been common; but during his term, which lasted from 1923 to 1945, such articles became largely the purview of the General Sunday School Association (GSSA). The GSSA's annual appeal, which appeared in the *Leader* from 1918 on, was the key component in the American Friendship Offering, which included updates about the Suffolk mission, stories, poetry, and activities, and lists of things the school needed. The *Leader*'s editorial pages, however, reflected van Schaick's bias.

Van Schaick's bigotry was so self-evident that in August 1939, Llewellyn Jones, the editor of the *Christian Register*, the official journal of the AUA, felt called to respond. The *Register* published an editorial titled "Is Color Appearance or Reality?" after one of its readers asked its editor to "attack, confute, condemn, and annihilate" van Schaick's position. The editorial pointed out the absurdities of the arguments van Schaick used in supporting the Daughters of the American Revolution after that organization had denied permission to the renowned African-American contralto Marian Anderson to perform for a racially integrated audience in Constitution Hall. It went on to imply that van Schaick's mean-spirited editorials attacking the mixed marriage of seminarian Francis Davis and Marguerite Campbell and disparaging her brother, Jeffrey Campbell, the only African-American Universalist minister, laid bare his prejudice.[13]

For more than three years the debate in the *Leader* over race continued. In 1942 van Schaick explained his position in an editorial addressed to "Dean Atwood, Mr. Perry, et al.":

> There are two ways of dealing with race discrimination.
>
> One is by forcing the issue, taking colored students into white schools, training colored people to be ministers for denominations without colored churches, making some of these students despise their own race and refuse to have anything to do with it, promoting all the social contacts which lead to marriage and working for a day when the colored peo-

ple will be absorbed in the white race or the white race in the yellow race. We admit freely that the process of absorption is going on now, and not usually with motives as high-minded as those of the young couple under discussion.

The other way of dealing with race discrimination is by encouraging each to help itself, to take pride in its achievements, and to be fair and kind to people of all other races; by the strong bearing the infirmities of the weak; by generous giving to schools like Hampton and Tuskegee; by legislation to correct injustice and by definite, patient effort to help young people of all races to secure an education and to find jobs.

We do not believe that one has to be unwise in order to be kind or unkind in order to be wise.[14]

Who was the Mr. Perry to whom this was in part addressed? A letter from Oscar Hoyt Perry had appeared in the *Leader* under the headline "The Universalists and the Negro." Perry wrote, "As applied to our brothers of Negro blood, this ostracism is political, economic, and social—and most deplorable. We Universalists might well take a leading part in this reform; in fact, as exponents of brotherhood, we *must* take this stand or else be guilty of rank duplicity and hypocrisy. In that case our Church will rot and die, and it will well deserve its fate."[15] His words were prophetic.

The dispute was still going on in 1944 when Clarence Skinner, dean of Crane Theological School at Tufts University, wrote about "racial universalism" as part of a series titled "A Religion for Greatness" that appeared in the *Leader*:

Suppose everywhere I went I had to be constantly on guard because I had white skin! Suppose I could not eat where I wanted to, ride where I wished, go to a hotel of my choice, or sit with others in a theater or church! Suppose I could not work at the occupation of my choice at wages equal to others doing the same thing! Suppose at every turn in my career I was forced to think of myself as the *white problem!* . . . Suppose every day other people dinned into my ears the epithets "white trash," "no 'count white man," "lazy, good-for-nothin' white," "sneakin', lyin' white"! Could any reasonable person expect me to behave as a normal human being?

. . . Prejudice thus defeats itself, and the longer it operates the more disaster it creates. . . .

The religion of the unities and the universals is [the] radical cure. It gets down to the root of which prejudice grows. It digs into the soil of man's selfishness, superstition, and distortion. It destroys the vicious partialism which would lock men into divisive cells of race, denying them the common rights of humanity. . . . Man *must* enlarge the borders of his consciousness to include the human race.[16]

The long-running debate came to a close with the resignation of van Schaick in 1945. In the following years, even though there were not many articles on race, an attitudinal shift became apparent in editorials such as "First Year of Desegregation." Reflecting on the progress made since the 1954 Supreme Court decision on school desegregation, it said, "We are a long, long way from achieving the abolition of racial segregation in the United States but we are on the way. . . . In this process our churches have a heavy responsibility. . . . We, who talk about brotherhood, must revise our policies and our practices to make brotherhood a reality in our parishes."[17] Indeed, the denomination would have to do more than revise its policies to achieve these high aspirations; it would need to change its practices and behavior.

The Unitarians

Jeffrey Worthington Campbell, an African American of mixed heritage, held ministerial fellowship with both the American Unitarian Association (AUA) and the Universalist Church of America (UCA).[18] This may have given the editor of the *Register*, the Unitarian journal, additional impetus for responding to van Schaick's

writings in the *Universalist Leader*. Unitarians could protest, but
they had no mission in the African-American community comparable to the Universalist effort in Suffolk, and never attempted
to have one. Indeed, for the first third of the twentieth century,
official Unitarianism showed little concern for the issue of race.

Meadville Theological School, however, building on a commitment to race relations it had pursued since the 1870s, held an
extraordinary event. In 1915 its Convocation included eight well-
known speakers addressing the topic of race and immigration.
Foremost among them was Booker T. Washington, who addressed
"Immigration and Race Adjustment." Rev. Jenkin Lloyd Jones
spoke on "The Negro in the South," and Rev. Celia Parker Woolley delivered two addresses: "The American Color Problem" and
"Democracy and the Negro." In the 1916 *Meadville Quarterly* her
two presentations appear to have been combined into one article
titled "Democracy and the Race Problem":

> In the study of the Negro question we naturally look back to
> the days of abolitionism, that era of high, transcendental faith
> whose tide-water mark was reached in the lives of Emerson,
> Garrison, Channing, and Parker, but the spirit and methods of
> one age cannot be incorporated into another. The Color Prob-
> lem must fit into the age in which it has risen. . . . The present
> day problem is one of slow adjustment, patient endeavor and
> hopeful waiting. It is the white man's problem as much as the
> black man's. The sin of white complicity is very marked. . . .
>
> The present most serious aspect of white complicity is seen
> in the growing spirit of segregation, the disposition to dis-
> criminate against the colored man, woman and child in every
> walk and calling of life.[19]

Samuel Atkins Eliot II and Louis C. Cornish, AUA presidents
from 1900 to 1927 and 1927 to 1937, respectively, were imbued
with the racial prejudice of their era. As a young man Eliot
believed "negro and Chinese and various half breeds—are more

nearly brutes than anything I have ever known," while Cornish was "sympathetic to [the negroes'] temperamental peculiarities" and found them to be "very lovable people and often very child-like."[20] However, as a three-decade-long battle between him and Egbert Ethelred Brown escalated, Cornish's attitude turned from patronizing to defamatory.[21]

Given Eliot's and Cornish's beliefs about blacks, it is not surprising that in 1908 they discouraged Brown, who was Jamaican, from enrolling at Meadville Theological School to prepare for the Unitarian ministry. Nor is it surprising that the AUA eventually withdrew its funding from the congregation Brown had gathered in Jamaica upon his return in 1912. In 1920 Brown emigrated to the United States and established a Unitarian church in Harlem. The Boston blue-bloods (including Eliot's father, who was president of Harvard) greatly admired Booker T. Washington but Brown's forthright style so irked them that the AUA tried repeatedly to drop him from ministerial fellowship. And in 1929 they succeeded.

The AUA's treatment of Brown was replicated elsewhere. In 1927, Rev. Lewis A. McGee, an African American, was dissuaded from applying for Unitarian fellowship. In 1930, when Harry V. Richardson, an African-American student at Harvard Divinity School, asked to be fellowshipped, he was denied. Throughout the 1930s William H. G. Carter, who had founded the Church of the Unitarian Brotherhood in Cincinnati, was ignored. When, in 1934, Ethelred Brown secured help in getting his ministerial fellowship reinstated, one denominational official complained in a memo to another that Brown had "a Jewish lawyer of the type you might expect to be active in the affairs of" the American Civil Liberties Union (ACLU).[22] It seems that along with racial prejudice, some at the AUA found it acceptable to drop anti-Semitic remarks as well.

Following his presidency, Eliot served as minister of Boston's Arlington Street Church. There, in 1933, he preached the sermon "The Blight of Prejudice." He said, "Race prejudice has not a single scientific leg to stand on. Negro inferiority has no scientific justification."[23] However, he went on to say, "I suppose that there will always be race problems,—races are different and the difference persist [sic] in spite of change of environment."[24] On other occasions, he spoke with compassion for Native Americans and African Americans and expressed outrage at their treatment. He had supported the educational approach used at the Hampton Institute and Tuskegee, with its emphasis on vocational training and moral development, since he had first visited Hampton in 1887. He served as trustee at several black schools as well. But how can this be reconciled with the way he treated Ethelred Brown? Correspondingly, why did Eliot choose to promote the spread of Unitarianism in a half dozen new immigrant communities yet not among African Americans? We can surmise that his response was rooted in *noblesse oblige*: African Americans deserved charity and fairness, but "racial differences" allowed no place for them in the Unitarian church, just as he believed that women were unsuited for ministry.

At the 1934 AUA annual meeting, the program of social action put forward by the Department of Social Relations and voted on was so "controversial" as to require the caveat that it "in no wise binds the denomination." Concerning race relations, it stated,

1. As believers in the brotherhood of man, we affirm that all men everywhere, regardless of race, creed or color, are entitled to equal social, political, and economic opportunities.

2. We protest all discrimination against Negroes or members of other races and we favor all legislation which aims to eliminate such discrimination.

3. We unqualifiedly condemn organizations which have as their basis racial or religious prejudices, and we pledge our utmost effort to the development of a co-operative spirit between racial and creedal groups.[25]

The publication of *Unitarians Face a New Age* by the AUA Commission on Appraisal in 1936 signaled denominational renewal. For Frederick May Eliot, who had chaired the commission and followed Cornish as AUA president, it served as an outline of the new administration's priorities. It was a blueprint that mentioned neither race nor diversity in the context of extension or ministry. Indeed, race was mentioned nowhere. Its significance must be read into the phrases "sense of human brotherhood," "the struggle to create a just social order," and "concern for betterment of social condition." Tables show these values were rated by survey participants second, third, and fifth in relative importance, with "free exercise of intelligence in religion" standing first.[26]

In reviewing the resolutions passed at AUA annual meetings, we see a different sensibility emerging. In 1942, amid the Second World War and five years into Frederick May Eliot's presidency, the AUA, at its 117th annual meeting, passed a resolution on race relations with the following preface:

> Whereas: All race prejudice, particularly anti-Semitism and anti-Negro feeling and anti-Orientalism, threatens not only our national morale but also our unity as a people in this grave hour of crisis;
>
> And Whereas: Such prejudice and fanaticism are fundamentally opposed to all high morality, to the spirit of true religion, and to every principle of democracy, and therefore cannot be condoned nor tolerated by a free people committed to the proposition that "All men are created free and equal"; . . .

The resolution goes on to call Unitarians to practice "those principles of brotherhood on which the liberal church is founded," to become knowledgeable about racial discrimination, to take action to end it, and to condemn all forms of prejudice.[27]

During the nineteen years between the 1942 resolution on race relations and the consolidation of Unitarianism and Universalism, the AUA passed twenty-four resolutions regarding race.[28] Nonetheless, in its 1947 report to the AUA General Conference, the Commission on Planning and Review touched on the issue of race in only one paragraph. In section 5, under the title "Church

Maintenance and Extension," the commission recommended that the Department of Maintenance and Extension direct its "future extension efforts" toward establishing interracial churches and that the AUA form a special committee to study the policies of Unitarian churches regarding members of minority groups and "make specific recommendations to stimulate [congregations] to achieve a more inter-racial character."[29] Five years passed before the AUA board created such a commission.

Established in 1952, the Commission on Unitarian Inter-group Relations was charged to study the "discrimination against Negroes within our churches" and make recommendations. The commission members included Lillian Smith, a Southerner and author of *Killers of the Dream*. In his letter soliciting her participation, Frederick May Eliot confessed, "The American Unitarian Association, which comprises some four hundred fifty Unitarian churches and fellowships in the United States and the Dominion of Canada, has been increasingly concerned and troubled in recent years because of our failure to make what seems to us an adequate contribution to the solution of what is commonly called 'the race problem.'"[30] In May 1953 the commission issued an interim report which asked, "Are we Unitarians providing the leadership in inter-group relations that we should? Are the scattered non-whites in our church merely tokens with which we quiet our consciences or are they the beginnings of more adequate integration?"[31]

The final report, published in the April 1954 *Christian Register*, described the purpose of the beloved community:

> When brotherhood is limited, real self-hood is hard to attain, perhaps impossible. For man is a social being; the denial of brotherhood is a limitation upon the self. A man's uniqueness must be recognized by his friends. The liberal church accepts this challenge: It preaches and practices, if imperfectly, both fellowship and individualism. It recognizes modern man's dual need— the need to be in the fullest sense a person and the need to be a brother, to find vital human fellowship across all boundaries.

The report challenged Unitarians to hold firm to principles in "universal brotherhood, undivided by nation, race, or creed." It said, "An honest implementation of these principles within the parish life of our churches would go far to clear our collective conscience, and to enrich immeasurably our individual experience as members of churches." It called upon the AUA administration to provide "strong leadership": "It must set the tone for member churches to a greater degree than ever before, and the position of the Association must be unmistakably clear not only to member churches but to every fellowship which proposed to join it." Finally, the report offered nineteen recommendations, beginning with "a door that's really open." Merely opening a door was insufficient, it argued, because racial minorities expected to be excluded. Churches and fellowships should make special efforts to publicize themselves in black newspapers, invite black participation, and serve the black community. In conclusion, the commission opined, "It is not enough to help the Negro, it is not enough to provide for him; it is the responsibility of the local liberal church to welcome him, to respect his dignity, and treat him as an equal. . . . It is the obligation of the liberal church to take leadership in the integration of all groups in its community."[32]

The commission's report also lauded the *Christian Register*'s "long series of vivid articles on group and race relations." The editorial policy of the *Register* had shifted with the hiring of Rev. Stephen Fritchman as editor in November 1942. In the years prior to the Second World War, the publication intermittently mentioned race—usually to decry anti-Semitism in an era when Jewishness was seen as a racial issue. The January 1943 issue, grounded on the AUA's 1942 "Resolution on Race Relations," was devoted to the question of race. This emphasis continued throughout Fritchman's increasingly stormy tenure. The *Register* published articles by Paul Robeson; by Walter White, the executive secretary of the National Association for the Advancement of Colored People (NAACP); and by Edwin (Bill) Berry, the executive secretary of the Portland, Oregon, Urban League. It printed articles about the persecution of

Japanese Americans. More photos of people of color appeared. It started including a Brotherhood Week section each February.

When Fritchman's editorship was terminated in 1947, the *Christian Register* did not retreat from the issue of race.[33] The cover photo of the February 1953 "Brotherhood" issue depicted Doris Scott, an African-American industrial nurse who was a member of the Tennessee Valley Unitarian Church in Knoxville, Tennessee. In addition, the issue contained an article by Unitarian minister Homer Jack titled "Sunday at 11: Segregation Hour." The cover photo of the October 1954 *Register* showed fourteen-year-old Charles Vernon Bush, the first African American to serve as a page boy in the Supreme Court, and whose family belonged to All Souls (Unitarian) in Washington, D.C.

While racial justice was not high on the list of reforms Frederick May Eliot set out to make when he became president of the AUA in 1937, by 1955 he saw things differently. "We must make our way to a pluralistic concept of race, culture and religion," he said, "and it is no longer a symptom of an alarmist spirit to say that the hour is growing late."[34]

How late and how urgent became clear to D.C.-area Unitarians on Sunday, October 19, 1958, when the First Unitarian Church of Arlington, Virginia, was evacuated after receiving a bomb threat. Since the late 1940s the 350-member congregation had taken the lead in challenging segregation in northern Virginia; it had even run a summer program that brought African-American and white children together and which, if called a school, would have been illegal. The evening following the bomb threat, Unitarian ministers of four suburban congregations issued a statement:

> We view this threat as part of the pattern of lawlessness and violence which is being created on a national scale and which will grow to dangerous proportions, threatening both our democracy and our freedom of religion unless it is checked by the protest of our citizens and the work of law enforcement. . . . We appeal to those who have been segregationists with a ques-

tion mark in their minds. We ask them to join the people of good will who believe in equal rights for all men everywhere.[35]

The Unitarian Universalists

In 1959, six years before Selma and two before the consolidation of the Universalist Church of America and the American Unitarian Association into the Unitarian Universalist Association (UUA), the AUA established six commissions. Four years later these commissions jointly issued a book-length report, *The Free Church in a Changing World*, to help with the transition. In the book's preface, Dana McLean Greeley, first president of the UUA (1961–69), paraphrased Proverbs 29:18, "Without vision we would perish."[36] The report outlined the goals of his administration, just as *Unitarians Face a New Age* had done for the goals of Frederick May Eliot in 1936.

The report first mentions race on page 7: "The Negro membership in some of our congregations is a demonstration of our inclusiveness, but, except in a few large city churches, it is essentially token if it exists at all. We have not yet drawn Negroes in any number into positions of lay or ministerial leadership." Two pages later it states that membership should be open to all. And toward the end of the report the Commission on Ethics and Social Action asks two pointed questions: "Did we not criticize the German churches that failed to stand up to Hitler? Do we not rightly criticize the churches in our own South which fail to oppose segregation?" Equal opportunity for all, it argued, was a pressing issue, and Negroes faced the most acute problems. Therefore they should receive "a special kind of attention," and once their difficulties had been solved, "other intergroup problems" might become more solvable.[37] The commissions that reported on theology, leadership, and worship gave little or no attention to the issue of race. This could be a reflection of the fact that among the sixty-five commission members serving on the six commissions there appears to have been only one African American—Rev. Howard Thurman.

Silence about the issue of race had also been evident a year earlier in a report issued by the Committee to Study the Theological Education of Unitarian Universalist Ministers, "A Plan of Education for the Unitarian Universalist Ministry." The AUA board had also appointed that committee in 1959. Its mandate was to evaluate both the content of theological education and the possibilities for consolidation of Universalist and Unitarian theological schools. In discussing ministerial recruitment and selection, the committee's report did not mention race, and its only relevant recommendation was that when possible students should have "experience in [sic] foreign country in a social service post . . . preferably in Asia or Africa."[38]

Conversely, elsewhere Unitarian Universalists trumpeted their commitment to racial justice. At the first General Assembly following consolidation, the UUA reaffirmed its stance by passing four resolutions, one each on African independence, desegregation, public school integration, and freedom of residence. Over the next three years general assemblies passed four more: on civil rights (1962), admission of members to Unitarian Universalist congregations without discrimination (1963), the establishment of a Freedom Fund (1964), and civil rights yet again (1964).

Why the inconsistency? Why did commission reports rarely mention race, while general assemblies passed a plethora of resolutions about it? In general, the commissions focused on the workings of the UUA itself, while the resolutions targeted society at large.

The exception was the 1963 resolution on non-discrimination regarding admission to membership. Submitted by ten Southern congregations, this resolution called for an amendment to the UUA bylaws that would require congregations wishing to be voting members of the UUA General Assembly to have "maintained a policy of admitting persons to membership without discrimination of race, color, or national origin." The proposal reflected a dilemma over the differing understandings of what it meant to be a Unitarian Universalist. Debate over the amendment raged for three hours.

Kenneth Marshall, the minister of Davies Memorial in Washington, D.C., called the amendment a threat to "congregational freedom" and warned, "we must think not only of 1963, but also of 1993." Donald S. Harrington, the minister of the Community Church of New York—at that time the UUA's most successfully integrated congregation—countered that freedom must not become a "sacred cow": "This association can set certain standards of common conduct and common acceptance." The executive secretary for the Southern Unitarian Universalist Regional Office, Clifton Hoffman, worried that, rather than promoting integration, "if this amendment is forced upon unintegrated churches, it will force them out of membership and out of the Association and preclude any possibility of their ever being brought into full [membership] or integrated possibilities." And Greta W. Crosby, the minister in Roanoke, Virginia, asserted, "The ultimate purpose of congregational polity is to protect the individual from ecclesiastic tyranny, not to protect the local church in its exercise of ecclesiastic tyranny."[39] In the debate, some saw the freedom of congregational polity as sacrosanct, others saw that freedom as a license to discriminate. Some felt it had to be addressed locally, others insisted the UUA needed to take a stand by setting policy for all its member congregations. Some wanted to engrain non-discrimination in the association's bylaws, others felt the issue would be best addressed through persuasion. Alfred Hobart, a longtime resident of the South, introduced the resolution, and Southerners both opposed and supported it; likewise, African Americans spoke for and against. Many who were both for and against it would go to Selma.

In the end, 436 voted in favor and 379 against; the motion failed because changes to the bylaws required a two-thirds majority. A motion to reconsider passed and the debate continued, only to end in a second defeat, with 459 in favor and 383 against. The amendment was sent to committee, and what eventually emerged was a resolution that congregations "welcome into their membership and full participation persons without regard to race, color, or national origin" and that the UUA establish a "Commission on Religion and Race . . . to promote the complete integration of Negroes and other minority persons into our congregations." The amended resolution passed, 583 to 6.

Afterward Dana McLean Greeley said,

> Yesterday I voted against the amendment. I did it with a heavy heart. I was concerned about it then; I am concerned about it now. My worries were somewhat resolved at the luncheon, however, by Oliver Pilat [an author], who spoke to us and said it was the first debate he had ever listened to where both sides were right. When I voted yesterday as did others who voted against the amendment, we voted for freedom, we did not vote against brotherhood. And those who voted for the amendment yesterday, did not vote against freedom, they voted for brotherhood.[40]

Like the assembly debate, news reports on the meaning of the vote were divided. The *Springfield Union* of Springfield, Massachusetts, announced "Church Adheres to Basic Tenet," while the *Chicago Daily News* headline read "Unitarian Universalist Assn. Defeats Attempt to Spell Out Anti-bias Stand."

The Commission on Religion and Race acted quickly. In July, at its first meeting, the commission voted to support the March on Washington for Jobs and Freedom. When that historic march took place on August 28, 1963, Dana McLean Greeley led a Unitarian Universalist contingent of about sixteen hundred, nearly 1 percent of the association's total membership. On September 15, when the Sixteenth Street Baptist Church in Birmingham was bombed, the local UU congregation responded immediately. Members with medical training went to the hospital to help, others gave blood, still others went to visit the families of the four girls who died. Three days later Walter Royal Jones, the chair of the commission, flew to Birmingham to represent the UUA at the funerals, and the Civil Rights Disaster Fund, which the denomination established, raised nearly $13,000.

Not surprisingly, the 1964 annual report of the Commission on Religion and Race contained stronger language than the report issued by the Commission on Intergroup Relations a decade earlier: "It is unthinkable . . . that any shadow of a doubt should be permitted to stand. . . . A segregated Unitarian or Universalist church is a contradiction in terms."

The UUA also became active legislatively. In the midst of a congressional filibuster by the "Southern Bloc," which was holding up the Civil Rights Act (H.R. 7152), the Unitarian Universalist Ministers Association submitted a petition urging it to be passed without being weakened by amendments. Illinois senator and Unitarian Universalist Paul Douglas introduced the petition to the association on May 19, 1964, and it was signed by 386 UU ministers (three expressed opposition). Already in February Dana Greeley, Walter Royal Jones, and others had lobbied five UU members of Congress to support the act. Three voted for the legislation. The two who voted against it were Rep. William R. Poage of Texas's Eleventh District—a fourth-generation Universalist who attended Universalist National Memorial Church—and William Henry Harrison, who, when interviewed by fellow Wyomingite James Reeb and Jones, said, "he had left the Unitarian church because of its becoming involved in social and political issues."[41] When the bill finally passed, the 71 senators voting for it included Leverett Saltonstall of Massachusetts, a moderate Republican and lifelong Unitarian. The bill was enacted on July 2, and nine months later more than a hundred of the 386 ministers who signed the petition would participate in the march from Selma to Montgomery, including Reeb, Orloff Miller, Clark Olsen, and Farley Wheelwright.

At the 1964 UUA General Assembly in San Francisco, 150 ministers marched on the San Francisco Real Estate Board, protesting California's Proposition 14.[42] Repealing the Rumford Fair Housing Act and giving homeowners and landlords the absolute right to sell or rent to whomever they wished amounted to a license to discriminate. However, it was a one-man demonstration in support of the proposition that received nationwide publicity. The demonstrator was Rev. James Madison Barr III, minister of the First Unitarian Church of Memphis.

The UUA made its position on and engagement in the civil rights movement clear in its new journal, the *Unitarian Universalist Register-Leader*. A month did not pass without multiple articles about UU civil rights actions. One described how a local chapter of Student Religious Liberals (SRL), the UUA-affiliated organization of college students, had participated with other students from Florida State University in picketing segregated off-campus restaurants. The journal also carried a report on the 1964 Mississippi Summer Project, organized by the National Council of Churches, which brought twelve hundred students to Mississippi to organize freedom schools and support voter registration. The *Register-Leader* estimated that about a dozen ministers and thirty-five UU college students were involved.[43] Its coverage prompted a debate, with letters pro and con in the subsequent issue. In November the *Register-Leader* included the article "Our Church in Birmingham Has Not Kept Quiet," highlighting the ways that congregation had combated racial injustice since its founding in 1954.

In the years leading up to Selma, the Universalists supported the Suffolk mission and issued the lofty 1957 "Declaration of Social Principles," but beyond that only a few people seem to have striven to keep race relations on the UCA's agenda. This inattention must be partly attributed to the reality that from the turn of the twentieth century onward Universalism was hemorrhaging churches and membership. Among Unitarians, however, the 1942 "Resolution on Race Relations" seems to have signaled a growing concern with racial justice. After the denominations merged in 1961, that emphasis continued to build, until the events of Selma galvanized the Unitarian Universalist commitment to racial justice.

The public declarations made by Unitarians and Universalists about equal opportunity, integration, and racial justice sharpened during the two decades leading to Selma. However, when we pinpoint the locations and relocations of their congregations, analyze their religious education materials and hymnbooks, dissect the cultural proclivities of the burgeoning fellowships, add up the number of African Americans in leadership positions, and survey the experiences of the African-American ministers, we see clearly that the *espoused values* of Universalists, Unitarians, and Unitarian Universalists were rarely matched by their *values in practice*.

WHAT UNITARIAN UNIVERSALISTS DID

An assessment of liberal religion's *values in practice* must examine the humdrum of congregational life. There its principles can be seen in action; revealed, not in aspirational statements, but in the everyday business-as-usual decisions made by individuals, congregations, and denominational departments. The worship resources and religious education curricula they used, the books they published and the historical scholarship they pursued, the geographic location and movement of congregations, the impact of the fellowship movement, the details of who did—and did not—sit on denominational committees, and the near impossibility of settling African-American ministers tell their own story.

Worship

Worship is central to congregational life. It is a time set outside ordinary time, into which community members bring their spiritual yearnings. There, stirred by the sacred, they find comfort, hear the unexpected, and are lifted by inspiration. It is a time to meet what is at other times pushed away, to find hope, express gratitude, and be reminded that we are in this together.

During worship, what did religious liberals proclaim and to whom did they speak? What did they sing, and not sing? What do the images, language, and rhythms of Unitarianism, Universalism, and Unitarian Universalism tell us about who their adherents were, who was welcomed and who not? When they affirm aspirations and sing songs, they give voice to and bring together intellect and emotion, the self, and the community. What do these elements of worship reveal?

During the 1893 World's Columbian Exposition, Frederick Douglass regularly attended Unitarian services at All Souls Church in Chicago. On his last Sunday in attendance he bade farewell to the minister, Jenkin Lloyd Jones. "I am now going away," Douglass said. "I have been here more often than I meant to be. . . . But I could not stay away. You are standing for a great and holy ideal. My brother, keep the standard as ever so high as now and the world will come to it by and by."[44] Douglass was accustomed to mingling with Euro-Americans, but for many African Americans such a foray into Anglo-Saxon culture would have required courage. In the segregated society which prevailed during much of the twentieth century, a black person could never have casually decided to attend a Unitarian church. But perhaps knowing that the minister stood unequivocally for equal rights made it possible for some, even if they found the customs of the church foreign.

On the issue of race there was no doubt where Jones stood. A few, following in his tracks, held that standard aloft with equal passion. Foremost among them was John Haynes Holmes. W. E. B. Du Bois spoke as highly of Holmes and his Community Church of New York as Douglass had of Jones. In 1948, looking back, he said that "the Community Church welcomed Negroes; discussed the Negro Problem, and evidently did not believe that the white race was the only race on earth worth saving. That was a difficult creed to live up to in early twentieth century New York."[45] From the beginning of his ministry in 1907 at the Church of the Messiah (renamed the Community Church of New York in 1919), Holmes went beyond merely preaching about the race problem. He invited Dr. Adam Clayton Powell, the minister of Abyssinian Baptist, the largest African-American church in America, into the pulpit.

Another champion of civil rights was John H. Dietrich, a signer of the Humanist Manifesto and minister of the First Unitarian Society of Minneapolis. He proclaimed, in a 1929 sermon "The Myth of a Superior Race," "The fact is that there is only one race—

the human race."[46] In 1946 Holmes's successor at the Community Church, Donald S. Harrington, preached a sermon "The White Problem." He said, "Our race problem is a white problem. Until white people are ready to face the white problem, beg forgiveness for their crimes against humanity and God, turn and make amends for past errors and follies, no white man in this land can live a healthy spiritual life."[47] A year later, in a sermon "Declaring for Color" and broadcast on the radio, Kenneth Patton, minister of the First Unitarian Society of Madison, Wisconsin, resigned from the white race.[48] His announcement lit up the wire services. Another widely publicized sermon on race was delivered by A. Powell Davies at All Souls Church (Unitarian) in Washington, D.C. On February 1, 1953, in "The Shelter of Good Intentions," he declared, "I shall myself, from this time on, not knowingly eat a meal in any restaurant in the District of Columbia that will not serve meals to Negroes. . . . I invite all who truly believe in human brotherhood to do the same. We have talked enough. It is time for action."[49] And in 1957, Robert Raible, minister in Dallas, in a sermon "Advice to the Dallas School Board" which was reported on by Dallas newspapers, radio, and TV, "accused the Dallas Board of Education of subterfuge and defiance of the law in postponing racial integration in the schools."[50] These sermons show how the Unitarian ministers who preached them at mid-century engaged the issue of equality.

However their stance was far from universal. These were big-city ministers, delivering sermons that had little resonance in the lives of congregants living in small, lily-white communities. Other ministers, like James Madison Barr III, abhorred the Civil Rights Bill, and some, such as Seth R. Brooks, eschewed their colleagues' prophetic style. In 1939 Brooks became the minister at the Universalist National Memorial Church in Washington, D.C., the same congregation where John van Schaick had been settled. After serving there for nearly a quarter century, and living through the assassinations of Medgar Evers and John F. Kennedy, the March on Washington, and the bombing of the Sixteenth Street Baptist Church in Birmingham that killed four girls, Brooks nonetheless said of his approach, "We can talk about crusades and causes but when it comes right down to basics you must be able to talk to people out of your life and their lives. Otherwise these other things do not mean much. . . . I do not believe in the spectacular."[51] While there is truth in his comments about preaching from experience, we must wonder whether he addressed any of these events. If so, what did he say? Perhaps nothing. "Brooks avoids controversial subjects," commented an observer of his preaching style. And Brooks himself admitted, "I am fearful of the biased sermon. . . . I have tried to say things that would not be unjust to people. I try to talk in a timely way about timeless themes."[52] His ministry stood in contrast to that taking place at All Souls (Unitarian), less than a mile to the north, a congregation known for its outspoken, activist ministers, and where Frederick Douglass "not infrequently attended."[53] Perhaps Brooks's approach explains why the conservative Democratic Congressman William R. Poage from Texas, who voted against the 1964 Civil Rights Bill, felt comfortable attending National Memorial.

While the sermon is central to worship, it is only a part of the experience. It must be woven together with readings and prayers, music and hymns to create a worship service. Hymnody has always played a role in liberal religious worship. Twenty years after Douglass's visits to All Souls (Chicago), the Abraham Lincoln Centre, where All Souls gathered, held a fiftieth-anniversary celebration of the Emancipation. Naturally, the celebration ended with the singing of "The Battle Hymn of the Republic," a song written during the Civil War by Unitarian Julia Ward Howe at the request of her minister, James Freeman Clarke. In 1971, reflecting on this hymn, Dana McLean Greeley remembered singing it at the 1963 March on Washington and lamented that "our Hymnbook Commission left it out of the new hymnbook. Even the earlier commission, in 1937, put it in the back of the book in a sort of inferior class."[54] It held a special place in Greeley's heart and in that of many African Americans; but while the 1937 *Hymns of the Spirit*, a joint venture of the Unitarians and Universalists, had included the song, in 1964 it was left out of *Hymns for the Celebration of Life*.

Both the American Unitarian Association and the Universalist Church of America issued program guides during the 1940s and 1950s suggesting worship resources to use during Brotherhood Week. Hymns from *Hymns of the Spirit* were recommended. However, since the hymnbook contained neither spirituals nor gospels, the suggested songs, while praising brotherhood and comradeship, were written by white composers.[55] This situation was partly remedied when the Ethical Culture Society published a children's hymnal in 1955 called *We Sing of Life*. Edited by Rev. Vincent Silliman, it was widely used by Unitarians and Universalists and included two African-American spirituals: "Sometimes I Feel Like a Motherless Child" and "Go Down Moses."

Unitarians and Universalists, seeing their consolidation in 1961 as a new beginning, consummated the union with a new hymnbook. This enabled worshippers to join together in affirming their new identity. In an essay for *The Free Church in a Changing World*, the Commission on Religion and the Arts confessed, "We can scarcely boast that we are a singing people. And now we are faced with the challenge and opportunity of a new hymn book [*Hymns for the Celebration of Life*] about to appear among us. The Commission predicts that this book can lead to a rejuvenation of our congregational singing, but only if the people are patient with the novel features of the new collection and are willing to work at learning to master its unfamiliar parts."[56] Since religious liberals had been occupied with civil rights for a decade, the new hymnal might have been expected to address the issue of racial justice.

The members of the hymnal commission had already shown their commitment to race relations. The chair of the commission, Arthur W. Foote, was minister at Unity Church–Unitarian in St. Paul, one of the congregations that had been identified in 1953 as having "five or more Negroes attending."[57] A member of the local NAACP and the Urban League, Foote had also been a member of the Unitarian Commission on Intergroup Relations from 1952 to 1954; there he worked alongside Howard Thurman, mystic, African-American minister, and prolific writer. Rev. Christopher

Moore sat on the commission; in 1956 he had founded an interracial children's choir at the First Unitarian Society of Chicago. The commission included Rev. Kenneth Patton, who had made headlines in 1947 by resigning from the white race.

Given these ministers' commitments and their relationships to black culture; given the ethos of the 1960s; given the Unitarian Universalist general resolutions supporting integration, desegregation, and African independence, one would expect to find in the new hymnal material by and about African Americans, and songs calling for racial justice. There is nothing—not one reading, not one song. Because Patton was interested in world religions, the hymnal included writings by Rabindranath Tagore, Lao-Tzu, Kahlil Gibran, and Mahatma Gandhi, but nothing by an African American. The commission members, all white, lived out their values by working for racial justice; yet they lived in a Euro-American cultural hegemony. Indeed, two of them were also members of the Commission on Religion and the Arts, which wrote in *The Free Church in a Changing World* that worship at its best offers "the wisdom of European culture and faith."[58] Apparently they couldn't imagine, from inside their cultural bubble, that the African Americans who were coming to UU congregations in increasing numbers would be more comfortable if their own culture were reflected in worship. It also seems not to have occurred to them that Euro-Americans could benefit from the meditations by Howard Thurman or poems by Langston Hughes or Gwendolyn Brooks, or from singing spirituals or the African-American anthem "Lift Every Voice and Sing."

Including African-American material would have required breaking an unwritten, and largely unconscious, rule about singing only "good music"—code for classical Euro-American, English, and Continental music. Beyond this cultural myopia lay another reason for ignoring non-Eurocentric musical traditions: Unitarian Universalism's cutting edge lay elsewhere. *Hymns for the Celebration of Life* represented a significant departure from *Hymns of the Spirit*; the prior book was biblically oriented, the latter was not. A review of the new hymnbook in the *Inquirer*, the weekly journal of the British Unitarians and Free Christians, observed that the new American hymnal "reflects a strong swing to humanist worship."[59] This transformation preoccupied the commission's attention. Trying to create a hymnal that could speak to humanists, theists, and those who still identified as Christian presented a formidable task. The struggle between competing orientations and the effort to reach the necessary compromises—while managing the temperamental Kenneth Patton—consumed the commission members. Since the commission lacked an African-American voice and considering that the Commission on Religion and the Arts did not mention race in its report, it is possible that the issue never came up.

The *Free Church* report admitted, "Our common practice shows that many, possibly most, of our people do not sing lustily and do not enjoy hymns in their musical quality."[60] This was not a ringing endorsement of UU worship. Reflecting on UU worship, Alfred W. Hobart, while serving the congregation in Charleston, South Carolina, wrote, "Negroes are not knocking upon the doors of the Unitarian church demanding entrance. . . . Even intellectuals among Negroes find our type of service lacking in warmth and emotional content, and I don't wonder at that, either, after having attended services in a Negro church."[61] Unitarian Universalism may have appealed to their intellect, but only a handful of African Americans were willing to cross the barrier that American society had built into people's minds and souls and walk into a UU congregation that did not reflect, much less affirm, their experience or stir their hearts.

Religious Education

How did Unitarians and Universalists express their values through religious education? What curricula did their congregations use? What did these curricula teach about racial and ethnic diversity? Who was left out and what was invisible?

The backbone of religious education in Universalism, and thus of the way race was addressed in the denomination, was the General Sunday School Association (GSSA). From 1917 onward it focused its efforts in the racial arena on the Suffolk Normal and Training School. Universalists held up the school as an example to its children of a living model of interracial understanding and respect. The GSSA provided a small budgetary support to the mission, supplemented by the American Missionary (later Friendship) Offering collected in Universalist Sunday schools. The publicity for the Suffolk school also prompted many individual gifts of money, books, and school supplies. In the early twentieth century, when racism and violence against blacks was rising and the Ku Klux Klan was growing, the Suffolk mission represented a revolutionary program and an antidote to the racist stance of *Christian Leader* editor John van Schaick—the only regular mention of the Suffolk mission in that publication appeared on the Church School page.

The GSSA also sent resource materials to its congregations. The information on the American Friendship Program disseminated to Universalist Sunday schools in 1947 defined the program's purpose as "to recognize the worth of individuals as persons. To appreciate Negro people and their contributions to our country's life. To become acquainted with the work of our church among the Negroes. To do something to foster better race relations." The GSSA enclosed sample worship services and suggestions for class activities, a poster depicting Jordan Neighborhood House with information about it, a label for a dedicated collection box, and a long list of resources, including a story about how one teacher dealt with a child singing "Eenie, meenie, minie, mo, catch a nigger by the toe" and a true-false test about Negroes.[62]

By 1957 the name of the program had changed to Brotherhood Week Programs; it was administered by the Universalist Service Committee (USC) and had a broader focus. In addition to discussing Jordan Neighborhood House, it suggested ways to demonstrate support for Hungary and for refugees, for integration in the South, housing rights in the North, and the Universalist social project in rural Nagano, Japan. Brotherhood, the USC declared, required good will and a sacrificial spirit.

Since the mid-1940s Universalists had been using the Unitarian New Beacon Series in their religious education programs. The Unitarians produced the series between 1939 and 1966, guided by Ernest Kuebler, director of religious education for the AUA, and the religious educator and author Sophia Lyon Fahs. The program was revolutionary in its non-creedal theology and exploratory approach to religious education.

In the 1942 book *Growing Bigger* by Elizabeth M. Manwell and Fahs, one story, "The Engine Dance," depicts Roger and his mother visiting a nursery school where she volunteers. She tells him beforehand that many of the children will have "dark brown skin." She calls them Negroes and Roger is curious. That day they are to make a special trip to a train station. The father of one of the children is a porter on a Pullman car. He shows them around. Roger likes him and thinks that perhaps someday he will be a porter. It ends with Roger feeling, "He liked the boys and girls with the brown skin." The story is structured so that Roger learned from children who are both younger than him and Negro. Its message is that you can learn from and like anyone.[63]

This story was an anomaly in the Beacon series.

The first books in the series said nothing about racial issues. *Martin and Judy in Their Two Little Houses*, the first of three books that offered the Unitarian and Universalist counterpart to Dick and Jane, came out in 1939, three years earlier. Fahs said, "The stories are meant to encourage in small children a sensitivity to the intangible values that are basic to all real living which deserves to be characterized as spiritual in quality." Based on exploration and questioning, it was religiously non-doctrinal. But the particulars of Martin and Judy's lives make it clear that they are middle-class Euro-Americans, living in the suburbs, with their father ensconsed as the breadwinner. That is the hidden curriculum. Neither the original collection of stories nor its first revision depicts any ethnicity or culture other than Euro-American. That is the missing curriculum. Nor does the issue of race appear in *Child of the Sun: A Pharaoh of Egypt* (1939), *Joseph: The Story of Twelve Brothers* (1941), or *Moses: Egyptian Prince, Nomad Sheikh, Lawgiver* (1942). The assumption, since nothing is said, is that these Middle Easterners are white. Africans are not completely absent; the book *From Long Ago and Many Lands* (1948) includes three stories from Uganda. The 1958 book *Beginnings: Earth, Sky, Life, Death* describes the Bushmen before telling their myth of creation, and the stories that follow are from Australian Aboriginal, Native American, Chinese, and Japanese culture, making it a truly multicultural collection.[64]

The 1944 revision of the Martin and Judy books depicts no one of discernibly non-white ethnicity. In 1959 the editors revised the stories extensively. While there were no black characters in the stories, each new volume included a depiction of a single boy with Negroid features among its illustrations. In contrast, *Dick and Jane* included black characters, but not until 1965. *The Family Finds Out* (1951) is another book in the New Beacon Series. Gearing it to five- to seven-year-olds, Edith Hunter wrote it in the spirit of *Martin and Judy*. It includes two illustrations with an African-American boy. His name is either David or Philip, and he speaks. However, both times he appears paired with the same white boy, and the reader cannot tell which words are spoken by which boy. This was more typical, a drawing of a single black child without reference to race or culture.

Books produced for older age groups also demonstrate obliviousness to African Americans and their culture. *The Church Across the Street,* written by Reginald D. Manwell and Sophia Lyon Fahs in 1947 and revised in 1962, was a remarkable text meant to teach about other American faith traditions, including the Catholic Church, the Latter-Day Saints, the Baptists, the Society of Friends, and the Methodists. The chapter on the Methodists tells about John Wesley at length before ending with a single short paragraph noting the existence of "Negro Methodist" denominations. Revised in 1962, it mentions the African Methodist Episcopal Church, the African Methodist Episcopal Zion Church, and the Colored Methodist Episcopal Church, but it fails to tell of Richard Allen. In 1794, Allen, with the support of Universalist Benjamin Rush, founded one of the first independent African-American congregations in the United States, and in 1816 was elected the first bishop of the AME Church, the first black denomination. The curriculum also fails to mention the Nation of Islam. Founded in 1930, it was widely known by 1962, when the revised edition appeared; indeed, by then Beacon Press had published the first major study of the Black Muslims.

In 1962 the UUA also published *Unitarianism and Universalism: An Illustrated History,* written for teenagers by Henry Cheetham, the director of the UUA Department of Education. The book offers no mention of African-American Unitarians or Universalists. The same was true of *These Live Tomorrow: Twenty Unitarian Universalist Biographies* (1964); moreover, although it includes biographies of Benjamin Rush, Jenkin Lloyd Jones, John Murray Atwood, and Clarence Skinner, it fails to address their progressive attitudes on race. Another book for teens, *Tensions Our Children Live With: An Anthology of Stories Raising Ethical Issues* (1959), did include two stories about racial segregation, and in *Worshiping Together with Questioning Minds* (1965) Sophia Lyon Fahs devoted four chapters to the life of George Washington Carver. Fahs had first introduced Carver to the Sunday School program she directed at the Riverside Church in New York City in 1936. Indeed, on that occasion she wrote a poem titled "To a Little Dry Peanut." But not until the end of her career did she write these chapters about Carver. Why did it take thirty years for her to return to this project? Clearly, serving a congregation a mile and a half west of Harlem under the pre-eminent liberal minister of that era, Harry Emerson Fosdick, was more conducive to addressing the issue of race than working with lily-white, Boston-centric Unitarians.

In 1954 the Commission on Intergroup Relations, evaluating the AUA's education program, said, "The open-minded, experimental and reasonable approach to all human relations that we advocate tends to make for flexibility in thinking and feeling and to discourage the formation of stereotyped opinions."[65] The Commission on Education and Liberal Religion offered a more critical assessment of the New Beacon Series in 1963, finding the materials "deficient not only as regards to symbolism but also in terms of realism." The commission wrote, "One might ask how typical are [Martin and Judy] or more important, how meaningful are they and their neat white house in the suburbs to children whose world includes all the blood and thunder, as well as the sophisticated reportage, of television."[66] When, in 1964, the Commission on Religion and Race approached the UUA Department of Education, its director told them that for financial reasons the department could not "scrap its present stock of books despite the fact the texts and illustrations are 'pure white' but that new materials will reflect intercultural and interracial situations. The issues of city life, multi-ethnic groups and poverty, will be featured in contemplated new materials."[67]

Prior to Selma, the AUA and UCA produced almost no religious education resources relevant to race. However, the denominations did disseminate useful materials developed by individual congregations.[68] Nor was the topic of race relations confined to Sunday school curricula. Camps, congregations, and both the Unitarian and Universalist Service Committees offered summer programs.[69] When considering the limitations and failings of religious education programs in both denominations, it is important to note that until the mid-1970s there was virtually no historical scholarship on African-American contributions to or experiences in Unitarianism or Universalism.[70] Therefore, religious educators had few resources specific to Unitarian Universalism to draw upon.[71] Carter G. Woodson had helped establish African-American history as a legitimate field of study in 1915, and Negro History Week had existed since 1926. Although Meadville, Harvard, St. Lawrence, and Starr King School for the Ministry had admitted African-American students, supported local integration efforts, taught the imperative of seeking racial justice in social ethics classes, and encouraged students to participate in the civil rights struggle, their faculties had never paid attention to the relationships between liberal religion and African Americans.[72]

There was certainly history to research and expound upon. Meadville Theological School had matriculated Alfred Amos Williams, its first of five students from the African Methodist tradition, in 1871; Universalist missions to African Americans in the Tidewater region of Virginia dated back to 1887; S. Laing and Fannie Barrier Williams, intimates of Booker T. Washington and W. E. B. Du Bois, joined the interracial All Souls Church in Chicago in 1888; and in 1920 the founding members of the Harlem Unitarian Church were among the most prominent political activists in Harlem. None of this garnered notice.

Only one effort received attention, albeit in a very limited way: the Suffolk mission. For decades Universalist children learned the lesson that all people were of dignity and worth and all were sacred to God while engaging in hands on projects, sending books and other supplies they gathered, hearing stories about children like themselves who were African Americans, sending cards and receiving them. Some even traveled to Suffolk to see the school and meet Miss Annie, the director of Jordan Neighborhood House. As progressive as the New Beacon Series was, it offered nothing comparable. Indeed, the Universalist program was exceptional on two counts: It engaged children in doing something for, and with, others that made a difference in the world; and it stood against what was the norm for most Universalists and Unitarians. Both faiths were heavily concentrated in the Northeast, where their members had little contact with African Americans, held black intelligence in low regard, and were ignorant about black contributions to America. The American Friendship Program served as a corrective.

One of the reasons the lack of material and skewed perspective were not called into question was that only a handful of African Americans held positions in religious education. The first African-American Universalist or Unitarian religious educator, other than

Joseph F. Jordan and Annie B. Willis, seems to have been Rev. Maurice Dawkins, who served from 1948 to 1954 as the minister of education at the Community Church of New York. When in 1950 the First Unitarian Universalist Church of Detroit considered and then voted against hiring Rev. Eugene Sparrow, it was for the position of director of youth activities. In 1954, William Y. Bell served as director of adult education and social relations for the Council of Liberal Churches (Universalist Unitarian) for about a year; in 1956 Pauline Warfield Lewis became the director of religious education (DRE) at the First Unitarian Church of Cincinnati; in 1957 Bernice Just became the DRE at All Souls (Unitarian) in Washington, D.C.; and in 1958 Rev. William R. Jones, newly graduated from Harvard Divinity School, was hired as assistant minister and DRE at the First Unitarian Church of Providence.

Few as their numbers were, there were more blacks working in Unitarian and Universalist religious education than in any other arena of church leadership. Why was the realm of religious education the first place African Americans found professional employment within Universalist and Unitarian congregations? Perhaps religious education of children was seen as ancillary and thus an acceptable arena for women and black leadership.

The African-American experience within Universalism and Unitarianism points to racism's insidiousness. The distortions of the overt curricula, and the omissions that created the hidden ones, supported a Euro-American worldview that was implicitly racist. Even the well intentioned, living as they did in a cultural milieu of racial isolation and educationally buttressed ignorance, found it difficult to see their way free. Earnest affirmations of brotherhood were not enough.

How did the children raised with these programs in the 1940s and 50s become the change agents of the 1960s and 70s? Perhaps the stark disparity between the earnest espousals of the supreme worth of every person, which they recited like a mantra, and these anemic religious education materials nurtured an impatience with the status quo emanating from the congregations in which they were reared. Raised to question the status quo, they saw what their elders did not: the hypocrisy of affirming racial justice and then doing so little about it in their own lives. The world was changing and young UUs were changing with it and changing it as they ventured south to work for racial justice in the lead-up to Selma.

Beacon Press

Beacon Press, wholly owned by the AUA and then by the UUA, published the New Beacon Series. It also published scholarly works about Unitarianism—but none about Unitarianism and African Americans.

The Commission on Intergroup Relations and the Commission on Religion and Race described the press as "effective" in publishing "excellent books on the Civil Rights movement, Negro aspirations, and other ethnic and religious minorities." Yet early in the twentieth century Beacon also published works on eugenics, and it offered little in the 1940s regarding African Americans or topics to which African Americans would have been drawn.

A shift took place in 1946, when Mel Arnold became the editor and began seeking more controversial books. The number of titles grew. Some, like James Baldwin's *Notes of a Native Son* and Kenneth Clark's *Prejudice and Your Child,* both published in 1955, were seminal. With the 1960s came a wave of new books, many by prominent writers. In 1960 Beacon published *Theodore Parker: An Anthology*, edited by Henry Steele Commager, who wrote about and offered examples of Parker's uncompromising opposition to slavery and all who supported it. However, Commager neglected to mention Parker's thoroughly racist attitude toward African Americans and Mexicans. In 1961 C. Eric Lincoln's *The Black Muslims in America* came out, and in 1963 Kenneth Clark's *The Negro Protest.* The latter, comprised of Clark's interviews with Martin Luther King Jr., Malcolm X, and James Baldwin, came with a study guide prepared by the UUA Department of Adult Education and distributed to UU congregations. In 1964 Bea-

con published *SNCC: The New Abolitionists,* in which the histo-
rian Howard Zinn recounted the birth of the Student Non-violent
Coordinating Committee, and also the paperback edition of John
Hope Franklin's *The Militant South, 1800–1861.* A year later it
released the paperback edition of E. Franklin Frazier's *Race and
Culture Contacts in the Modern World,* which joined an already
substantial backlist.[73]

Location, Location, Location

The relationship of Unitarian Universalism to the African-
American community cannot be understood without examining regional and residential demographic patterns. Three factors
militated against Unitarian Universalists developing an African-
American membership and integrating their congregations: In
the South there were lots of blacks but few UU congregations; in
the Northeast there were plenty of UU congregations but hardly
any African Americans. Finally, although both UUs and African
Americans gravitated to the burgeoning cities, white flight to the
suburbs confounded that opportunity. Understanding the roots of
why these two communities were so isolated from one another is
the first challenge; the second is reconciling that isolation with the
UU response to Selma.

Rooted in New England, Universalism and Unitarianism
spread during the nineteenth century into the middle and upper
Midwest and along the West Coast. Membership in both denominations declined at the end of the nineteenth and during the first
half of the twentieth centuries, more severely among the Universalists than the Unitarians. Following that decline, the growth that
did occur took place in suburban and university communities.
However, all attempts to gather black congregations were made in
urban centers, and were welcomed tepidly at best.

In 1946 Lon Ray Call, minister at large for the AUA Department
of Extension and Maintenance, submitted a report to the department asking "when and under what conditions groups should be

encouraged to organize a new church." Among the factors to be considered, he said, were "such things as the percentage of foreign born and negro."[74] He did not specify whether these were positive or negative indicators, but it is difficult to imagine that he viewed them positively. Eight years earlier, after visiting Cincinnati, Call had recommended against supporting the only African-American Unitarian church outside Harlem or its minister, William H. G. Carter. In a memo he said that the Church of the Unitarian Brotherhood, which had been founded in Cincinnati in 1932, was in the wrong neighborhood.[75] When interviewed in 1982 about his philosophy of and experience with church extension, Call mentioned neither diversity nor race, but he did voice his astonishment that so many congregations had been born in "unpromising locations."[76]

A 1942 effort to establish an African-American congregation in Miami also encountered troubles, but different from those in Cincinnati. Frederick Fay chronicled the events in a report to the AUA. It began when Rev. William H. Floyd, a fundamentalist minister who had come to hold liberal views, "gathered a group to listen each Sunday afternoon" to radio broadcasts by Rev. Joe Barth, the minister of the First Unitarian Church of Miami. With a population of over 170,000 in 1940, Miami was growing rapidly. Within its confines was a "compact Negro community of some 30,000 people living in abject slum conditions." However, Floyd's initial effort was located a few miles south of the city center in Coconut Grove, an African-American community of 3,000. A theological liberal, Floyd found himself "battling against tremendous odds because of his liberal views." An "Episcopal minister talked him down" at the "colored ministerial meeting."[77] When he organized a junior choir, local ministers spread the word among the girls' parents that their daughters would go to hell. The choir disbanded but, with a contribution of hymnals and $500 from the AUA, Floyd shifted his focus to establishing a church in the larger black community in the center of Miami. He envisioned it including a nursery school. Floyd's undertaking resembled similar approaches in similar types of locations both before and after. Each attempt offered liberal religion with an emphasis on "social betterment" and was located in big to mid-sized cities among black populations living on "the other side of the tracks."[78] But the Miami effort, like those in Harlem, Cincinnati, and Des Moines (an even more short-lived attempt), died and was forgotten.

In 1952, when the AUA Commission on Intergroup Relations was beginning its research, the majority of Unitarian and Universalist congregations outside New England were found near a university or college community.[79] Indeed, Call believed a congregation needed to be located in a city with a population of over 100,000, and in a neighborhood close to cultural centers (i.e., universities). This tendency had become more pronounced after the Second World War when many new fellowships sprang up in college towns, drawing former soldiers using the GI Bill to further their education.

One hundred and seventy Unitarian congregations (one-third of the total number) responded to the Commission's survey; two-thirds of them were in New England or the Middle Atlantic states. The South, on the other hand, contained only twenty-five congregations in all, or 5 percent of the total number. The Commission found that "nearly all the Southern churches are in communities of 100,000 or more. Most of the churches in the Middle and Far West and Canada are also in communities of 100,000 or more, and about three-fourths of the churches in this area are in communities which have Negroes in the population. As might be expected, none of the Southern churches report that there were no Negroes in the community."[80] This meant that in the region with the highest concentration of African Americans the UUA had the fewest congregations.

Congregations in the Unitarian Universalist heartland had the same dearth of black members; however, the demographic profile in the region was the reverse. There were few blacks in New England; in 1940 its population was 1.2 percent African-American, in 1950 1.5 percent, and in 1960 2.3 percent. These percentages were kept low by design. African Americans were often prohibited from working in the area's mills; in general, the few jobs available to them were as domestic servants or unskilled labor. And even if they found employment, restrictive ordinances kept them from living in many towns. In 1960 Waltham, Massachusetts (one of the towns that prohibited black mill workers) had a population of 55,000, of which 209 (0.37 percent) was black. Dana McLean Greeley was born and raised in Lexington, Massachusetts; in 2010, a hundred years after his birth, African Americans made up just 1.5 percent of the town's population. These numbers are consistent with the report of the AUA Commission on Intergroup Relations, which found that 25 percent of the congregations responding to its survey, and 50 percent of those in the Northeast, reported having no African Americans in their community.[81] It could not be otherwise. The 1960 U.S. census reported only 111,842 blacks in Massachusetts, 3,313 in Maine, 1,908 in New Hampshire, and 519 in Vermont.

In 1964 the Commission on Religion and Race conducted a survey, finding that only 54 percent of the respondent congregations "declared the presence of a significant Negro minority," while 25 percent reported that no minority made up more than 5 percent of their community. Examining both its own survey and the one done ten years earlier, the commission concluded that "in both surveys the greatest percentage of thin or 'unstructured' answers (that is, the greatest degree of evasiveness or indifference) was in New England. . . . The greatest degree of these 'thin' answers were from smaller communities, with a population of less than 100,000. A large portion of the congregations in these smaller communities were, of course, [sic] New England."[82]

In small communities, the pressures of class and clan are more acute than in a metropolis, which offers anonymity and with that freedom. In the Northeast, particularly in Massachusetts for the Unitarians and New York State for the Universalists, most of the congregations were in small communities; indeed, only one-sixth of the Unitarian congregations in the Northeast were in communities of 100,000 or more, and of these only Arlington Street Church in Boston reported having more than five African-American members. This was the insular cultural milieu from which Unitarianism and Universalism spread and in which Samuel A. Eliot, Louis C. Cornish, and Dana McLean Greeley were reared. This would have consequences as the UUA tried to integrate in the years before Selma and even more so in its aftermath.

A demographic shift involving both African Americans and Unitarians was taking place. Until the First World War, 95 percent of African Americans lived in the South. Then came the Great Migration. Following the railroad trunk lines north, they congregated in major urban centers. Between 1910 and 1970, 6 million African Americans headed to industrial cities large and small. Similarly, as Unitarianism spread across North America, it moved into urban centers. Even after the 1961 merger, 74 percent of Unitarian Universalists resided in urban environs, a percentage which matched that of Catholicism and gave Unitarian Universalism the highest urban concentration of any protestant faith.[83] But, by and large, this did not bring Unitarians or Unitarian Universalists into closer contact with African Americans, because as blacks moved into city centers, Unitarian congregations moved to or arose in the suburbs.

In 1920 after he was called to the Universalist Church of the Restoration in Philadelphia, Clinton Lee Scott was told that one African American had been attending regularly for several years. Scott became acquainted with the man and the next Sunday his sister and her husband came. Scott "began including Negro families in parish calling with the result that one Sunday eighteen adults of black skin were in the congregation and their seven children in church school." The members called each other about this situation and at the next board meeting Scott "was closely interrogated." He "reminded the board that the word 'welcome' was on the mat . . . and that Universalists professed to believe in brotherhood." However, Scott never won the congregation over to his point of view.[84] In 1936 Restoration sold its building to an African-American Baptist group and moved eight miles north to Mount Airy, a white suburb. When Rudolph Gelsey arrived in February 1964 to serve the congregation it was "lily white" and members knew nothing about what happened during Scott's three-year ministry.[85]

Suburbs were the seedbed of the Unitarian fellowship movement. The number of fellowships grew from 22 in 1949 to 247 in 1958 and most were in suburbs.[86] In Washington, D.C., Detroit, and Buffalo, established congregations helped seed congregations in nearby suburbs. Large churches in city centers remained (in New York, Boston, Baltimore, Brooklyn, Philadelphia, Albany, Chicago, Oakland, San Francisco, and Los Angeles), but most of these began to struggle. In mid-sized cities many established congregations moved out of the city center.[87] Others, such as the First Unitarian Church of Cleveland, Third Unitarian in Chicago, and the Unitarian Church of Berkeley, split over whether or not to move.

Congregations moved for complex reasons. Their buildings were often old, in disrepair, hard to maintain, and unsuited to the kind of less sermon-centric worship style that was evolving. Some had to relocate because of urban renewal. In Harrisburg, Pennsylvania, the church building was demolished when I-81 ran through the neighborhood. The site that had been the home of the First Unitarian Church of Rochester, New York, was sold in 1959 to make way for Midtown Plaza, the first urban indoor mall in the United States.

Members who had moved to the suburbs had to drive to church, and so parking became an issue in America's increasingly auto-dependent culture. As neighborhoods changed, church members became more afraid of crime. As their membership moved to the suburbs, some congregations felt they had little choice but to move the church buildings there as well.

Rarely was their intent racist. But the effect of their actions was. In 1954 the Commission on Intergroup Relations warned that Unitarian congregations were often located in communities "from which Negroes and other minorities are generally excluded."[88] Despite this, the AUA and UUA continued to systemically nurture congregations in areas where few African Americans lived, failed to develop a growth strategy aimed at African Americans, and acquiesced as congregations moved away from areas where African Americans were concentrated. In addition, the few attempts to start new congregations in African-American communities were under-resourced. In this way, the UUA and its predecessors helped perpetuate racial isolation and discrimination. Aron Gilmartin, the minister of the Mt. Diablo Unitarian Universalist Church in Walnut Creek, California, in a sermon asked his congregation to face this reality: "Are you aware of the almost complete pattern of discrimination in our suburban communities? . . . We have created these communities thus. You may protest that you had nothing to do with making it so. So much the worse: we accepted it then without a protest."[89]

Laile Bartlett, in *Bright Galaxy*, a history of the fellowship movement, framed the situation as a risk to UUs rather than a moral failing:

> While Unitarians engage in social action opposing class and racial discrimination . . . those living in suburbia are increasingly isolated from the objects of their concern. Further, many of the fellowships and new churches are themselves part of suburban developments, and so have a very limited population-arc upon which to draw. In communities having specialized composition, one finds fellowships which are almost totally comprised of engineers, atomic physicists, oil geologists, professors from one educational institution, or employees from a single factory or plant. Does this limited social perspective of the immediate neighborhood or the local religious group constitute a serious hazard?[90]

Bartlett sounded the alarm: we cannot separate the question of location from the reality of UU social isolation and its impact on fellowship culture. Her phrase "objects of their concern" meant African Americans. People with whom you do not have a significant relationship are people you work *for*, not *with*. Selma would turn this on its head. Furthermore, the hazard Bartlett identified can be explored in more depth by investigating the role race played in the fellowships that sprang up in the 1940s, '50s, and '60s. Lay-led fellowships represented the primary source of denominational growth and developed in parallel to Unitarianism's and Unitarian Universalism's deepening concern with race issues.

The Fellowship Movement

In *The Fellowship Movement,* Holley Ulbrich mentions race twice: first while noting that fellowship members shared a passion for social justice, including racial justice, and second while observing that, in working for civil rights, many Southern congregations alienated their white neighbors without attracting new black members.[91] Undoubtedly, fellowships in the Southeast and elsewhere were open to African Americans. Fellowships in Tuscaloosa and Huntsville, Alabama, both founded in 1958, took courageous stands; so did the Chico Unitarian Fellowship in California when it hired Rev. Lewis A. McGee, an African American, in 1961.

In Chico three of the strongest financial supporters of the congregation went to Dick Boeke, who had been serving them as a circuit rider, and asked him to resign so that McGee could fill the position. McGee then became just the second African American to serve as senior minister of a white congregation. Nevertheless, race does not seem to have been a significant issue for fellowships, perhaps because of the neighborhoods in which they established themselves and the way they worshipped.

In 1954 all thirteen Unitarian congregations known to have more than five African-American members existed in urban settings. Meanwhile, the fellowship movement carried Unitarianism into suburbs, exurbs, and university communities in the Midwest, Southwest, West, and Northwest. Some congregations, like those in Hobart, Indiana; Decatur, Illinois; and Appleton, Wisconsin, were in "sundown towns" that forbade Negroes to spend the night—more than ten thousand towns enforced such ordinances, most located outside the South. Other fellowships, such as those in Walnut Creek, California, and Deerfield and Winnetka, Illinois, were founded in segregated suburbs;[92] and some in the Southwest had substantial nearby populations of Native Americans and Mexican Americans but failed to attract members from those groups.[93] Other fellowships sprang up in states like Oregon, which forbade African Americans from living there until 1926, and until 1951 outlawed interracial marriage. White members would have been unaware of this, because it would not have affected them in any obvious way. Many congregations and individual UUs worked on open housing, but in reality the places where fellowships took root reinforced patterns of segregated housing and racial isolation.

When fellowships could reach out to African Americans, other elements of fellowship culture militated against it. They did so in many different ways.

Fellowships were known for their informality; among other things, this meant dressing casually for worship services. The tradition in the black church, often made up primarily of laborers, service providers, and people who had to wear uniforms, was for congregants to wear their Sunday best. To cross the color line to attend a fellowship would have taken courage for African Americans. Upon arriving as well-dressed visitors, they would have felt instantly out of place.

Ulbrich identifies four characteristics that, while not universal, are broadly typical of fellowship culture: resistance to growth, "flat-earth humanism," a particular style of worship, and resistance to authority. Each of these conflicted, generally speaking, with African-American sensibilities.

In 1964, UU congregations were evenly divided about whether congregations should deliberately try to attract members of racial minorities. Some respondents to the Commission on Religion and Race's survey "all but 'scorched the paper,' with such comments as . . . 'we do not proselytize,' 'we do not *seek* any members,' 'we avoid getting minorities on any kind of racial basis.'"[94] This common and longstanding rejection of perceived evangelism was magnified by many fellowships' ambivalence toward growth. The more a fellowship functioned like an extended family and embodied "the closeness of the group" that Lon Ray Call extolled,[95] the more difficult it became for members to welcome and incorporate diversity, and for someone perceived as an outsider to come in—perhaps especially an African American venturing across the color line. As the Commission on Intergroup Relations had warned in 1954, a church that claimed to have an "open door" but made no particular effort to urge minorities to walk through the doorway would simply uphold the status quo. Good intentions were irrelevant if not backed up by statements and actions beyond the fellowship walls. Fellowships' resistance to making such public proclamations hindered their becoming more racially diverse.

During the era when fellowships emerged, humanism was becoming the dominant theological stance in the denomination. Ulbrich uses the tongue-in-cheek phrase "flat-earth humanism" to describe an attitude akin to Christian fundamentalism in its dogmatism and rigidity. Vociferously rejecting God, the humanists were hostile to Christianity and spurned traditional religious language and ritual. This was not a theology or attitude that attracted many African Americans. The 1954 Commission on Intergroup Relations report opined that some African Americans found it difficult to theologically reconcile their ongoing oppression by Christian America with an "expectation that Jesus would be pleading their cause at the throne of grace, bringing them relief and solace,"[96] and hoped they might be attracted to Unitarianism. But as a later survey showed, such doubt did not lead to a complete rejection of Christianity. In fact, a 1989 study by the UUA Commission on Appraisal found that African-American UUs were more likely than others to identify as Christian or Christian-Humanist (28 percent, compared to an overall average of 20 percent) and less likely to call themselves Humanist-Existentialist (36 percent, compared to 54 percent). Only one African-American survey respondent deemed the word *God* irrelevant.[97] As early as 1926, Ethelred Brown had assailed black churches for encouraging believers to transfer their "interest in the here and now to some existence in some other world," and embraced "servile contentment instead of provoking rebellious discontentment."[98] It was this docility, not Christianity itself, that African Americans were now rejecting.

The prevailing theology in a fellowship naturally manifests in its worship life. The 1954 commission report also averred that "to many Negroes the highly emotional content of worship services is objectionable and often embarrassing."[99] To the commission this suggested that a "highly intellectual" service, focusing on a talk and subsequent discussion, might appeal; that seems not to have been the case. Charles Patterson, an African American who became a Unitarian in Fort Wayne after the Second World War, told of his experience in a sermon delivered decades later. He was raised in the African Methodist Episcopal Church, but as an adult was attracted to liberal religion. "It brought me tears of joy to sing in the Gospel Chorus with my mother. . . . I loved the church—but I discovered I [was] having trouble with the theology . . . [yet] I did not wish to lose all of that warmth—all of that joy of expression." Patterson resolved his predicament by making "peace with both" and finding "glory in ambiguity."[100]

African Americans did not want to reject emotional elevation, or space in which to grieve, or a message of hope and solace. They were seeking a different kind of emotional expression, not the absence of emotion. Survey results indicate that arid intellectuality did not appeal to, nor meet the needs of, African-American UUs. In both the 1967 survey by the Committee on Goals and the 1989 survey by the Commission on Appraisal, 74 percent of Unitarian Universalists ranked "intellectual stimulation" as the most important aspect of worship. However, for African-American UUs, what was most important was "celebrating common values." This option was ranked most important by 69 percent of African-American respondents in 1989, followed by "hope," "fellowship," and "music." These all point to the importance of affect in worship, and they all preceded "intellectual stimulation," chosen by only 47 percent of African-American respondents. The 27-percentage-point difference between African Americans and all respondents regarding "intellectual stimulation" was the largest such difference in the survey. The next largest was regarding "hope"—its ranking among African Americans was 23 percentage points higher than among all respondents. This makes sense considering the African-American experience in the United States. Add to that the confession made in *The Free Church in a Changing World*: "We can scarcely boast that we are a singing people." What, then, did Unitarian Universalism have to offer to African Americans? More often than not, those who ventured into a UU fellowship found an intellectual club struggling with an ambivalent relationship to worship. Even when the sermon was pertinent, little else affirmed the black experience and eased an African-American newcomer into feeling at home.

Resistance to authority in fellowship culture kept African Americans away as well. On the positive side, fellowships empowered the laity, placing the clear location of spiritual authority within the community, rather than in the clergy or denomination. This fueled an engagement with social action. On the other hand, as Ulbrich writes, "Resistance to authority often extends to distrust of denominational leadership. . . . Many fellowship members express a mixture of disdain, ignorance, and indifference to the Unitarian Universalist Association."[101] In the black church, the situation was the opposite. From early in the African-American experience, the church was the one place meant for and controlled by black folks. Congregants held ministers and deacons in high regard. Accustomed to being treated with deference, some African-American ministers who later transferred to the UUA ran aground on the shoals of UU anti-authoritarianism. Anti-clericalism and the insistence on congregational autonomy, which characterized fellowships, were foreign to most African Americans. Indeed, the urban churches to which they gravitated tended to have strong ministers: John Haynes Holmes, Jenkin Lloyd Jones, and Clarence Skinner—followed later by the equally prophetic A. Powell Davies, Tracy Pullman, Stephen Fritchman, Donald Harrington, and Leslie Pennington.

The fellowship movement—in breaking with tradition, in its creativity and emphasis on freedom, in carrying liberal religion into environs it had not entered before, and in today accounting for a significant number of UUs—invigorated Unitarian Universalism and, Call claimed, saved the denomination. But in significant ways, fellowships were less attractive to racial minorities than traditional congregations. Fellowships represent one more example of how Unitarianism and Unitarian Universalism promoted principles of openness, tolerance, and integration while at the same time fostering behavior that ran counter to those aspirations.

Boards, Committees, and Commissions

Universalism's relationship with African Americans dates back to its origin in North America, but with one exception: no African American is known to have represented the denomination or served on any of its state or national bodies. Unitarians fared only slightly better. In 1947 it passed a resolution titled "Toward an Unsegregated Church and an Unsegregated Society" which specifically urged the denomination to examine its practices regarding membership, church administration, and staff employment. Despite this, it is difficult to identify more than a handful of African Americans who served on the national boards, commissions, or committees of the AUA.

In 1937 Jeffrey Worthington Campbell attended the International Religious Fellowship conference in England as a delegate from the Young People's Christian Union. At the conference, he was elected president of the fellowship. He didn't learn until forty years later that an effort had been made to draft another American delegate to run against him. Recognizing that the effort was motivated by racial prejudice, the candidate who had been propositioned refused.[102]

In 1952 Howard Thurman and Dr. Errold D. Collymore, DDS, were appointed to the AUA Commission on Intergroup Relations. In 1954 the commission recommended that the new Council of

Liberal Churches (Unitarian-Universalist) (CLC), a transitional body, should be interracial and include a specialist in interracial relations on its staff. Notably, the commission did not recommend recruiting African Americans as volunteers or members of regional or continental boards and committees, even though all eighteen members of the CLC governing board were white.

Collymore, however, did serve on the AUA's board of trustees from 1954 to 1957 and was the first person of color to do so. In 1959, when the six study commissions that went on to write *The Free Church in a Changing World* were established, Howard Thurman was the only African American among the sixty-five commissioners. Two years later, at the time of the merger, there was no black presence on either board. The lone African American sitting at the national level was Marcella McGee, the wife of Rev. Lewis McGee. She served on the joint board of the Alliance of Unitarian Women and the Association of Universalist Women (combined in 1963 as the Unitarian Universalist Women's Federation).

In 1956 the *Christian Register* surveyed 514 Unitarian congregations. Of the 287 that replied, 80 had African-American members, and 49 had African Americans serving as officers. This means nearly 10 percent of Unitarian congregations had African-American members holding leadership positions.[103] Indeed, if the sample was representative, the overall percentage could have been higher. These individuals included some of the most highly educated and accomplished people in America. By 1961 several congregations claimed memberships that were as much as 10 percent African American. African Americans served on congregation boards and as presidents; they were judges, dentists, educators, scientists (including two who participated in the development of the atomic bomb), social workers, and administrators, as well as postal workers like Nathan J. Johnson. Johnson joined University Church in Seattle in 1946 and went on to serve two terms as its president.[104] Nonetheless, as late as 1964, the list of those appointed to committees by the UUA board seems to include no African Americans, except that the Commission on Religion and

Race initially had five African Americans and one Hispanic among its ten members. The first African American to serve on the UUA board was Judge Wade H. McCree, who had served on the board of the First Unitarian Universalist Church of Detroit, and who was elected to national office in the wake of Selma.

Despite the high caliber of black leadership in UU congregations, before 1963 no one except Howard Thurman, Errold Collymore, and Marcella McGee had been recruited into national leadership. Whatever formal or informal networking process led individuals to be chosen to serve on the governing bodies of the UCA, AUA, and UUA, African Americans were—whether intentionally or otherwise—not included.

The composition of the board (and of the field staff of the twenty-one districts) during the Greeley administration makes it clear that, despite the presence of three women on the board, Greeley and the "old boys' network" were in control.[105] Once again, while their intent was not racist, the effect of their actions was so. The continuing omission of African Americans, probably unnoticed, gives insight into Dana McLean Greeley. He sat *ex officio* on the nominating committee[106] and also participated in the annual appointment of Board committee members. Yet not until eight years into his eleven-year term as president was an African American nominated for an elected position. His inaction suggests that until late in his presidency Greeley did not see the need to promote African-American leadership within the UUA, even though it was identified as an issue of concern in *The Free Church in a Changing World*. Nor did he seem to understand the consequence of not doing so. The absence of African Americans on the UUA's boards, committees, and commissions meant that any expertise, insight, or guidance African Americans could have contributed never made it to the table. African Americans were largely without a voice in the administration's discussions and decision making, nor did they hold influential positions on UUA committees and commissions.

In an era when race represented America's most pressing domestic issue, the UUA was not attuned to the subject and not prepared for what was to come. But leadership in a denomination comes not only from its governing bodies but also from its ministry.

Ministerial Settlement

The Universalists escaped addressing the issue of ministerial settlement as long as they had missions in Virginia. Thomas Wise began working with the first Joseph Jordan in Norfolk, Virginia, around 1889 and then, in 1894, began a mission school in nearby Suffolk. In 1902 Joseph Fletcher Jordan was recruited by Quillen Shinn and trained at the Canton Theological School with Virginia in mind.

In August 1911 Jordan met with denominational leaders at Murray Grove and proposed a way to help Universalism grow across the South. These leaders included William H. McGlauflin, the general superintendent; Frederick A. Bisbee, the editor of the *Universalist Leader*; the presidents of Tufts and St. Lawrence; and John van Schaick, minister of the Church of Our Father in Washington. Jordan proposed building a theological training center and school in Suffolk for African-American Universalist ministers and lay leaders. The project won enthusiastic support, except from van Schaick, who voiced the lone dissenting opinion. That fall and winter, as Jordan traveled from congregation to congregation, the *Leader* chronicled his progress and called for contributions to support his efforts. It produced meager results, even after McGlauflin wrote a special appeal. Only $1,491 was raised of the $6,000 sought, enough for an addition to the existing school, but that was all; and when Jordan died in May 1929 there was no one to replace him.

That same fall, Jeffrey Worthington Campbell, a member of the Universalist Church in Nashua, New Hampshire, entered St. Lawrence University. In 1935 he graduated from its Canton Theological School, and the challenge of settling him commenced. Energetic and outspoken, Campbell served as president of the International Religious Fellowship from 1937 to 1939, while running for governor of Massachusetts in 1938 as a Socialist. Unable to find a settlement, he left the country in 1939 to study in England. Not only couldn't the Universalists find a settlement for Campbell, three years later they couldn't settle his white brother-in-law, Francis Davis. In a letter to the editor in the *Christian Leader* in April 1942, a dismayed Dean Atwood asked how it was that, with ministers in short supply, a settlement could not be found for "one of the best equipped and qualified men we have ever sent forth. . . . We think there is something wrong with the Universalist Church if it cannot find a place for a man of the parts and spirit of Francis Davis."[107] A position for him was never found.

With Campbell in England throughout the war and Davis working for the Boston Urban League, the issue of settlement receded. Then late in 1954, perhaps because Campbell had returned, the UCA Department of Ministry surveyed Universalist congregations in order to determine which ones would consider settling a female or African-American minister. Twelve congregations replied that they would consider a woman and twenty-five that they would consider an African American.[108] One response came from Gwendolen Willis, daughter of Rev. Olympia Brown and president of the congregation in Racine, Wisconsin. She wrote, "Women were never not allowed to preach in our church, and as for negroes, they could be members, but would not be called to fill our pulpit as that would further complicate our foremost problem, that of survival." The congregation's trustees concurred.[109]

Among the Unitarians, the AUA Commission on Appraisal had not mentioned race or diversity in its 1936 report *Unitarians Face a New Age*. But in 1937 Jeff Campbell received ministerial fellowship as a Unitarian, and so they faced the challenge of settling him as well. Campbell said later that whenever he dropped in at 25 Beacon Street "Frederick May Eliot would start making excuses as soon as he saw me."[110] In 1942 the AUA's "Resolution on Race Relations" explicitly called on the association to practice the principles of brotherhood. As the war came to an end and a handful of African Americans began training for the Unitarian ministry, it became even clearer that the AUA could not ignore the issue of their settlement. Nevertheless, although the AUA Commission on

Planning and Review mentioned the issue in its initial report in 1947, the topic seems not to have surfaced again before the commission was dissolved in 1954.

In December 1945 Alvin Neeley Cannon, former Tuskegee student and graduate of the University of Chicago, received a BTh from Starr King School for the Ministry. On the occasion of his graduation the speaker—probably the school's dean, Edward W. Ohrenstein—spoke directly to Cannon saying, "you, [as] the representative of a minority people, . . . are essential to that which makes America distinctive among the nations. America fought a civil war to make herself internally free. . . . America fought another war to make the world safe for democracy. In the present conflict drawn now to its close [the challenge before us is to] make democracy safe everywhere for minorities." Ohrenstein concluded his address to the graduating class with a biblical reference: "It may therefore come to pass, as in the ancient East, that a minority, having known sorrow and become acquainted with grief, will transform the larger world, recalling to the larger soci ety its own ancient ideals, and saving that which could not save itself."[111]

These prophetic words foreshadowed the struggle that would unfold in the United States and in liberal religion over the next twenty years and more. Soon the difficulties confronting Cannon became evident. On January 24, 1945, he appeared before the Fellowship Committee and was denied fellowship; the committee decided it was "unfair to grant fellowship because [sic] no opportunity for Negro minister."[112] Nonetheless, that spring Cannon went to Des Moines, Iowa, to help the minister there, Grant Butler, start an African-American Unitarian congregation. In 1940 Des Moines had a population of 160,000 and was home to several colleges, but the black population was only 6,400—which itself should have indicated a low chance of success. In addition, Cannon reportedly did not hit it off with leaders sympathetic to Unitarianism in the African-American community. The attempt failed, and Cannon disappeared from the Unitarian scene.

In November 1948, nine ministers serving in the South gathered in the Magnolia Conference and issued a statement challenging practices that "stultify the whites and repress the Negro": "As ministers of southern churches we recommend that our churches re-examine their constitutions and present policies . . . and recommend that our brethren in the North do likewise. At the time of the selection of a minister, a positive commitment to these principles and objectives should be made by both the minister and the congregation."[113] A few months later, twenty-six ministers at the mid-winter conference at Meadville Lombard Theological School petitioned Frederick May Eliot, challenging the AUA to find a settlement for Eugene Sparrow, who was due to graduate from Harvard Divinity School in June. Eliot and those in the Department of Ministry, working as they did alongside Sparrow's wife, Donna, at the AUA, would have been reminded of his position every day. Nevertheless, not until six months after his graduation, and after he had been appointed dean of men at Texas College and had moved his family to Texas, did one of the many churches the AUA courted express a willingness to consider him. The Church of Our Father in Detroit agreed to put him forward as a candidate for director of youth activities. Excitement on one hand met resistance on the other, and turned to acrimony in June when the vote to call him was defeated. Ten years passed before Sparrow, who remained involved in Unitarianism, was settled as director of field services for the Midwest Unitarian Universalist Conference, only to have that position eliminated by the conference two years later following the consolidation of Unitarianism and Universalism. Amid the politics that marked the transition, the sole African American holding an administrative position in the UUA was left out in the cold.[114]

In December 1949, as the unwillingness of any Unitarian congregation to consider Sparrow became increasingly obvious, Edward Redman, the minister in Ann Arbor who had befriended Sparrow, wrote to Frederick May Eliot, "If Eugene Sparrow is now where he is, it is my fault. I must plead guilty for having given a young student encouragement in the decision to sacrifice some years of his life in preparation for the liberal ministry. Both of us knew that the way would not be easy for him, but both of us had great confidence in the integrity, the vision, and the moral earnestness of Unitarianism."[115] Just over two years later, probably in response to Sparrow's experience in Detroit, the AUA board voted to discuss with some congregations the giving of "unbiased consideration to Negro candidates for pulpits."[116] Having read about the matter in the *Register*, Charles Mason Jr. wrote to Frederick May Eliot to say that he was disturbed by the implication "that some churches, at least, have shown indications of discrimination against Negro candidates for pulpits. It seems rather inconsistent for a church to consider itself a member of the Unitarian family and yet fail to follow [sic] 'fair employment' principle when employing a minister. Selection, it seems to me, should be based on ability —not race." Eliot replied, "To date the record is one of repeated effort to find such a practical solution without any real measure of success . . . but the record also testifies to the widespread feeling among our people that what has thus far been accomplished is very far indeed from satisfactory."[117]

This exchange seems to have been the catalyst for the formation of the Commission on Intergroup Relations. Mason anonymously gave the AUA $2,000 toward the ill-defined project of discussing Negro candidacy with congregations, which the AUA board had handed off to the Denominational Planning Council. Eliot responded that he was not sure what the next step should be, but that he wanted to meet with Mason as soon as possible and then wait and see what emerged from the resolutions going before the 1952 General Assembly. At that meeting, the assembly passed a resolution titled "Racial Discrimination and Exclusion" by unanimous vote, urging churches and conferences "to promote an intensive educational program to the end that the practices of racial discrimination and exclusion be eliminated." The board then voted to appoint a commission "to make a study of the relation of the Unitarian movement to racial discrimination and segregation."[118] Eliot and Mason were among its nine members.

In 1951 Jeff Campbell returned from teaching in England and was hired to teach at the Putney School in Vermont. Denominational leaders had found no settlement for him, but still talked of possibilities. Perhaps he could work in Suffolk. Perhaps he could take over the Harlem church when Ethelred Brown retired. In September 1953, Lewis McGee, who in 1948 had been the founding minister of the predominantly African-American Free Religious Fellowship in Chicago, left to take the position of field secretary for the American Humanist Association, and Alfred McClung Lee, chair of the Commission on Intergroup Relations, suggested to Grant Butler, who was working at AUA headquarters in Boston, that "Campbell looks like an excellent possibility [to replace McGee]. The fact that he is married to a white woman would, in my estimation, be an asset in the FRF."[119] Lee and Butler also considered Maurice Dawkins, who since 1948 had been the minister of education at the Community Church of New York. He declined to apply. Instead he was called by the People's Independent Church of Los Angeles, said to be the oldest and second-largest community church in America. Finally Benjamin Richardson, an African-American 1939 graduate of Harvard Divinity School, was granted fellowship and called to the FRF in 1954.

When the commission issued its report in the April 1954 *Christian Register,* it made two recommendations on ministry. The first addressed congregations: the commission insisted that "Unitarian churches should be 'color blind' in their consideration of candidates for their ministry. There is no place in liberal religion for 'Negro churches' or 'white churches.' Negroes should be trained for the Unitarian ministry and then given opportunities to serve in Unitarian churches." The second addressed the AUA: "In the use of its funds and placement services, the Association should do all that it can to make the Unitarian clergy more substantially interracial."[120]

The next opportunity to settle an African American came in spring 1957. Lewis McGee was asked to candidate for the pulpit in Flint, Michigan; it seemed like a possible fit. Four years earlier, the congregation had told the Commission on Intergroup Relations that it had seven African-American members, including a board member and the president of the choir. The former minister, John H. Morgan, was an activist who had served on the boards of the local NAACP and Urban League. McGee spent the second week of April in Flint, and when a special church meeting was convened to, among other matters, vote on his candidacy, the vote was 34 for and 41 against. The meeting went on to approve all the resolutions that were to be presented at the upcoming AUA annual meeting, including one that encouraged congregations to work against housing discrimination.

The vote went against calling McGee for complex reasons. McGee was a humanist; the church was Congregational and Unitarian. Morgan was later told that some Congregationalist members, who seldom attended the services, "came out of the woodwork to vote against McGee."[121] The uneasy relationship between the two camps only ended months later, when the Congregationalists departed. The congregation was also in the midst of a building campaign, which elevated the general anxiety level. In addition to the congregational dynamics, racial tensions in Flint were high. Its population was approaching 200,000, and an increasing number of African Americans were arriving to work for General Motors and pushing into Flint's segregated neighborhoods. Cross burnings had begun. But the facts remain: the Pulpit Committee resigned *en masse* after the failed vote, and less than three months later the congregation called Rev. Karel F. Botermans, a thirty-four-year-old Dutch immigrant, fresh out of Meadville Lombard. The whole affair screams of racism. Some said the congregation wasn't ready for a black minister;[122] the same had been said seven years earlier after Sparrow's failed candidacy in Detroit.

"Not ready" is also what Dana McLean Greeley told African-American seminarian David H. Eaton. During his second year at Boston University School of Theology, Eaton approached Greeley, the new president of the AUA, to inquire about the possibility of serving a Unitarian congregation. Greeley said, "Personally, I would love to have you, but I am afraid we could not settle you."

Years later, Eaton said he was not offended but took it as "honest advice because in 1957 racism was alive and well in America."[123]

Greeley was not alone in his assessment. In 1958, while Ralph Stutzman was serving as the acting minister at All Souls (Unitarian) in Washington, D.C., a former classmate from Oberlin Theological Seminary—an African American—called him. The classmate felt that he could not continue in his own tradition and wanted to talk to Stutzman about the possibility of transferring to Unitarianism. Stutzman called the Department of Ministry and the director Leon C. Fay told him, "Ralph, unless he is truly truly exceptional, don't encourage him. We will just break his heart." Perhaps that is what Isaiah Jenkins had realized as well. Granted preliminary fellowship in 1956, he resigned it after only one year. The settlement situation was hardly better for women. When, in 1955, Greta W. Crosby approached Frederick May Eliot to express her desire to abandon her career in law for ministry, he told her, "It's as hard to be a woman in the Unitarian ministry as to be a Negro."[124]

In 1958 the situation of African-American ministers was dire and Fay, facing the necessity of settling two of them, knew it. William R. Jones was about to graduate from Harvard Divinity School, and Lewis McGee was still in search after his failed candidacy in Flint. Robert H. Schacht, minister of the First Unitarian Church of Providence, Rhode Island, was a member of the AUA Fellowship Committee, which had just granted Jones fellowship. He went to his congregation's Prudential Committee with a proposal to hire Jones as assistant minister. The congregation had hired new graduates before, but never a black one. It was the congregation's decision to make, but both Schacht and the Prudential Committee knew that the entire denomination would be watching. A few members resisted, but the majority voted for Jones, and called him as their assistant minister.

That same year, Lewis McGee answered the call to serve as associate minister of the First Unitarian Church of Los Angeles, a left-wing congregation led by one of the most radical Unitarian ministers, Stephen Fritchman. McGee left three years later to serve the Chico Unitarian Fellowship in California, marking the first time a congregation had knowingly called an African American to be its senior minister. (Clarence Bertrand Thompson was the first African American to be called. When the Peabody, Massachusetts, congregation hired him in 1906, it appears that they thought he was white.)[125] But not until 1969, when David H. Eaton accepted the call to All Souls Church (Unitarian) in Washington, D.C., did an African American fill a major Unitarian Universalist pulpit.

Settling African-American ministers in these two overwhelmingly white denominations was a Sisyphean task, and this small success took more than a generation to achieve. In 1927, when Lewis McGee was first attracted to Unitarianism, he was told he would need to bring his own congregation. In 1930, Harry V. Richardson, a student at Harvard Divinity School, was refused fellowship. In 1939, Jeff Campbell gave up and spent over a decade in Great Britain. In 1945–46, the AUA tried to found an African-American congregation in Des Moines. They identified possible funding sources and the black professionals who might be drawn to join; the catch was finding an African-American minister to lead it. Alvin Cannon was about to graduate and available, but the effort's backers in the AUA did not feel "confident enough in Al to request him to undertake a new movement of this kind."[126] Correspondence indicates that the AUA searched for other candidates. Failing to find one, they hired Cannon, and their concerns proved warranted; the effort failed. "I was wrong about Al," wrote Grant Butler. "He hasn't the experience and the ability to make the personal contacts necessary to build a new group."[127]

When Maurice Dawkins became minister of education at the Community Church of New York in 1948, the congregation—having been integrated for nearly forty years—was ready to accept him. Sparrow's and McGee's track records, before and after their failed candidacies, indicate their suitability, yet Detroit rejected Sparrow in 1950 and Flint rejected McGee in 1957, even though both congregations were integrated. Repeatedly the AUA turned promising young ministers away, and only by extraordinary means did it manage to settle William R. Jones.

In Jim Crow America most white Universalist and Unitarian congregations, despite proclaiming brotherhood, refused to consider calling an African-American minister, or even a white man married to a black woman, like Francis Davis. In their deliberations denominational officials, struggling to address this moral challenge, didn't understand that some of their plans could not work and that they were sending African-American ministers to fill positions for which they weren't suited and in which they couldn't succeed. Sending Jeff Campbell, born and bred in New England, to the Universalist mission in Virginia would not have worked; neither could Campbell, a boisterous Socialist, follow the gentle, staid army chaplain McGee into the FRF, a start-up on Chicago's South Side. Equally inappropriately, the Department of Ministry asked Dawkins, who was serving the large, thriving Community Church off Park Avenue in New York, to consider the small, underfunded FRF. Sparrow reported that Harlem was the only place to which the Department of Ministry would recommend him. "My God," he told a colleague, "they'd kill me there."[128] And both Campbell and Ben Richardson, after speaking at the Harlem Unitarian Church, realized Ethelred Brown had no intention of retiring, nor did anyone seem to consider the potential for the culture clash of an African American leading a largely Caribbean congregation. Good intentions notwithstanding, denominational officials understood neither these ministers nor the particularities of their situations. To them, Negro America was a black box, and most often they must have thought, "He's one of them," and no further.

In 1935, a caricature of a black-faced bellboy with bulbous lips appeared in the *State Messenger of the Illinois Universalist Convention*. The caption read, "Call for Mr. Delegate," and the bellboy was saying, "Yassuh. De Publicity Chairman done tole me to be extry special careful in deliverin' this here notice to prosperective delegates to the convention you all is havin'. I don't know nothin' about it but dat program sure does look mighty awful interestin'." In December 1964, the announcement of a fund-raiser in the *First Parish News* in Framingham, Massachusetts, appeared below the title "What Type of Slave Do You Need?" In March 1965, while the world watched the events in Selma, a follow-up to that announcement appeared: "Slaves Waiting to Hear from Owners: Some of the slaves purchased at the Slave Auction in January have not yet heard the cracking of the whip." It is fanciful to believe that UUs were an enlightened cultural anomaly in America. Given the overwhelmingly Euro-American ethos they embodied, they could not have stood above their times regarding race.

Delving into the contrasts between the actions and attitudes of the Universalists and Unitarians and the principles they proclaimed lays bare the deep-seated, pervasive, and unconscious culture of racism within both individuals and institutions during the decades preceding Selma:

- Hymnals were devoid of worship materials that reflected the African-American experience.
- Black life and culture were rarely depicted in the religious education curricula, and African-American achievements were not acknowledged.
- Congregations were routinely located at a distance from black population centers and were averse to calling African-American ministers.
- Fellowships tended to be anti-clerical, vehemently humanist, intellectual cliques located in suburbia, and thus did not align well with the sensibilities of African Americans seeking a liberal religious community.
- African Americans rarely served on denominational governing bodies.

Unitarians and Universalists celebrated an exclusively Euro-American worldview that was implicitly racist, while convinced that their congregations were open and accepting. Unable to imagine anything else, they championed *assimilation* while calling it *integration*. Although they were good people with noble intentions, these dichotomies and tensions advanced the disconnect between both denominations' *espoused values* and their *values in practice*. The ideals, aspirations, and values they proclaimed were rooted in their belief in freedom, tolerance (in the form of acceptance), and human fellowship (universalism), while their behavior was conventional, blinkered, aloof, and, beneath its cosmopolitan veneer, apprehensive.

The African American was a mystery to most Unitarians and Universalists, yet many, in the words of the Commission on Intergroup Relations, thought they knew "all about Negroes because they have had a sequence of Negro employees."[129] Prior to the 1960s most members of both denominations had little contact with African Americans as equals, knew nothing substantive about their culture, and the awareness that they should be concerned with racial injustice and inequality was only slowly dawning. Universalists and Unitarians naturally and routinely embraced contemporary mores.

In truth, most African Americans had heard of neither Universalism nor Unitarianism. The revulsion UUs felt toward evangelism, reinforced by an unwillingness to persistently and unequivocally proclaim that people of all colors were welcome, guaranteed it would continue that way. How often were the few African Americans who were drawn by the message of liberal religion to enter a congregation welcomed with insidious slights and jaundiced assumptions? How many were told, as three black visitors were in Louisville in 1959, that "they were welcome 'but' that they would make some [people] uncomfortable"?[130] How many never returned? Unitarian and Universalist behavior was shaped by white discomfort: ignorance and anxiety about people and cultures that seemed different from their own; an inability to step too far outside cultural norms; and a fear of ceding control, which venturing into unfamiliar situations would have required.

In their complacence, Unitarians and Universalists unwittingly continued to support American apartheid. The liberals' version was just white supremacy–lite. How, then, can this behavior be reconciled with the Unitarian Universalist response to Selma?

HOW THE WORLD CHANGED AND HOW
UNITARIAN UNIVERSALISM CHANGED WITH IT

Unitarian Universalism's impulse to hold African Americans at arm's length seems incompatible with the magnitude of the UU response to Martin Luther King Jr.'s call for clergy to come to Selma. But in fact, in Selma the Unitarian Universalists' *values in practice* snapped into alignment with their *espoused values*. Something must have changed to account for this.

The global struggle to preserve freedom and democracy against fascism was implicitly anti-racist, and so the war accelerated a cultural change that spurred Unitarians and Universalists to live lives more consonant with liberal religion's principles. Necessity drove this behavioral reversal: for the war to be won, race relations had to change. Prior to the Second World War a prophetic minority heralded a shift. This led the transformation of Unitarian Universalism's values in practice toward closer alignment with its espoused values. The most influential of these figures taught social ethics in the seminaries Unitarians and Universalists attended. Their students would join the institutional networks that worked for racial justice; and within these networks, Euro-American UUs began building relationships with African Americans.

The Second World War

"The war we have dreaded for so long has broken out," began a letter from the American Unitarian Association's board of directors in the October 26, 1939, *Christian Register*.[131] The United States wouldn't declare war on the Axis powers until December 1941, but the AUA was a continental organization and Canada, as part of the Commonwealth, was now at war. In the months leading up to the outbreak of hostilities *Register* editorials, articles, and letters had been full of foreboding and division. Contributors repeatedly voiced the need to combat anti-Semitism abroad and at home: "The time to put on the brakes is before you have too much momentum. Anti-Semitism in America is already beyond the point where the brake ought to have been employed."[132] Other writers decried what had happened to Czech Unitarians since the handover of the Sudetenland to Hitler at the 1938 Munich Conference. Some supported intervention, some opposed it, and some advocated pacifism under all circumstances. Their arguments filled the "Family Circle"—the letters section of the *Register*. Aware of these strong differences of opinion, in its October letter the AUA board counseled its congregations to "stand like a great rock for the elementary principles of spiritual liberty and the ultimate sovereignty of individual conscience."[133]

In the years between 1938 and 1941, mentions of race in the *Register* focused largely on anti-Semitism. "Suppose the Jews WERE Wiped Out" proclaimed the headline of an editorial on March 1, 1940; on April 15 an article appeared called "Can the Ghetto Return?" The degree to which Jews were seen as a race is evident in the 1953 survey conducted by the Commission on Intergroup Relations. Asked about "racial minorities," congregations mentioned Jews along with the French, Italians, and Scandinavians. The First Unitarian Church of Philadelphia reported "one person of colored ancestry" and twelve of "Jewish extraction"; the only racial minority mentioned by the First Unitarian Church of Denver was "Jewish." Even in 1963, when the Commission on Religion and Race inquired, "thirty-seven different groups were named."[134] The homogenization of these groups into "white" was still in process; before the Second World War, American Jews were far from being considered white.

To some, the similarities between the situation of the Jews in Germany and of African Americans in the United States were obvious. Clare and Winnie Pineo, members of the Winthrop, New York, congregation where Jeffrey Campbell had served as student minister, made the comparison in the letter they sent to the *Christian Leader* in response to John van Schaick's attack on the marriage of Marguerite and Francis Davis. "We can but conclude from your article that you are willing to place limitations upon human liberty such as are paralleled in Germany by Jewish persecution," they wrote. "Is it too much to expect that in times when freedom of every kind suffers from narrow and bigoted attacks, the Christian Church should concentrate its valuable organs of propaganda upon spreading doctrines of true brotherhood of race and nation, instead of wasting time on small and malicious attacks upon idealistic individuals?"[135]

After the Great Depression had exposed the shortcomings of *laissez-faire* capitalism, people sought alternatives. The economic collapse tainted the Anglo-American liberal approach and to an extent discredited democracy. This provided an opening for National Socialism, which attracted some Americans. Its appeal largely ended with *Kristallnacht* in November 1938. In the aftermath of such violent anti-Semitism, the nature of Nazi ideology became clear and support for it all but vanished. From that point on, America had no choice but to define itself as against all that Hitler stood for.

This stance was nearly universal; it resounded in pulpits, press, and popular culture. The comic book superheroine Wonder Woman appeared in 1941; in the comic's inaugural issue the goddess Aphrodite, Wonder Woman's patron, sent her to fight for the Allies with the declaration "American Liberty and Freedom must be preserved. . . . America, the last citadel of democracy, and of equal rights for women, needs your help."[136] Frederick May Eliot declared much the same. Unitarians, he said, "stand in full commitment to the overthrow of totalitarian power wherever it seeks to dominate free people."[137] It became increasingly evident that the term *free people* applied to all, including women and African Americans.

With the United States entry into the war on December 8, 1941, the conversation about race broadened. In February 1942 the article "Racism vs. Americanism" by Donald G. Lothrop, minister of the Community Church of Boston, appeared in the *Register*. Lothrop began by describing the difficulties African Americans faced in finding work in the defense industry. He went on to equate racism with Nazism, to call on churches to form action committees, and to encourage people to work with the Urban League and the NAACP. "It would be the supreme tragedy of our day," he concluded, "if in defeating Hitler upon the field of battle, we should give him victory at home, in our domestic habits, and in our hearts."[138]

Lothrop was not alone in seeing this connection. The African-American press had already begun promoting the phrase "Victory at Home and Abroad," and in the black community everyone knew what "Double V" meant. In June the *Register* returned to this theme in the article "A Stake in Democratic America." Written by Malcolm S. MacLean, the chair of the President's Fair Employment Practice Commission (FEPC), it began by calling for "victory at home and abroad" and went on to elaborate: "Unless we strengthen our democratic foundations here, we may win the military victory abroad, but lose the home front and have to fight another war or wars. To have security at home, we must make America secure for all our people."[139]

In 1942 Samuel Atkins Eliot preached a sermon "From Slavery to F.E.P.C." Unlike Lothrop, Eliot was anything but a radical, yet in this sermon he sounded like one: "Certainly ours is an ironic situation. We cherish in this land the same demon of racism that we vigorously condemn in the Nazi creed. Democracy is denied in its own house. I heard just now a virile young American saying that he wanted to knock hell out of the Japanese—well, I sometimes feel that way too, but I'd like also to knock hell out of some snobbish, narrow-minded, tyrannical, hypocritical Americans."[140]

Linking racism with fascism became a powerful tool for those fighting segregation. James Luther Adams, who began teaching at Meadville Lombard Theological School in 1936, recounts that in 1942 he and his wife, Margaret, were involved in integrating the University of Chicago Laboratory Schools that their daughters attended. After several parents circulated a petition discussing equal opportunity and calling for the school's integration, all the parents met. One speaker contended that allowing African-American children admittance would impinge on the fundamental American right of parents to "choose the associates of their children, namely, white children." In response, Adams rose and explained that he had recently been in Germany and needed a clarification. "I did not believe that this speaker held to a Nazi conception of white supremacy," Adams said. As he recalls, the man jumped up and threatened to "knock me flat on the floor [and] immediately, the people who had been associated with him turned against him and treated him like a leper."[141] That ended the discussion, and the Lab Schools were integrated. In the environment of the University of Chicago, at least, the debate was clear. Nazis stood for totalitarianism and racism. America was the protector of freedom, democracy, and equality.

Communists, both during and following the war, relished pointing out that inequality and racism were endemic to America. This strengthened Communism's appeal while compromising America's international image as defender of freedom. This, plus the need to utilize all the country's domestic human resources, forced the Roosevelt administration to begin the process of change. That change meant fair employment practices that opened positions in industry to African Americans and women. It put nearly a million black GIs, plus Native and Mexican Americans, in uniform. It saw the creation of the Tuskegee Airmen and the Nisei 442nd Regimental Combat Team, made up of second-generation Japanese Americans. The latter unit would go on to become the most decorated of any in the Second World War. African Americans also participated in the development of the atomic bomb. The 129,000 people who worked on the Manhattan Project included black laborers at the Hanford Reservation, where the polonium was produced; and at least eighteen African-American scientists filled positions in labs in Chicago and New York. The war forced America to more fully utilize its resources, including using African Americans in ways never before open to them.

Alongside the Double V lay a double dark irony—these dark years gave dark-skinned men opportunities that they would not otherwise have had. These defenders of democracy returned with changed expectations and a new confidence. Forged at a terrible price, their expanded vision gave momentum to the emerging civil rights movement. America had changed, and despite massive resistance, the nation's only option was to move forward toward equality of rights and opportunities. There could be no returning to the Jim Crow world that had existed before the war. But that dystopia didn't simply vanish; it suffered through prolonged and violent death throes. The need to refurbish the American ideology had been forced upon the nation by the Nazis and kept alive by the Cold War. But in Selma, Alabama, the old ideology was thriving when events made everyone aware of the change.

On the evening of Sunday, March 7, 1965, ABC interrupted the broadcast of *Judgment at Nuremberg*, a drama about the war-crime trials in Nazi Germany, to cut to footage of the vicious attack by Alabama state troopers and local vigilantes on six hundred black citizens of Selma. The connection couldn't be missed. Ethel Gorman, the president of the Unitarian Church of Birmingham, wrote that on Tuesday night, "before we got down to business, we expressed our horror at the scenes in Selma which we had seen on TV. We felt shame for our state as well as pity for the victims; and fear because law enforcement officers acted like Nazi Storm Troopers."[142] Carl E. Ulrich, minister of Thomas Jefferson Unitarian Church in Louisville, Kentucky, made a similar comparison in a letter to his brother, who had disapproved of his going to Selma:

> The tactic of the white power structure there, is to instill fear in
> the hearts of the Negro . . . and this has been the tactic for the
> last hundred years . . . and we in the rest of the country have

just ignored it. But after it was so vividly shown to us . . . when everyone saw it clearly on TV . . . and with the temper of the country . . . it was almost impossible to ignore it.

It is hard to believe, but the fact is that in Alabama there is a police state [and] the troopers are not there to protect the Negro.[143]

In March 1965 the twentieth anniversary of the end of the Second World War was at hand. The trauma of the war years, having touched nearly every adult, was easily evoked. Most remembered the sacrifices made, and many were aware of the consequences of inaction in the face of tyranny. Only in this context does what happened in Selma make sense.

Cultural Currents

Throughout the 1950s, religious liberals across the country became increasingly involved in the issues of fair housing, equal access, and integration. The backdrop for this was an American society undergoing a tumultuous metamorphosis. In June 1941 President Roosevelt, pressed by A. Philip Randolph's threat to lead a march of 50,000 African Americans on Washington, issued Executive Order 8802, establishing the FEPC; it aimed to promote full employment and to maximize available talent to win the war. However, since the war effort also demanded solidarity, the legal assault on Jim Crow laws was not made until the war had ended. In 1946, in *Morgan v. Virginia*, a case that the NAACP had appealed to the U.S. Supreme Court, the court ruled that segregation on interstate buses was illegal. The ruling came down in December, and by spring 1947 it was being tested by the first freedom riders. (Among them was UU minister Homer A. Jack, who in 1942 had been one of the co-founders of the Congress of Racial Equality [CORE].) The riders traveled through the border states on buses and trains. Some of those in racially mixed groups were arrested and served time in prison, but there was no violence. In 1948, in *Shelley v. Kraemer*, the Supreme Court declared restrictive housing covenants illegal. In that same year, President Harry S. Truman issued Executive Order 9980, which desegregated the federal work force, and 9981, which desegregated the armed forces. In 1954 the Supreme Court declared school segregation illegal in *Brown v. Topeka*. Then in August 1955 Emmett Till was killed. Fourteen-year-old Till was from Chicago, and while visiting his uncle in Mississippi he was kidnapped, tortured, disfigured, and murdered in a horrific act of racial violence that shocked the nation. That December Rosa Parks refused to move to the back of the bus, and the Montgomery bus boycott began. In March 1956, three Unitarian ministers—Homer Jack, David H. Cole, and Albert Harkin—went to Montgomery to offer moral support; they were among the few whites to do so. That summer Jack, who had edited *The Wit and Wisdom of Gandhi*, returned to Dexter Avenue Baptist Church, where Martin Luther King Jr. was pastor, to preach about the Indian holy man.

The Civil Rights Act that was passed in 1957 was the first since Reconstruction, but the legislation, having been gutted by Dixiecrats, proved ineffectual. Nonetheless it and the fact that President Dwight D. Eisenhower, whose administration had been reluctant to act, sent federal troops to Little Rock, Arkansas, to enforce the desegregation of Central High School, sent a message to civil rights leaders that the federal government was becoming more willing to take a stand. By then the Southern Christian Leadership Conference (SCLC) had taken shape, with King as its president.

Activists began their sit-ins in February 1960, and soon thereafter students founded the Student Non-violent Coordinating Committee (SNCC). In December 1960, in *Boynton v. Virginia*, the U.S. Supreme Court extended the 1946 ruling in *Morgan v. Virginia* to all bus terminal facilities. CORE again tested the ruling with freedom riders, and as soon as they reached the deep South violence erupted. The administration of President John F. Kennedy didn't act. As local authorities defied court orders, the president, not wanting to alienate Southern voters, hedged and hoped that some accommodation could be reached. But violence and defiance only mounted, until the admittance of James Meredith to the University of Mississippi (Ole Miss) in 1962 and Gov. Ross Barnett's recalcitrance forced the administration to act and Attorney General Robert Kennedy sent in 500 U.S. marshals and, when rioting commenced, federal troops. The following June President Kennedy announced that he had federalized the Alabama National Guard, that two black students had peacefully enrolled in the University of Alabama over the protest of Gov. George Wallace, and that his administration would soon submit civil rights legislation to Congress.

The March on Washington for Jobs and Freedom took place on August 28, 1963. More than 200,000 people took part, including 1,600 Unitarian Universalists, led by UUA president Dana McLean Greeley. Among them was Orloff Miller, director of the Office of College Centers and staff advisor to Student Religious Liberals (SRL). SRL had moved its annual meeting from California to Washington, D.C., to enable its members to participate. John M. Wells, minister of the Mount Vernon Unitarian Church, bore the overall responsibility for the UU contingent. Wells later recalled that after the march had set off down Sixteenth Street, "Dr. King came back along the line and marched with us a while. It surprised us all. And our picture, side by side, was on the front of the *Washington Post* the next day."[144] One out of every hundred Unitarian Universalists marched that day.

Later, when civil rights leaders met with the president, the room was thick with UU connections. President Kennedy and Dana Greeley were both Harvard graduates, and civic events in Boston occasionally brought them together.[145] Kennedy's speechwriter, Ted Sorenson, was a UU. The vice president of the AFL/CIO, A. Philip Randolph, had been active in Harlem politics and would have known Ethelred Brown and the many members of the Harlem Unitarian Church who, like himself, were Socialists. Roy Wilkins, the NAACP's executive director, had been hired into his first position there in 1931, when Mary White Ovington, a Unitarian, was its chair. Whitney M. Young Jr., the executive director of the National Urban League, was a Unitarian Universalist. And King himself had many UU connections. Some of them dated to his attendance at the Boston University School of Theology in the early 1950s, while his friendship with Homer Jack had begun when Jack came to Montgomery in 1956, and grew in 1957 when Jack and King traveled to Ghana together to participate in its independence celebrations.

The Civil Rights Act of 1964, which Unitarian Universalists had lobbied for, was followed the next year by the events of Selma and the signing of the Voting Rights Act. In 1967, in *Loving v. Virginia*, the Supreme Court declared all laws prohibiting miscegenation illegal. In 1966 the California State Supreme Court ruled that Proposition 14, which allowed discrimination in the rental and sale of property—and against which the UU ministers had marched during the 1964 General Assembly—violated the state constitution. The U.S. Supreme Court not only upheld that decision but also ruled, in *Jones v. Mayer*, that an 1866 federal civil rights law barred such discrimination. In 1968, the federal government passed Title VIII of the Civil Rights Act, commonly referred to as the Fair Housing Act. In just over twenty years the legal underpinnings of Jim Crow and discrimination were demolished. This achievement didn't end prejudice or discrimination; far from it. Continuing inequality and grinding poverty ignited the discontent smoldering in black ghettos, and it erupted into urban conflagration. Nonetheless, after over a half century Jim Crow was no longer entrenched in and reinforced by law.

Forerunners and Mentors

Change was at hand. But with a few exceptions, Euro-American Unitarians had not been at the forefront of the battle for African-American civil rights; and among the Universalists, there were few reformers beyond Lothrop, Atwood, Patton, and Skinner, and none of national note. The Unitarian minister Jenkin Lloyd Jones had founded the interracial All Souls Church in Chicago in 1883, and

in 1905 he established an interracial social agency, the Abraham
Lincoln Centre, as an extension of the congregation. In New York
Mary White Ovington and her minister, John Haynes Holmes, were
among the five incorporators of the NAACP in 1910. Holmes served
as its vice president for decades, and Ovington gave it everything,
including her soul. "I can see now the dingy little office—a table, a
few chairs, a feeble electric light—in which we met for our deliberation," wrote Holmes. "Mary White Ovington was there—a young
woman who was giving her life as an offering to the Negroes, who
had called this conference on her own responsibility, and herself
assumed the sole direction of this new Association."[146] She served
first as secretary but later in every imaginable position, including
chairperson, from 1917 to 1932. On the NAACP Advisory Committee sat Rev. Celia Parker Woolley, as well as an African-American
Unitarian, Maria Baldwin. Woolley and her close friend Fannie
Barrier Williams, another African-American Unitarian, together
founded the interracial Frederick Douglass Center, with Woolley
serving as its director. But besides these individuals, no other Uni
tarians of national stature joined the struggle for civil rights until
Homer Jack.

There were, however, forerunners. In 1922 Leon Birkhead,
the minister of All Souls Unitarian Church of Kansas City, was
quoted by the *Kansas City Times* as saying, "The negroes of Kansas
City do not want racial equality but the cooperation of the white
people in solving their problems. They do not want alms but justice."[147] Birkhead, who had a taste for controversy, grew increasingly concerned about the Ku Klux Klan, its far-right splinter
group the Black Legion, and fascists of all kinds. Seeing Nazism
taking root in America, he founded the Friends of Democracy, a
group that exposed Nazi sympathizers and, later, Communists.
Consumed by this cause, he left parish ministry in 1939 to give all
his energy to the organization. He also served on the board of the
Council for Democracy and has been credited with authorship of
the widely distributed booklet *The Negro and Defense: A Test of
Democracy* (1941).

In 1929 Rev. John Dietrich, a leading humanist and, like Birkhead, a signer of the Humanist Manifesto, proclaimed truths most whites were not ready to hear. In "The Myth of a Superior Race," a sermon he preached at the First Unitarian Society of Minneapolis, he offered a cogent and prophetic analysis of white supremacy:

> We always dislike anything that is different, and to bolster up this emotional attitude we rationalize and seek solid foundations for its existence. . . . This is lately become prominent in the so called Nordic propaganda, which is an assertion of the superiority, not only of the white race, but of a section of this race inhabiting Northern Europe. . . . They get their satisfaction from proclaiming the superiority of the group to which they belong . . . and we cannot view the characteristics of our own race impartially because they are also our own inherited traits. The idea of our own race involves the idea of our own ego.[148]

Others acted on their conviction. In 1929 John Murray Atwood, dean of the Canton Theological School of St. Lawrence University, admitted Jeffrey Campbell as a student over the protest of the superintendent of the New York State Universalist Convention. Later Atwood strongly defended Marguerite and Francis Davis when their interracial marriage was attacked in the *Leader*. In 1942, when it appeared that the denomination was about to rescind Davis's ministerial fellowship, Atwood threatened to resign his own. Two years later, as the Second World War raged on, he said in the keynote address at the Pennsylvania Universalist Convention, "If the world is to be saved the church must go in for the salvation of all without regard to race or state. This includes the Germans and the Japs as well as others. Under God there is but one people. He makes no distinction as to race, color, sect or creed."[149]

Kenneth Patton, minister of the First Unitarian Society of Madison, Wisconsin, was moved by Sinclair Lewis's 1947 novel *Kingsblood Royal*. Set in post–Second World War middle America, the novel depicts a white man whose innocent explorations of family genealogy lead to a shocking discovery: a black ancestor. Through his initially faint-hearted efforts to build relationships with African Americans, the protagonist develops the courage to publicly claim his heritage. But when he does so, he is shunned by his extended family and becomes a pariah in his all-white suburb. After reading *Kingsblood Royal*, Patton felt compelled to speak out. In September 1947, first on a Sunday morning radio broadcast and then in his sermon, he resigned from the white race. His statement made national headlines and brought praise, threats, and opportunities. A major magazine asked him to visit establishments around Chicago to see whether he and a black companion would receive service or, if he was alone, what would happen when he announced he was black. Patton wrote of this experience, "I begin to see that no 'white' man can know what it is like to be one of a marked group. He cannot experience a life-time of frustration [and] blocked hopes and ambitions. . . . But I was coming as close to an inside glimpse as any of my group could. . . . I have 'crossed the line' through a deeply emotional experience and I have no desire to cross back."[150]

More than 177 Unitarian Universalist ministers and seminarians journeyed to Selma or Montgomery. Understanding why they went requires assessing the influence of their seminary professors. Much as *dharma* is transmitted from teacher to student in Buddhism, students of UU ministry seem to have internalized the lessons of their mentors, generating a response to the call to Selma that was nearly instinctual.

One of these teachers was Clarence Skinner. Early in his ministry he established a forum at his church in Lowell, Massachusetts, to which he invited radicals like W. E. B. Du Bois. When he founded the Community Church of Boston in 1920 he followed the same pattern of holding forums and again invited Du Bois to speak. In 1915 he published *The Social Implications of Universalism*, a text that was rooted in the Social Gospel movement but went beyond it. His this-worldly orientation led him to proclaim that Universal Brotherhood was "the great social dynamic of the twentieth century."[151] An outspoken pacifist, he also decried the conviction of Sacco and Vanzetti and defended the Scottsboro Boys—nine African-American youths unjustly charged with raping two white women. But above all he thought of himself as a teacher. He taught at Crane Theological School, the Universalist seminary at Tufts University, from 1914 to 1945 (and became dean in 1933), and in his social ethics class he often took up the situation of African Americans in the United States.[152] His students included David H. Cole—who graduated from Crane in 1947 and was one of the three Unitarian ministers who went to Montgomery during the 1956 bus boycott—as well as Ernest Brown and Eugene H. Adams. All three would go to Selma. When Skinner died in 1947, Cole and John Ratcliff, who succeeded Skinner as dean, eulogized him for "his love for his fellow men and his constant defense of human rights and civil liberties. His untiring effort to erase racial and class barriers. His uncompromising support of principles he felt to be right, in the face of severe criticism and hostility."[153]

Still, twenty years would pass between the end of Skinner's teaching career and the events of Selma. Important as his influence was, the impact of James Luther Adams overshadowed it.

James Luther Adams, often known as "JLA," had a greater impact than anyone else on those training for the Unitarian ministry. His career spanned four decades. After serving as a parish minister from 1927 to 1935, he accepted an offer to teach at Meadville Lombard Theological School in Chicago. But, before commencing his career as a teacher, he spent a year studying in Germany (his second visit). There he interviewed religious leaders, engaged with the underground resistance, and witnessed the Nazi suppression of dissidents. Subsequently, he taught at Meadville Lombard until 1956, when he joined the Harvard Divinity School faculty, where he served until 1968. In retirement he taught at Andover Newton Theological School and again at Meadville Lombard.

His experience in Germany, which included being interrogated by the Gestapo, framed the themes not just of his classes, but of his life. His involvement in race relations, civil liberties, and housing problems reinforced his conviction that for a democratic society to survive, voluntary associations had to assume civic responsibility. By contrast, in "the structure and power of the American business corporation community, and the largely centralized control of the mass media of communications," he saw "the dimensions of domination in American society." He believed that the church is a significant locus of power and morality, and that "Christian ethics must be promoted in direct confrontation with these principalities and powers."[154] For those taking his classes at Meadville Lombard, the University of Chicago Divinity School, Harvard, or Andover Newton, this meant critiquing "the gradualist, simple, optimistic doctrine of progress" and rejecting "philanthropy-cum-reform."[155] Individuals need to be fully engaged in organizing centers of power dedicated to shaping a just, democratic society, while resisting those seeking dominion over others.

Beyond the classroom he taught by example. He spent untold hours organizing and taking action: he was active with the Independent Voters of Illinois; he was on the board of the First Unitarian Society of Chicago when the battle to integrate that congregation was fought; and he joined Wallace Robbins, president of Meadville Lombard from 1944 to 1956, in initiating the meeting of the University of Chicago faculty senate that led to the desegregation of the University of Chicago hospitals. Homer Jack, who studied under him, called him his mentor, and many of those who went to Selma became ministers under his tutelage, including Clark Olsen, who was attacked and beaten with James Reeb in Selma.

On that fateful March evening, Orloff Miller was walking between Olsen and Reeb. Miller had attended Boston University School of Theology (BUST) and among the teachers who most influenced him was Howard Thurman. Thurman had been a contemporary of Rev. Martin Luther King Sr. at Morehouse College, and then in 1953 he was at BUST when Martin Luther King Jr. enrolled. That was Thurman's first year as dean of Marsh Chapel, and King's last year as a PhD candidate before he accepted the call to Dexter Avenue Baptist Church in Montgomery, Alabama. They hung out together. They watched the New York Yankees and the Brooklyn Dodgers battle in the World Series. They talked. And Thurman's religious perspective deeply influenced King. In his 1949 work *Jesus and the Disinherited*, Thurman paraphrases Jesus's message to those with their backs to the wall: "Love your enemy. Take the initiative in seeking a way by which you can have the experience of mutual worth and value. It may be hazardous, but you must do it."[156] King carried this little book with him wherever he went. Walter Fluker wrote, "I don't believe you'd get a Martin Luther King Jr. without a Howard Thurman."[157]

Thurman also helped prepare the UUA for Selma. He had a longstanding relationship to Unitarianism. In 1944 the inaugural service of the interracial Church for the Fellowship of All Peoples, where he was co-minister, had been held at the First Unitarian Church of San Francisco. In the ensuing years Starr King students did field placements at Fellowship Church. In 1952, just before beginning his tenure at Marsh Chapel, Thurman was invited to serve on the AUA Commission on Intergroup Relations. In 1956 he delivered the Ware Lecture at the AUA General Assembly. In 1959 he was appointed to the Art of Worship Study Commission, whose report was included in *The Free Church in a Changing World*. And in 1965 Anne T. Chiarenza, Thurman's daughter, was working at the UUA in Orloff Miller's department as editor of the *Liberal Context*, its journal for college students. Miller had taken Thurman's course on spiritual disciples.

Jack Taylor was one of Miller's close friends. Another BUST student, he was one of Thurman's assistants at Marsh Chapel and later served as the minister of Fellowship Church. Taylor went to Selma, as did Gene Reeves, another BUST student. (However, the person who most influenced Reeves during his student days was his African-American classmate David H. Eaton.) The BUST faculty also included Walter Muelder, called the "Red Dean," and L. Harold deWolf, one of King's mentors and his thesis advisor. BUST was the center of Personalist theology. In Muelder's words,

Personalism "held that the basic explanatory principle of reality is personality. Hence all persons are sacred and belong to a divine-human community. . . . The non-violence which King espoused was not passive nonresistance to social evil. It resists evil, but it distinguishes [what] evil persons do, as in racial injustice, from the persons who do the evil."[158]

Those who attended Union Seminary in New York City studied social ethics under the influential promulgator of Christian radicalism Reinhold Niebuhr. Early in his career, while serving as a pastor in Detroit, Niebuhr had chaired the mayor's Race Committee. In his teaching he called his students to minister at the intersection of love and justice, faith and politics. Those who attended Meadville Lombard following James Luther Adams's departure were radicalized by Gibson Winter and Al Pitcher, who taught social ethics at the University of Chicago Divinity School. At Canton Theological School, Robert B. Tapp taught social ethics. Richard S. Gilbert, who graduated in 1961, remembered Tapp leading the class on a field trip to Watertown, New York, to demonstrate at the national board meeting of Woolworth's, the department store chain. They protested Woolworth's refusal to seat blacks at its lunch counters in the South. Gilbert said this demonstration, his first, set him on the road to activism. When word of Reeb's death reached him five years later he not only left Chicago for Selma, he dropped out of a PhD program at the University of Chicago to begin four decades of parish ministry, fueled by a commitment to social justice.

These scholar-pastors lived through the Depression and the excesses of capitalism. They decried and sought to end America's racial caste system. They witnessed the rise of totalitarianism and lived through the Second World War. These experiences led them not only to teach radicalism but to model it to a generation of seminarians, challenging them to pursue ministries of radical engagement.

Civil Rights Organizations

Ministers put to work in their pastorates the tenets they had absorbed in seminary. In the 1940s, '50s, and early '60s many Unitarian and Universalist ministers became members of the NAACP or Urban League in their community, sometimes both. During and after the Second World War, people primarily turned to these two organizations to work for "brotherhood" and better race relations. In 1943, Homer Jack went to minister in Lawrence, Kansas, and, finding it "a racist town," he naturally "tried to befriend" the NAACP in his effort to foment action.[159] Before becoming president of Meadville Lombard in 1944, Wallace Robbins had been the minister of Unity Church–Unitarian in St. Paul and president of the local Urban League. After graduating from Meadville Lombard in 1942, Aron Gilmartin accepted a call to Fort Wayne, Indiana. Finding no NAACP branch there, he helped found one, becoming its first president. By the time he left in 1951, he was president of the local Urban League. His involvement in the Urban League continued in his new settlement at University Church in Seattle. In 1949 the Washington, D.C., branch of the NAACP recognized A. Powell Davies, the minister at All Souls Church (Unitarian), for his work in fighting segregation. In 1954 the Urban League chapter in Oklahoma City received an award from the national organization; Frank Holmes, the minister at First Unitarian, had been the chapter's president the year before. The majority of the board members of the Urban League Guild of Oklahoma City were Unitarian women. When David H. Cole arrived in Champaign-Urbana in 1959 he joined the NAACP, became a board member, and later cofounded and was secretary of an Urban League chapter. In Meadville, Pennsylvania, the NAACP met in the parish of the Unitarian church and its minister, Neal W. Ferris, was vice president. Dozens of ministers served on local boards, and many more were members.

The relationship between these civil rights organizations and liberal religion was more fluid and symbiotic than coordinated. In the case of the NAACP, the relationship had existed from the beginning—partly because at its inception its national leadership was white, the only African-American officer being W. E. B. Du Bois. When the NAACP was incorporated, two of the five signatories were Unitarians, Mary White Ovington and John Haynes Holmes; two other Unitarians, Maria Baldwin and Celia Parker Woolley, sat on the organization's advisory committee. Jenkin Lloyd Jones, numbered among the sixty people who in February 1909 called for the meeting that led to the formation of the NAACP, and the association invited him to speak at its fourth annual meeting in 1912. His friend S. Laing Williams, who with his wife Fannie were members of All Souls, was vice president of the newly formed Chicago chapter (1916). In 1949, on the occasion of the NAACP's fortieth anniversary, the AUA General Assembly passed a resolution of congratulations and esteem, and in 1963 the Commission on Ethics and Social Action suggested that all church members should be annually urged to join the NAACP.[160]

Two of these early reformers were also involved in the formation of the Urban League; neither has ever received the recognition she deserves. Mary White Ovington sat on the board of the National League for the Protection of Colored Women, one of three groups that merged in 1911 to form the National Urban League. Celia Parker Woolley was a founding member of the board of the Chicago Urban League in 1916; in March 1918, as director of the Frederick Douglass Center, she invited the Chicago Urban League to move its headquarters into the center, rent-free.[161]

CORE, which focused its energies on direct non-violent action, was organized in 1942. Its constituency was different from those of the NAACP and the Urban League, and its approach reflected the fact that it was founded by students and young radicals rather than middle-class institutionalists. To open up opportunities for African Americans, CORE sent freedom riders to the South, held sit-ins at lunch counters, and stood on picket lines rather than relying on polemics, persuasion, and the law. Homer Jack, while still training for ministry, was a founding member. In April 1947, he participated in the first wave of freedom rides.[162]

While CORE's style was different from that of the NAACP or Urban League, the pattern of UU involvement in CORE was similar to what it had been in the more established civil rights organizations. In March 1961 the CORE national office approached the Mount Vernon Unitarian Church (MVUC) about the possibility of holding its annual training in nonviolent direct action, known as the Interracial Action Institute. CORE sought a location that was ' "liberal' enough to permit interracial centralized living" as well as "a site that has real problems which can be tackled."[163] MVUC was ideal, located in northern Virginia on an eleven-acre hilltop estate that included a mansion (which had been a guest house), carriage house, green house, and gardens. The board voted unanimously in support of the three-week conference.

CORE was not well received by some in the surrounding community. Midway through the institute, which had thirty participants and five trainers, complaints to the Fairfax County Zoning administrator led to an effort to shut the gathering down. The headline in the August 23 *Northern Virginia Sun* read, "County Official Denies Threatening to Arrest Leaders of Core." The MVUC board refused to comply and appealed. The trouble didn't end there. Following the news stories, someone strewed tacks across the wooded driveway leading up to the church.

One month before MVUC hosted the CORE institute, the Seattle chapter of CORE held its organizing meeting at University Unitarian Church. Among its leadership were members of University Church, including organizing secretary Ken Rose, a nineteen-year-old member of Liberal Religious Youth (LRY).[164] When CORE established a chapter in Denver, Unitarian Ruth Steiner was among its founders. In 1962 Charles Blackburn, newly graduated from Starr King School for the Ministry and in his first settlement, organized a chapter of CORE in Hayward, California, and took on the issue of fair housing.[165]

The continuing relationship between liberal religion and these civil rights organizations didn't just provide Euro-Americans ways to engage with the concerns of African Americans. It also furnished black leaders with a means by which to reach white audiences. In 1917 W. E. B. Du Bois delivered the talk "World Problem of the Colorline" to the Lowell Forum, which had been founded by Clarence Skinner. Later Du Bois spoke at the Community Church of New York and at All Souls (Unitarian) in Washington, D.C.; he also addressed the Community Church of Boston, as did two successive executive secretaries of the NAACP, James Weldon Johnson and Walter White. The newsletter of the Community Church of New York carried a column written by Johnson in 1925, and it reviewed White's first book, *The Fire in the Flint.* In 1936 Roy Wilkins, the editor of the NAACP's journal *The Crisis,* spoke to the Ridgewood Unitarian Church about "the black-white situation" and DuBois spoke at the Universalist Church of Peoria, at that time the largest Universalist congregation in America.[166] In 1943 Walter White, still NAACP executive secretary, delivered the AUA's Ware Lecture. In 1944 Rev. Chester L. Marcus, pastor of the Washington Street Presbyterian Church in Reading, Pennsylvania, brought greetings from the NAACP to the Pennsylvania Universalist Convention. During the 1950s Miller Barbour, secretary of the Denver Urban League, occasionally spoke at First Unitarian of Denver.

In addition to delivering presentations, black leaders reached Unitarians through the *Christian Register.* In 1939, the *Register* published a letter from John Caswell Smith Jr., the executive secretary of the Boston Urban League. It thanked the journal for its editorial "Is Color Appearance or Reality?" criticizing John van Schaick's attack in the *Leader* on the marriage of Marguerite and Francis Davis. Smith wrote, "Those of us who are greatly concerned for the programs of Negroes welcome an ally such as you."[167] During the 1940s, under the editorship of Stephen Fritchman, the *Register* lauded the NAACP and the Urban League and published articles by Walter White and by Edwin (Bill) Berry of the Portland Urban League.

As a result of the give-and-take with these organizations, a few African-American compatriots became Unitarians. In 1910 John Haynes Holmes recruited an African-American associate from the NAACP to join the Community Church of New York. Dana McLean Greeley said that in 1935, when he became the minister at Arlington Street Church, he found the "heads of both the Urban League and the NAACP in the congregation."[168] J. Westbrook McPherson, who became executive director of the New Orleans Urban League in the early 1950s, was a lifelong Unitarian. During the 1950s Frank J. Corbett, secretary of community relations for the Flint Urban League, became a member of the Unitarian Church of Flint, and in the 1960s Richard L. Traylor, the president of the Flint branch of the NAACP, joined as well. Gwendolyn Thomas, who in 1976 would become a UUA board member, discovered liberal religion while working on open housing with members of the Unitarian congregation in Denver. Charles Patterson was a member of Cleveland's First Unitarian Society while serving as secretary of industrial relations for the Cleveland Urban League between 1951 and 1957, and Whitney M. Young Jr., who eventually became the executive secretary of the National Urban League, first became involved with Unitarianism while serving as the executive secretary of the Omaha Urban League in the early 1950s. Francis Davis made the connection in reverse. When no Universalist church would call him because of his interracial marriage, he went to work for the Boston Urban League.

The relationship seems to have been broadly embraced and to have worked well. Augustus Granville Dill, the office manager and associate editor of *The Crisis* between 1913 and 1928, played the organ at the Community Church of New York. In 1945 when Ernest Kuebler, the director of the AUA Department of Education, needed advice on how to more efficiently distribute certain funds to black schools, he wrote to Walter White.[169] In 1954, at the time he was hired by the Council of Liberal Churches, William Y. Bell was a member of the executive council of the National Urban League. In 1958 the Unitarian Church of Flint sponsored the play *Mississippi Mud*, about the slaying of Emmet Till, and the president of the Flint NAACP branch served as a resource person for the discussion that followed. *The Free Church in a Changing*

World recommended the establishment of a Department of Social Responsibility, which would stay in "close touch" with the NAACP, CORE, and similar national organizations.[170] In Seattle the local CORE newsletter was produced on the mimeograph machine in a church member's basement. In Cincinnati in 1963, over two hundred Unitarians participated in an NAACP March for Justice, and in 1964 the St. John's congregation in Cincinnati made a large contribution to the NAACP Legal Defense Fund.[171]

In 1963 Rev. Felix D. Lion delivered the sermon "A Letter to James Baldwin" to the members of the Palo Alto Unitarian Church, saying, "I plead with you, drop your guard, let the barriers fall, speak the word of friendship, do the deed of love. Participate in groups like CORE and the NAACP which work to overcome this injustice. Bring them to church with you and make them welcome."[172] Deeply compassionate and committed, Viola Liuzzo joined the NAACP in Detroit in 1964 after an African-American friend, Sarah Evans, took her to its meetings. And James Reeb, having decided to leave his position as associate minister at All Souls in Washington, D.C., asked Sterling Tucker, the executive secretary of the Washington Urban League, about job opportunities.[173]

In the sermon "Race in Rochester," delivered on February 7, 1965, Robert West, the minister of the First Unitarian Church of Rochester, New York, praised the Urban League for its programs in jobs, education, and housing and declared, "An Urban League chapter is long overdue in Rochester, and we wonder what kind of blindness has caused our community to feel it does not need this kind of assistance. . . . I believe we should have an Urban League here, and we should have it now."[174]

West's first settlement had been in Knoxville, Tennessee, in 1957. There he collaborated with the Unitarian Service Committee (USC). In 1960 the USC began addressing the desegregation of schools and other public facilities, and its staff person, Galen Martin, assisted in founding the Knoxville Area Human Relations Council (HRC). The energies of most Human Relations Councils went into bringing blacks and whites together, promoting dialogue, disseminating information, and sometimes spinning off autonomous groups that would take more direct action. Although they were biracial and thus radical by segregationist standards, HRCs did not take to the streets and were thus moderate enough that some white business and church leaders could participate.

The NAACP, the Urban League, and the HRCs had similar goals. But some of the younger, more militant civil rights workers in SNCC and CORE, who called for activists to put their bodies on the line, saw all three as middle-class organizations, irrelevant to poverty-stricken black masses. Nevertheless, most white Southerners deemed the NAACP and the Urban League too radical—meaning they were black-run, black-dominated, and focused firmly on the needs of the black community. While individual church members might have been involved in the NAACP, or Urban League, or occasionally SNCC, in southern communities with a Human Relations Council the involvement of Unitarian Universalists was often substantial. Sometimes there were official ties between the councils and the church.

Unitarian and Universalist ministers and laity built connections to the black community through the NAACP, the Urban League, CORE, and HRCs, while leaders of those groups found allies and gained access to Euro-American audiences through Unitarian and Universalist connections. In a racially divided country these organizations gave members of both denominations the opportunity to develop personal and institutional relationships with African Americans. These developments are evident in the 1954 report of the Commission on Intergroup Relations and the 1964 report of the Commission on Religion and Race. The former stated that of the nine churches that had "instituted special techniques" for attracting African Americans, four "actively participated in the local NAACP," and of these, one had made its church the NAACP's meeting place.[175] The latter found that 40 percent of the responding congregations had made attempts to influence their communities regarding "the present social revolution in America." The report goes on to encourage UUs "to take part in integrated functions, Council of Human Relations, League of Women Voters, etc., so as to gain first-hand experience with the problems and satisfactions of such fellowship."[176] Three years later a different survey found that 9.7 percent of Unitarian Universalists belonged to the NAACP or the Urban League, and 4.3 percent to CORE or SNCC. By comparison, 16 percent belonged to the Memorial Society, 12.5 percent to the ACLU, and 11.3 percent to the League of Women Voters.[177]

The activities of congregations and their members varied. In the 1940s, the Oklahoma City congregation's "young people's group went on a tour of the Negro slum district with representatives of the Urban League and NAACP."[178] In 1947 a similar tour of minority housing in Seattle, sponsored by the Urban League, so shocked Dorothy Hopper that she sought out a religious community that was as outraged as she was. Thus she found Unitarianism and married a Unitarian minister; in 1957 they moved east to a Boston suburb, where she joined the NAACP and organized its Fair Housing Practices Committee.[179]

These organizations didn't encompass all UU civil rights work. In Chicago in 1949 Leslie Pennington, minister of the First Unitarian Society, founded and served as the first chairperson of the Hyde Park–Kenwood Community Conference (HPKCC). The HPKCC, which worked to promote better race relations and build a stable interracial community, was recognized as one of the new and prophetic interracial movements in America, and won city-wide, national, and international recognition.[180] In Atlanta a relationship grew between the United Liberal Congregation (later renamed the Unitarian Universalist Church of Atlanta) and Ebenezer Baptist Church, where Martin Luther King Sr. served as minister. In the 1960s, the two congregations arranged joint Sunday evening programs for their youth groups, alternating location between the churches, so black and white young people could get to know one another. When the Southern Christian Leadership Conference (SCLC) leaders Martin Luther King Jr., Ralph Abernathy, and Fred Shuttlesworth spoke before thousands at Wrigley

Field in Los Angeles in May 1963, the First Unitarian Church of Los Angeles choir joined with choirs from local black churches.

Many UU congregations worked for open housing. Members of the Ridgewood Unitarian Society participated in a program in which whites would act as "testers," visiting properties where blacks had been refused the opportunity to buy.[181] And the Social Action Committee of the congregation in Plainfield, New Jersey, placed an article in the church newsletter seeking homeowners willing to sell to a "Negro buyer." Unitarian Universalists could fight for equal access to housing on their own (suburban) turf, and it fit so well with UU values as to be almost *de rigueur.*

The groundwork for the Unitarian Universalist response to Selma was in place. During the two decades that followed the Second World War, the UUA and its predecessors increasingly articulated their strong support for racial justice. Unitarians and Universalists supported school desegregation, open housing, equal access, and integration. Furthermore, the majority of their ministers engaged with the cause of racial justice in some way.

The liberalization of laws, the amelioration of cultural mores, and UU largesse notwithstanding, Unitarian Universalists still held a narrow, often self-serving understanding of race relations. Going to committee meetings with black folks and earnestly working for change enabled them to identify with the solution to the problem. It also impeded their awakening to the ways in which they themselves perpetuated it. The insularity of their lives as Euro-Americans produced a skewed view of the world and blinded them to how little they truly understood about the realities of African-American life.

Nonetheless, the Unitarians and Universalists strove to turn good intentions into action, and in doing so began to build relationships with African Americans and their institutions. By March 1965, enough UUs were embedded in a web of relationships that these connections—whites to blacks, and liberal religion to the cause of civil rights—compelled them to respond.

WHAT HAPPENED IN SELMA

Dana McLean Greeley's early engagement with race relations had been, in his own words, "moderate," but he would come to judge the matter to be "the second most important social problem in the world today," after peace.[182] *The Free Church in a Changing World* had recommended the establishment of a Department of Social Responsibility, and Greeley hired Homer A. Jack in 1964 as director of the new department. At the time, Jack was the executive director of the National Committee for a Sane Nuclear Policy, and his pacifism and pursuit of disarmament fit well with Greeley's own pacifism and passionate commitment to peace. Just as important, Jack was respected and well connected in the civil rights movement (although a few people considered him an arrogant know-it-all and opposed his appointment). In 1943 he had helped to organize the Chicago Council Against Racial and Religious Discrimination, and from 1944 to 1948 he was employed as its executive secretary. Greeley's choice of Jack thus compensated for his own heretofore limited engagement in race relations.

Prelude to Bloody Sunday

In the summer of 1964, dozens of Unitarian Universalists were involved in the Mississippi Summer Project to organize freedom schools and register voters. Among the hundreds of other volunteers were James Chaney, Mickey Schwerner, and Andy Goodman. On June 20, they disappeared. Greeley announced that the UUA Commission on Religion and Race was offering $1,000 for information leading to their whereabouts and safe return, but their bodies were found six weeks later.

That fall, after many of the volunteers had departed, some local whites who were displeased with the black community's growing assertiveness began to take reprisals. In response, the National Council of Churches (NCC) appealed to ministers to come to McComb, Mississippi, to support the Delta Ministry Project. By early October, UU ministers Melvin Van de Workeen, Albert D'Orlando, John Papandrew, and Walter Royal Jones were there, and Charles B. Blackburn arrived before the end of the month. They were followed by Arthur Graham, Kenneth MacLean, Peter Raible, Carl Scovel, and two Meadville Lombard students, Allen Wells Jr. and Ralph Mero.

Charles Blackburn had just arrived in Alabama as the first minister called by the UU Fellowship of Huntsville. A Southerner raised in northern Florida, Blackburn's route to activism had begun six years earlier, when he heard King speak at Howard University. Soon thereafter, in the wake of the bomb threat to the Arlington Unitarian Church, he wrote to the *Washington Post*, "We Americans seem always to need the blast of a bomb to lift us out of our apathy, and perhaps this incident and the many others so fresh in our minds will start a chain reaction of new thinking; a moral break-through of which we as a people are infinitely capable if we desire and will it."[183] When, a year later, he enrolled at the Howard University School of Divinity, he was the only Euro-American on campus. That year reinforced his commitment to civil rights. He spent four years in California, and then his calling led him first to move to Alabama and then to go to Mississippi. He wrote,

It was a lonely, frightening trip to McComb by myself by plane, bus and taxi, unlike the camaraderie of the mass demonstrations that came later—alone with the knowledge of self and what I stood for, knowing that integrity could mean death. . . .

We received instructions on driving techniques for civil rights workers: disconnect all interior lights of the car so as not to provide a clear target at night, drive down the center line of the highway, and without lights if possible, in order to thwart moves to run you off the road. It was like a bad "B" movie thriller—but, oh so real!

Our task was to assist a group of Negroes in nearby Magnolia, Mississippi, to register to vote. . . . I escorted a 94-year-old black Baptist minister and his 80-year-old wife to the county house to register. We were arrested for "trespassing on the courthouse grounds."[184]

Blackburn and the forty others who had been arrested were released two days later, without explanation.

Between January 1 and January 9, 1965, Homer Jack; Orloff Miller; Clifton Hoffman, the executive secretary of the Southern UU Regional Office; and Charles N. Vickery, program director of the Unitarian Universalist Service Committee, toured Mississippi to gain firsthand knowledge of civil rights projects in the state and understand how to get involved in them. They covered 902 miles, visiting sixteen projects and talking to seventy-three key people in Mississippi and another twenty-one in other states. Among the plethora of recommendations in their report was the expansion of UU involvement, especially in "the Alabama projects of the SCLC."[185] Ira Blalock and Gordon Gibson, recent graduates of Crane Theological School, had already volunteered to spend a week to ten days with the Delta Ministry in Mississippi; Jack asked them to check out the SCLC project in Selma instead.

Blalock and Gibson were serving small Boston-area congregations. Gibson would leave for Selma the day after being ordained. At the ordination ceremony Orloff Miller delivered the charge to the minister, but what stayed with Gibson was advice Miller offered afterward: "Don't go to Selma unless it's more important that you go than that you come back."[186]

An extraordinarily complex situation awaited Blalock and Gibson. Selma, a city of thirty thousand, was split evenly between the races; yet there were twelve thousand whites on the voting rolls and only 325 African Americans. The city had a new administration under Mayor Joe Smitherman, who had appointed Wilson Baker, a former police captain, as public safety director. The two of them hoped to derail the protest, but to do that they had to keep the larger-than-life county sheriff, Jim Clark, and his posse under control.

King kicked off the SCLC voting rights project in Selma by holding a mass rally at Brown Chapel AME on January 2. Then the first march to the Dallas County courthouse took place on January 18. Unlike the SCLC, SNCC was not new to Selma, and most of its workers were seething about SCLC moving into a community they had spent two years organizing. They felt they had done the groundwork to create enough cohesion to make direct action possible and now SCLC was stealing the show.

On February 1, the day before Gibson and Blalock arrived, another march to the Dallas County courthouse led to the arrest of King, Ralph Abernathy, and 250 others. On Thursday, February 4, the situation became even more tense. While King was in jail SNCC workers, having gone to hear the Black Nationalist Malcolm X speak at the nearby Tuskegee Institute, invited him to speak in Selma. Gibson suspected "SNCC wanted to upstage Dr. King."[187] Malcolm X's arrival threw the SCLC leadership into damage control mode. As a counterbalance, they rushed Coretta Scott King and Juanita Abernathy to town. Gibson recalled that Malcolm X was "in full form . . . jabbing accusingly with his index finger, but [when] listening to Mrs. King he was attentive, respectful, and almost pensive."[188] Later, in a private meeting, Malcolm X assured Coretta Scott King, "I didn't come to Selma to make his job difficult. I really did come thinking that I could make it easier. If the white people realize what the alternative is, perhaps they will be more willing to hear Dr. King."[189]

On Friday, February 5, Gibson was still getting a sense of the situation while Blalock, an ex-Marine, joined that day's demonstration and was arrested. The following Monday, when the black citizens of Selma once again marched to the courthouse to register, both Blalock and Gibson joined them. Standing atop the court-house steps, Sheriff Clark jammed his billy club into the belly of King's aide, James Bevel, pushing him down the stairs. The protest-ers were surrounded and arrested by "deputized hooligans" wield-ing cattle prods and billy clubs.[190] That day fifty people were taken into custody, but it was the incarceration of the two white UU ministers and a white Catholic lay theologian that made headlines.

Sunday, February 7, the Revs. Donald S. and Vilma Harrington set out on their own to tour the deep South. They met student vol-unteers in Jackson and Hattiesburg, Mississippi, and were invited to witness the deposition hearings of the Mississippi Freedom Democratic Party (MFDP), where person after person testified about their repeated attempts to register. After several days, the Harringtons arrived in Selma. They were at Brown Chapel AME the morning of Friday, February 12, when word came that Sheriff Clark had been hospitalized with a heart attack. "Let's go pray for Jim Clark," someone said. Church members got to work making posters saying "Sheriff Jim Clark, get well quick." Donald Har-rington recalls what happened next: "Then we all walked together, Vilma and I with the minister of Brown Chapel Church, and we kneeled for five minutes in silence outside of the hospital to pray. . . . I want to testify that that was a simple, honest, open action and not cynical in the slightest degree. Selma, Alabama! One had the feeling that it has become the moral hub of the universe."[191]

Blalock and Gibson were not released from jail until February 15, so they never knew the Harringtons had been in Selma, nor is there any indication that the couple knew Blalock and Gibson were incarcerated. Donald Harrington did not mention them in the sermon he delivered after returning home. Had they known, the Harringtons would have visited them and raised an alarm within the UUA.

Three days after their release, which was covered in Northern papers, came an event that did not receive such attention. Dur-ing a nighttime rally and march in the nearby town of Marion, Jimmie Lee Jackson, a twenty-six-year-old Army veteran, was shot twice in the stomach by an Alabama state trooper. A police melee had disrupted the gathering. When a trooper began beating Jackson's mother and grandfather, Jackson tried to protect them and was shot at close range. He died of a massive infection on Friday, February 26. That Sunday James Bevel preached at Zion United Methodist Church in Marion and in that sermon put forward an idea he'd been mulling over: a march to Montgomery, Alabama's capital.

Earlier that week Charles Blackburn had received a call from Joseph Ellwanger, a Lutheran pastor in Birmingham and native of Selma. To protest the brutality, he was organizing a group called Concerned White Citizens of Alabama. He requested that Blackburn organize a group in Huntsville, and Blackburn recruited fifteen people. In all, seventy-two whites met the other protesters on Saturday and marched with them to the Dallas County courthouse; thirty-six of them were Unitarian Universalists from the congregations in Huntsville, Birmingham, and Tuscaloosa.[192] This was a historic moment. For the first time, white Alabamans were demonstrating for black equal rights. As they approached the courthouse they were jeered and taunted by a hostile crowd of five hundred onlookers furious with these "nigger-loving" traitors. The marchers sang "America the Beautiful." The crowd sang "Dixie." All that kept them in check was the city's public safety director, Wilson Baker.

At the rally that followed the march, the "fiery" James Bevel said that when he saw "the thin line of whites walking four by four, demonstrating in support of equal rights," he thought "Damn, the Kingdom's come." C. T. Vivian, another SCLC leader, praised them as well, and then queried, "But where have you been?"[193]

Called to Action

On the afternoon of Sunday, March 7, the march from Selma to Montgomery set off with John Lewis, the chairman of SNCC, in the lead. At the foot of the Edmund Pettus Bridge, the march ended abruptly and violently. Let loose, state troopers and Sheriff Jim Clark's motley posse—some of them on horseback—charged, trampled, clubbed, and tear-gassed six hundred peaceful African-American marchers.

This time, unlike when similar violence had erupted in nearby Marion, television cameramen recorded the attack. That evening it was broadcast across the nation. Orloff Miller and his wife, Mary Jane, happened to be having dinner with an interracial couple. They spent the evening watching the news from Selma; so did many others, including Jim and Marie Reeb. At 4:57 a.m. on Monday, King sent his telegram calling "on clergy of all faiths to join me in Selma." At 10 a.m. Dana McLean Greeley wrote in the right-hand margin of his copy, "See if Homer would alert some of our men to go. And tell Webb." Ted Webb was the district executive of the Massachusetts Bay District of Unitarian and Universalist Churches.[194]

When Homer Jack called up to Miller's office to say the UUA had received the telegram, Miller rushed down to Jack's office, on the first floor of UUA headquarters at 25 Beacon Street, Boston. Jack consulted with the SCLC, the National Council of Churches, and the Union of American Hebrew Congregations; Miller telephoned college center clergy from coast to coast, and Ted Webb also made calls—including one to James Reeb, with whom he had had dinner on Sunday night. Most of the district executives east of the Mississippi were asked to send ministers. Greeley was on the phone as well, to his first cousin, Roger Greeley, the minister in Kalamazoo and an outspoken activist. Roger said he'd be willing to go on one condition: Dana had to promise to lead a march in Boston afterward. When Dana demurred, Roger stayed home.

King was also making calls. He phoned Gene Reeves, a Unitarian Universalist he knew from BUST. Reeves had enrolled in 1956, when King was completing his doctoral dissertation. King came to Boston periodically to consult with his thesis advisor, and Gene and a few other students would have dinner with him. In 1959, when Reeves moved to Atlanta to work on his doctorate at Emory University, King proposed that he organize a college-age group to work on desegregation. Now King called on him again. "He wanted me there," Reeves said, "and I told him I could only miss one week of classes."[195]

Word spread quickly. In Concord Brad Greeley, Dana's nephew, called his colleague Arthur Jellis and asked, "Shall we go?" They did. The secretary of the Midwest UU Conference called Hunter Leggitt, minister at Beverly Unitarian Church, and at 2 a.m. Leggitt was on a flight to Montgomery with other Chicago-area clergy. Richard Leonard, the minister of education at the Community Church of New York, stopped on his way south to mail instructions for his memorial service to his secretary, just in case.[196]

Homer Jack was among the first to arrive in Selma. When he addressed the rally on Monday night, Brown Chapel AME was packed, with people crammed into the aisles, balconies, and windowsills. Ministers of all faiths arrived from across the country, and the assembled greeted each entry with cheers and waves of applause.

In Berkeley, California, Clark Olsen was listening to his car radio when he heard of King's appeal. He immediately felt the need to go, but had no money for airfare and knew he'd miss several committee meetings at the eight-year-old fledgling Berkeley Fellowship. He didn't see how he could make it. But at home a message awaited him: Two members of his congregation offered to pay his way. Early Tuesday morning he caught a flight east. Expecting to be back in a day, he left without a full change of clothes.

In Indiana the Social Action Committee of the Unitarian Church of Bloomington, augmented by board members, met at 8 Monday night. By 10:45 p.m. their minister, David Johnson, was packing. By 12:45 a.m. he was in the air. Renting a car in Atlanta, he and his travel companion found it reassuring that so many others were pouring into cars and station wagons, heading for Selma. Johnson recalled,

> Through the small hours we drove. We painfully observed the speed limits, wondering how the police felt about outside agitators. . . . We felt as though we were playing a deadly game

and the other side had the only rule book. . . . Dawn broke over the brick-red hills of Alabama and revealed a strangely desolate land—dry grass with patches of pale green and marshy hollows between the low, rolling hills. The leafless trees hung with decaying moss. Tiny shacks dotted the land—sagging between the brick pillars of their foundations. There seemed few substantial houses. We wondered what life was nourished on this unsubstantial soil.[197]

Henry Hampton, the UUA's associate director of information (and the only African American holding a professional position at the UUA), flew into Atlanta on the same 11 p.m. flight as Miller, Reeb, Jellis, Brad Greeley, and ten others. That night the group bunked down in the waiting area of a rental car agency.

When Clif Hoffman's telegram to John Papandrew arrived in Miami on Monday at 9:30 p.m., Papandrew was in a committee meeting at church. With the committee's support, Papandrew and congregation-member Bob Ross were on a flight to Atlanta by 1:15 a.m. Tuesday. Later that morning Jack Zylman and Ralph Mero, two Meadville Lombard seminarians, arrived in Atlanta from Chicago; the school had paid their airfare. They joined up with Miller, Reeb, and the others.

Tuesday afternoon, when the UUs caucused in Selma, they numbered about forty-five UU ministers and fifteen laypeople. Among them was Emily Taft Douglas, who had been the last moderator of the AUA. She was also the wife of Paul Douglas, a U.S. senator from Illinois. Lillian Crompton Tobey, the widow of Charles Tobey, who had been a New Hampshire Senator, was there as well.[198]

David Johnson remembered,

Before two days were out, approximately sixty [UU] ministers had made their pilgrimage to Selma—nearly ten percent of our active parish ministry. I was unutterably proud of our presence. But there was no time for pride. . . . We had come because we had to. We were late, very late, twelve years late.

The first voter registration drive was in 1952. They were beaten into submission, beaten on street corners, on the steps of the courthouse, in their own churches, in their own homes—and we did not notice.[199]

Now UUs had noticed, but the march operated on civil rights time. They waited. King had spent most of the night and morning in discussions with federal officials. The White House wanted the march delayed. In addition, an injunction against it had been issued by the district federal judge, Frank Johnson. King had never defied an injunction before, but the protesters' mood, the momentum of events, and the rightness of the cause all said "March." As negotiations continued, SNCC workers offered the new arrivals training in non-violent defense. "We were told," said Ford Lewis, a UU minister in Sacramento, California, "that if we were attacked we should fall down in something resembling the fetal position, but with our hands over our heads curled up in as tight a ball as possible with our legs crossed; and remaining in that position praying while they beat upon us."[200]

While the SCLC leadership struggled with whether to march or not, the members of the Huntsville congregation also struggled with what to do. "There was an intense and painful consultation with the men from my church," Blackburn said. "[They] were all space-program engineers with top security clearances whose jobs might well be at stake in disobeying a federal injunction—an agonizing decision. Each went off alone. Each returned to say that he would march."[201]

Those gathered in the chapel debated hotly and at length over whether to obey the injunction or march in spite of it; they came to a clear consensus to march, but did not know what King would do. Finally, the marchers began assembling. Francis Anderson, the UU minister in Braintree, Massachusetts, found a place in line. As instructed, he positioned himself on the outside of a row of marchers; on the other end was a nun, Sister Joann, from Chicago. "Between us," he said, "stood an old man, his arm in a crude sling, and a boy, maybe twelve, thirteen, with a bandage around his head.

They had been there for the beating two days before, and now we were there with them, uncertain of everything but the dream. As Dr. King reminded us, it was a dream we were sharing with those between us, and we must stand on the outside, so they would have to beat through us to get to them. We were assured they wouldn't (though my confidence was a bit shaky)."[202]

At 3 p.m., singing "Ain't Gonna Let Nobody Turn Me Around," 2,500 marchers set forth. They passed ambulances at the ready, dozens of police cars—not there to protect them—and troopers with clubs in hand. No one knew what would happen, and no one knew what was going on in King's mind as he led the march from Brown Chapel AME back to the Pettus Bridge. Was his mind made up or was he still unsure, still seeking God's guidance?

"I was in the tenth or so rank," said Arthur Jellis. "A graying, small lady was on my left. To be in that procession was [a] frightening and unnerving action. I did neither weep nor tremble—or so I thought. But my marching partner knew it was bad going for me. She reached over the short distance between us, took my hand and said, 'We're going to be all right.' "[203]

Along the route a federal marshal stepped forward and read the injunction aloud. The marchers went on. As they went they saw no American flags. None. Only Confederate ones. They marched up and over the crest of the bridge. Before them a phalanx of five hundred blue-helmeted Alabama state troopers blocked the highway. King halted. Mrs. Douglas and Mrs. Tobey came forward on the arms of 6'4" Farley Wheelwright; behind them came nuns and priests, rabbis and ministers. They all knelt. They prayed. King rose—as he did so, the troopers parted. The way to Montgomery was open. If he hesitated, it was only for an instant; turning, he led them back to Brown Chapel AME.

During the rally back at the chapel, King explained his thinking in not pressing on to Montgomery. The state of Alabama was obviously reluctant to beat a mixed group, and more people were on the way. They'd use the time to work through the courts. He asked those who could to stay.

He had made the right decision. Responses to his telegram continued, with clergy and laity still arriving in Selma. The delay also offered a way out of the dilemma of whether to defy the injunction or not and a means of avoiding more deaths like Jimmie Lee Jackson's. Many of the protestors were relieved the march had turned around, some were disappointed and confused, and others felt angry and betrayed. While a few Unitarian Universalists must have sensed the tension between SNCC and the SCLC, they could not guess how deep it was or that it would fracture the civil rights movement. And they could never have conceived that when it finally erupted, it would nearly tear the UUA asunder.

After being released from prison on February 15, Gordon Gibson had returned to Boston. But when radio reports made it sound like the Tuesday march might be another bloodbath, he made a tentative airplane reservation and began phoning around, looking for a colleague to cover for him. He thought of a colleague who didn't have a church of his own, and therefore might be able to replace him in the pulpit if he went and didn't come back by the following Sunday—James Reeb. Reeb had recently left an associate minister position to become community relations director of the Boston Metropolitan Housing Program of the American Friends Service Committee. When Gibson called his house, Marie Reeb told him Jim was in Selma. Gibson offered his sympathy, saying he knew that "waiting in Boston and not knowing what was happening was an incredibly hard thing to do."[204] Early that evening, Reeb called home. Everything had gone well, he said. He'd be back soon.

The Murder of James Reeb

Tuesday evening, after returning from the Pettus Bridge, a group of UU ministers headed toward the restaurant recommended to them at SCLC headquarters. As they were on their way, a VW van pulled alongside and one of its passengers hailed them. The van held a contingent of Jewish men from New York, and one of them knew Ralph Mero. A seat was available: Did Mero want a ride to Montgomery? Mero hopped aboard.

At the same time, James Reeb and Gerry Krick, director of the Boston Ministry to College Students and Faculty for the Benevolent Fraternity of Unitarian Universalist Churches, were preparing to go back to Atlanta and catch a flight home. As they put their luggage in the trunk, Krick changed his mind. "Take care, Jim," he said. "I've decided to stay awhile."[205] As he took his bags back out of the trunk, a group of their colleagues gathered around and said, "Aw, Jim, stay with us."[206] Before Krick had gone far he heard Reeb call from behind him, "Hey, Gerry, wait for me, I've decided to stay awhile too."[207]

They headed for Walker's Café, which by then was full of black locals and white protesters. Mario Savio, a leader of the Berkeley free speech movement who had participated in the Mississippi Summer Project, was in an argument about religion. A year earlier, he had famously declared, "There's a time when the operation of the machine becomes so odious, makes you so sick at heart, that you can't take part, you can't even passively take part, and you've got to put your bodies upon the gears and upon the wheels, upon the levers, upon all the apparatus, and you've got to make it stop."[208] The UUs in the room included Richard Norsworthy, Francis Anderson, Homer Jack, Jack Kent, David Johnson, and Jack Wilkinson. They were huddled around postage stamp–sized tables when John Wells, David Cole, Jack Zylman, Orloff Miller, and Reeb and Krick crowded in—as well as Clark Olsen, who had arrived late after his plane was delayed. It took them a while to get seats, and then Hunter Leggitt joined them. With the jukebox playing, it felt like old home week. Famished, they dug into southern fried chicken, mashed potatoes, and collard greens. They relaxed.

"When he entered a room everything brightened up," one colleague said of Reeb. "He had a trace of mischief about him, and a deep sense of humour that endeared him to us all."[209] So spirits were good as Reeb, Miller, Olsen, and Krick shared a tiny table. Since the Berkeley UU Fellowship, where Olsen was minister, was next to the UC Berkeley campus, some of his time was spent serving students. Reeb had served campus student groups as the associate minister at All Souls (Unitarian) in D.C. Krick was working with students in the Boston area. Since Miller was the director of the Office of College Centers, they fell into talking about Olsen's impending trip to the Soviet Union with a group of twenty-two students.

Miller later recalled,

> After eating, each of us in turn phoned our wives from a booth in the restaurant to let them know of the day's events, that we were safe, and that we would be staying in Selma for at least another day. I phoned Mary Jane, then purchased a cigar and, while waiting for the others, stood outside leaning against the front window of the restaurant, smoking. It was just dusk on a warm spring evening, the downtown area felt quite peaceful, and I recall thinking this could be any downtown street of any town in America.[210]

When Olsen and Reeb joined him, instead of turning left and heading back the way they had come, they turned right, since that was the shortest way back to Brown Chapel AME. They walked three abreast: Reeb next to the curb, then Miller, then Olsen. They crossed an alley.

Four or five white locals came out of a variety store behind them on the opposite side of the street and began yelling, "Hey, you niggers." Olsen, Miller, and Reeb sped up, but the men ran at them. Olsen, who was furthest from the curb, saw them best. "They attacked us from behind, at least one carried a large club— possibly a baseball bat or length of pipe—with which he took a roundhouse swing at Jim's head."[211] He and Miller heard it land.

Having arrived in Selma late and not received instructions about what to do in a violent confrontation, Olsen backed away. But one of the men came after him, landing a punch that staggered him and sent his glasses flying. Miller dropped to the ground, doubled up, and tried, as he'd been trained, to shield his head, but one kick landed on his forehead, leaving an imprint that is still visible. Reeb was also on the ground, lying stunned; as their attackers kicked them, they yelled, "You want to know what it's like to be a nigger around here?"

The assailants landed a few more kicks, then fled. Miller and Olsen were bruised and Reeb dazed; they had to help him stand. By the time they had staggered to the SCLC office around the block to ask Diane Nash, the staffer there, for help, Reeb was in great pain.

Almost immediately an ambulance came and took them to the black infirmary. The physician, Dr. W. B. Dinkins (the same African-American doctor who had treated Jimmie Lee Jackson at Good Samaritan Hospital), quickly realized the seriousness of the injury and arranged for Reeb to be taken to the University of Alabama Medical Center in Birmingham. Reeb lay on a stretcher, grimacing. Olsen held his hand as the pain worsened. Reeb's grip tightened; then it went limp as he lapsed into unconsciousness.

Before the ambulance could leave for Birmingham, Olsen and Miller had to return to the SCLC office to get a check; the hospital would not admit Reeb without a $150 deposit. Then, with Dr. Dinkins and the driver, they set out on a desperate race that would turn into an ordeal. They ran several lights, but before long the ambulance got a flat rear tire. It was 9:30 p.m. Parked on the shoulder of the road, they had to decide what to do—call for a replacement ambulance or change the tire? The ambulance was equipped with a radio. They tried many channels, calling "Emergency, emergency" but got no response. Then a car full of white men pulled up. Olsen remembers thinking about the possibility of ending up in a ditch. Were he and his companions going to end up dead, like the Mississippi civil rights workers James Chaney, Andy Goodman, and Mickey Schwerner?

Finding that the radio didn't work and not daring to change the tire on that dark road, they turned back. The ambulance driver said he could drive on the rim of the wheel far enough to reach a radio station where he had once worked and where they could use the phone. They drove along with the clanging rim grating on their ears and fear in their guts. An unknown driver in a Nash Metro trailed behind them. Finally they pulled into the parking lot of WGWC, and the ambulance driver rushed inside to call for a replacement ambulance. Other cars cruised by and gave them the once-over. Olsen suggested an escort and Dinkins sent for his own car.

When the second ambulance arrived, it was followed by the Selma police. Reeb was transferred into it, but caution demanded that they not leave for Birmingham until Dinkins's car arrived. More cars drove by, checking them out. Then Dallas County sheriff's deputies arrived. They rapped on the windows, shone their flashlights into Olsen's, Miller's, and Reeb's faces, opened the ambulance's rear door, and began questioning them. Olsen requested a police escort, but they refused, saying, "We'll radio ahead—that's all you'll need."

The deputies told them to go on to Birmingham and drove away. But they waited, even though they feared that Reeb might die before they could get him to the hospital. In this hostile environment, civil rights workers always traveled in tandem. They needed an escort. The Metro driver came back and tried unsuccessfully to fix the siren on the ambulance, which was broken. They were never sure who he was or if he was really helping. Finally, Dinkins's car arrived—a radio-equipped Cadillac—and they departed for Birmingham via state route 22 at speeds of up to 70 mph. The road twisted and turned, and since the gurney brackets in the second ambulance did not match the gurney from the first, Olsen and Miller were left struggling to hold Reeb's stretcher steady. Finally, they did get a state trooper escort for the last few miles until they reached the interstate highway. Then, with Dr. Dinkins in the lead setting the pace, they sped toward Birmingham.

On hearing that Reeb was badly injured and on the way to Birmingham, Homer Jack went into overdrive. He called the Birmingham Church, interrupting meetings of its Finance and Nominating Committees. He told them Reeb was on his way. The Nominating Committee chair, Dr. Robert Hogan, immediately called Dr.

Joseph Volker, a member of the congregation who was the University of Alabama's vice president in charge of health affairs. Volker called the hospital to alert staff to Reeb's impending arrival, then rushed there himself. The top neurosurgeon in Alabama was called, and Hogan himself left for the hospital. Meanwhile, fearing the ambulance might be ambushed, Homer Jack called the FBI. Then he called Jack Mendelsohn, Jim and Marie Reeb's minister, in Boston. At 10:45 p.m., Mendelsohn called Marie to tell her of the attack, then drove to the Reeb home and sat through the night with her. Reeb reached the hospital at 11 p.m. and was wheeled directly into surgery.

In Alexandria, Virginia, Rollene Sumner Wells, John Wells's wife, was listening to the 11 p.m. news. The newscast reported that in Selma three Unitarian ministers had been attacked and that one was seriously injured, but it did not give their names. Terror gripped her. With no way to contact her husband, she called All Souls Church, which had been designated as the contact center for the local UUs who had traveled to Selma. She got the answering machine. All she could do was sit and wait, knowing that if he was alive he would call. Finally, just after midnight, he did.[212]

Earlier that evening, while Reeb and the others were congregating at Walker's Café, Charles Blackburn had been making the four-hour drive home to Huntsville, trying to put as many miles as possible behind him before dark set in. The phone rang just after he walked in the door. It was Clark Olsen. He told Blackburn that Reeb was gravely injured and asked him to come to Birmingham the next morning to help. With that on his mind, Blackburn headed to the church for a meeting. It was in progress when he arrived, full of heated arguments. Blackburn's arrest the previous fall, while assisting in the voter registration project in Magnolia, Mississippi, had received a lot of press in Huntsville. Now, in Selma, Blackburn and some church members had marched on Saturday with the Concerned White Citizens of Alabama, and marched again that very afternoon. This kindled the congregation's fears anew. Church members said they were afraid for the lives of their children. When

Blackburn arrived at the tail end of the meeting he found himself their target. Not expecting such an attack, and blindsided by the abusive language hurled at him, he "came close to breaking down."[213]

Wednesday Blackburn drove the hundred miles to Birmingham and spent the "morning helping to answer the hundreds of calls and telegrams as Jim lay dying."[214] Ken Marshall and Fred Cappuccino, who had been Reeb's colleagues in Washington, D.C., left for Selma as soon as they heard the news. Farley Wheelwright, who had just returned to Long Island, called Ralph Stutzman. "Farley's voice was more hurried than usual and Farley was usually in a hurry. 'If I can arrange it,' he said, 'are you interested in going to Selma?'"[215] They left the next day.

Those in Selma marched again. Hunter Leggitt said,

We went five abreast, down Sylvan Street from the Chapel, on our way to the Dallas County Court House, there to hold a prayer vigil for our fallen brother. But we were stopped at the first corner by a solid wall of troopers, backed up by posse-men. Confronted by a sea of blue helmets bearing Confederate flags. And they told us we could not march. That we could not assemble. And so we stood there, day and night, night and day, songs and prayers without end.[216]

Marie Reeb flew to Birmingham with John Sullivan, the director of the New England office of the American Friends Service Committee, Reeb's employer. En route, they met Duncan Howlett, senior minister at All Souls (Washington, D.C.), with whom Reeb had worked the previous five years. That evening Reeb's father arrived from Wyoming. By then it was clear that James Reeb would not survive.

Throughout Wednesday and all day Thursday the protesters stood on Sylvan Street, "and again through the night all night and all day," said Leggitt, and Saturday and Sunday until Monday the court order came through. . . . We stood in wind and rain and mud and for a few hours of sunshine. Often without eating, for days without sleep, sustained by the belief that we would overcome, we stood or we sat on the ground. For a while we had a raggedy plastic tent until they came and said it was against the fire ordinance to put up a tent in the street. People shot at us with pellet guns, and someone shouted from behind a fence at us, "You slab-sided egg-suckin' mother dogs, you." And the police put up a little clothesline across Sylvan Street, a puny little clothesline that came to be known as "the Berlin Wall of Selma."[217]

They sang and prayed and then sang some more. Leggitt and Kitty Jones, wife of an Episcopal priest from Chicago, put together a little twist on "Joshua Fit the Battle of Jericho":

We've got a rope that's a Berlin Wall, in Selma, Alabama.
We're gonna stand here till it falls, in Selma, Alabama.
Fear is the thing that built this wall, in Selma, Alabama.
Love is the thing that'll make it fall, in Selma, Alabama.

Others picked it up and added more verses as the night went on and they remained face to face with the police.

Thursday at 2 a.m., a bedraggled group of protesters stood steadfast at the Selma Wall. "It was cold and wet and my back was beginning to ache," said Leggitt, "when a Negro girl with a blanket came to me and asked, 'Are you cold?' 'Yes.' Without a word, she put half her blanket over my shoulders and her arm around my waist, and so we stood black and white together, male and female together, man and child together, through the long night and through other nights to freedom and to human community."[218]

At 12:15 p.m. on Thursday, March 11, Marie Reeb made the decision to stop using artificial means to keep her husband alive.

Meanwhile, Olsen, who had gotten the best look at the assailants, was spirited out of town. "The FBI wanted Jim's companions and witnesses to the fatal assault to be in safety and free from reprisals—and alive for testifying," said Clark Wells. "So Clark Olsen lay on the floor of a taxicab and we sat with our feet on him as we secreted him to the airport."[219] But Miller decided to stay on.

That evening, at 6:55 p.m., James Reeb died. President Lyndon B. Johnson called Marie Reeb to offer his condolences. Martin Luther King Jr. called, as well. And Homer Jack took off for Montgomery to meet with the SCLC leadership.

When Word Came

On Thursday evening, the board of trustees of the Birmingham Unitarian Church met, struggling to compose a statement. In this city where Eugene "Bull" Connor served as public safety commissioner, where between March and September 1963 there had been thirteen bombings, including the attack on the Sixteenth Street Baptist Church that killed four girls, where racial tensions were now higher than ever, the board wanted people to know who the Unitarian Universalists were and what they stood for. Ostensibly its members struggled over wording, but perhaps, without their being aware of it, their real conflict was between the differing sensibilities of the members raised in the North, for whom the congregation was a refuge, and those raised in the South. But when their minister, Lawrence E. McGinty, arrived with word that Reeb had died, they redoubled their effort and soon completed something that all but one board member could support:

> We in Alabama are at the crossroads in the maintenance of constitutional democracy. The events transpiring in Selma since Sunday, March 7, 1965, make this plain. The right peaceably to assemble and petition the government for the redress of grievance, indelibly written into the Constitution of the United States, has been obliterated by brutal police force.
>
> Widespread convulsion of protest against this display of inhumanitarian behavior has been demonstrated throughout

the United States. As citizens of Alabama, and Unitarians, we share the moral sentiments which have stimulated these outbursts of protest.

Our hearts are heavy with sadness at the tragic fate which overtook the Reverend James J. Reeb while acting in support of great libertarian principles. His death at the hands of civilian assassins illustrates that the use of violence by public authorities encourages violence by private citizens.

We will continue to dedicate ourselves to the eradication of this intolerable situation in our state and local communities.[220]

The lone dissenter was Edward Harris. He had been raised in Birmingham and wanted the statement more strongly worded.

In Selma, when word of James Reeb's death came, Public Safety Director Wilson Baker reportedly asked if the SCLC could control its people when they got the news. UU minister Richard Leonard from the Community Church of New York heard later that Baker "was told that there would be no problem on our side of the line [but] we wondered if he and Sheriff Clark could control their men."[221] Leonard said that when Reeb's death was announced, everyone on his side knelt and a service was held. Leonard delivered a brief eulogy.

Farley Wheelwright was on his way back to Selma bringing Ralph Stutzman and two other colleagues from Long Island when they got word of Reeb's death. They had flown into Atlanta and rented a car. "Driving to Selma was a nightmare," Stutzman said. "Farley didn't believe in speed limits nor in allowing anyone else to drive. We kept telling him to slow down. It was stupid to call attention to ourselves, four obvious clergy speeding through southern towns at night. All we needed was to end up in some red neck southern jail! Farley ignored us."[222]

Late that night, Homer Jack and David Johnson arrived in Montgomery to confer with King and the SCLC leadership. Because Johnson had rented a car, Jack had drafted him to serve as his chauffeur. But because King's location was kept secret, they had to rendezvous with an SCLC driver and leave their car behind. "We were driven a most circuitous route and couldn't guess where we were going or where this place was," Johnson said.

> There were guards outside, guards inside, guards everywhere. We were led to a back hotel room and that is when I first met Andrew Young. The room was cramped and spare with only one window and I stood in front of it. I was still a dumb kid from up North and didn't know it was the most dangerous place to be. Ralph Abernathy walked in first and he was friendly, next came the SCLC leadership and finally King. I was amazed. He was a very small man and when we shook hands his hand was very soft. He got right to the point. "What are the Unitarians going to do?" he asked. "We would understand when you have suffered like this if the UUs wanted to pack up and go home." Homer assured him no one was bailing out. King said he wanted several memorial services, including one in Brown Chapel. Homer readily agreed and said there would be other services, as well. The whole conversation was over in a few minutes and King left.[223]

On Friday morning, a jet sent by President Johnson flew Marie Reeb and Jim's father back to Boston. Orloff Miller traveled to Montgomery with Homer Jack to meet King and give him a detailed description of the events between being attacked and Reeb's death. In Selma the vigil at the Selma Wall continued. And across North America activists held marches and rallies—more than eighty in the forty-eight hours after the Bloody Sunday attack at the Pettus Bridge. Now, in the wake of James Reeb's death, countless more rallies, marches, sermons, and memorial services took place.

On Saturday Governor George Wallace flew to Washington to confer with President Johnson. The UUA Board recessed its meeting in Boston and flew to Birmingham. And around midnight, as Albert D'Orlando, minister of the Unitarian Universalist Church of New Orleans, worked on a sermon honoring Reeb, his home was firebombed.

On Sunday, March 14, like many clergy around the country, Ernie Pipes, the minister of the Unitarian Community Church in Santa Monica, California, preached about Reeb's death, "not really intending to go myself," he said, "but hoping to inspire perhaps a few members of the congregation to heed the call. Well, hardly had the last note of the closing hymn been sung when the congregation gathered itself to send a representative to the march [to Montgomery] and quickly decided it should be their minister. By such events are unintended and reluctant heroes created."[224]

In Tulsa, the response to Selma was influenced by the memory of the 1921 Tulsa Race Riot, when white rioters went on a rampage that destroyed the wealthiest African-American community in the United States. When John B. Wolf had been called as minister of All Souls Unitarian Church in 1960, a member of the Pulpit Committee told him, "John, we are careful not to get into racial relations here in Tulsa. You know, there was a race riot here. Something we don't talk about."[225] Against that backdrop, a group of clergy now gathered and decided to hold a city-wide service and march. As Pastor Clarence Knippa, a Missouri Synod Lutheran, put it, "God knows, it is needed as much here as anywhere." So it was that All Souls Unitarian hosted Tulsa's first truly ecumenical service. Wolf was joined by rabbis, priests, AME ministers, and other clergy, all of them leading seven hundred people of many faiths and races in worship. Following the service the crowd adjourned to the steps of Holy Family Cathedral and from there, joined by still others, they marched, now a thousand strong, to the Federal Building.[226]

Gene Navias, the UUA's religious education consultant, happened to be in Savannah, Georgia, to offer his expertise to the congregation's religious education program:

> I was visiting our churches and fellowships in the south at the time of the terrible trouble in Selma when James Reeb was killed. I was deeply depressed by the news that came hour by hour on the radio of my car as I headed through long stretches of the Carolinas on my way to our Fellowship in Savannah,

Georgia, and that feeling was not lifted when I stopped for gas in a small village. All conversation stopped in the gas station as I got out of my car with a Massachusetts license plate, and the air crackled with hostility as the woman attendant announced to the onlooker that my credit card said I was a minister.

But things were different in our little Fellowship in Savannah. Deeply distressed by the death of James Reeb, but moved by their conviction, the group decided that it had to declare, regardless of possible repercussions and reprisals, that it stood for freedom of all people. By the time I came upon the little rented downtown house where the fellowship met, the wayside pulpit had been draped in black crepe and a sign said IN MEMORIAM—JAMES J. REEB.

"Could we change the Sunday program," they clamored to know. "Would I relinquish my R.E. sermon for a memorial service, if they dared to hold one?" "Yes." They set to work inviting members of the black community, and they had never dared do that before. They invited the head of the local NAACP, and they had never dared do that before. The service was held with as high feelings as I have ever experienced in any Unitarian fellowship, and when the service was over, the head of the NAACP asked them if they, in turn, would come to a service and rally that afternoon in a black Methodist church in the heart of the ghetto where all the martyrs of the civil rights movement would be memorialized. They gasped. They had never traveled those streets. They had never been in a church like that. Did they dare? And once again, when the thought settled in, they said "YES." They committed themselves, and they went, twenty scared white Unitarians among 500 black people. . . .

I don't know what the curriculum was to have been that Sunday morning when we met in memoriam. I know not what words of what curriculum kits or books were never read. . . .

The children and youth of that fellowship were taught a more powerful lesson than anything from the books or kits. What the adults were doing as they struggled with their beliefs and their consciences spoke so loudly that words were not needed.[227]

In Memphis, Tennessee, the local branch of the NAACP organized a march to honor Reeb on Sunday, March 14. There Father Joseph Leppert offered a moving tribute. James Madison Barr III, the minister of the Unitarian Church of Memphis, boycotted the march. He explained why that Sunday morning in his sermon, saying that King shared in the guilt for Reeb's death, along with the assailants. "I will not join hands with those who help stir the cauldron of hatred and violence," he said. "Let us not confuse tolerance and decency with misplaced loyalty. Let us not unwittingly help destroy the very supports necessary to keep us a free people—respect for the courts of our land." Furthermore, he refused to participate in the march because Memphis ' "had done excellently' in race relations and such demonstrations 'harden the feelings of bigots.' "[228]

In Carbondale, Illinois, that Sunday, Henry Nelson Wieman, one of the leading theologians of the first half of the twentieth century and a Unitarian Universalist, preached a memorial service in which he strove to place James Reeb's murder in a broader context. "Such a death," he said, "gathers its power not merely from the man himself," but also from a "massive historic development." This development transforms

> the social order and the lives of men, and [gives] to James Reeb more power in his death than he could ever have had in his life. . . . It is a transforming power extending far beyond the bounds of the United States. It is world-wide in its scope. It is awakening all the down-trodden and oppressed and impoverished peoples of the earth to demand something like equality with those who have ruled over them, kept them in servitude and put on them the stamp of inferiority.[229]

In his sermon in Kalamazoo, Michigan, Roger Greeley did not repeat the condition he had laid on his cousin earlier in the week, when the president of the UUA had asked him to go to Selma. He focused, instead, on the limits of his own tolerance and what Reeb's sacrifice meant to him:

> Thus, my colleague and acquaintance went to Selma, Alabama, in the flesh and blood and was flown out as so many ashes in an urn. It would be criminal of me to overlook or ignore this momentous tragedy of our time. I cannot apologize to you for not going to Selma myself, for I am afraid. I am afraid that my devotion and belief in non-violence is very shaky. I am not anxious to be indicted for murder. . . .
>
> Yes, I knew Jim Reeb. . . . But knowledge, personal knowledge, . . . only sharpens the pain of this senseless tragedy. Any life that is given or taken in the cause of equality . . . is equal to every other life thus lost. Any man who suffers from man's inhumanity to man is my brother. When will we learn this?"[230]

In Lansing, Michigan, Bob Schaibly, a senior at Michigan State, was working as quarter-time secretary at the Unitarian church. Tom Smith, the minister, unable to go himself, made Schaibly an offer: "I'll give you $25 for your expenses if you will go in my place." Schaibly went, joining an ecumenical caravan that included a white Oldsmobile and a massive rented truck full of donated food for the marchers. Schaibly later recalled,

> I was a shy, middle-class boy from the suburbs and in Alabama I slept on the hardwood floor (for the first time in my life) in the choir loft of a Baptist church, using my jacket as a blanket and my sweater as a pillow. I saw the possibilities the church has in keeping values alive for decades until they can be realized, attained, and how the institution can help bring justice. The march changed my life. I saw the church as a place where good things could happen, and although I was a pre-law student I decided to enter the ministry.[231]

In Rochester, New York, that Sunday morning Robert West, the minister of Winton Road Unitarian Church and the person who three years later would succeed Greeley as president of the UUA, preached "Murder of Jim Reeb." He shared memories of Reeb, including of walking with him in the Washington March for Freedom two summers before. He concluded by saying, "I am leaving for Selma this afternoon. I am going, to attend the memorial service for Jim Reeb at 2 p.m. tomorrow afternoon. I am going as an individual to help people in our nation recognize that violence cannot destroy the movement toward equal opportunity and personal freedom."[232]

An hour and a half east, in Cortland, the front entrance to the church was draped in black crepe and a large sign read "WE ARE IN MOURNING FOR SELMA, ALA." In Binghamton, an hour south of there, the Unitarian minister Harry Thor sent a letter to the *Binghamton Press* announcing a rally at the courthouse; two hundred people came. A free-will offering was collected which enabled a group of six clergy—ministers, priests, and rabbis—to be their communities' witnesses in Selma. And downstate in Flushing, Dick Boeke, the minister of the UU church, helped organize a protest called "Flushing Marches with Selma." Two Congressmen and an array of clergy led a march from the Friends Meeting House to the Free Synagogue, where they addressed a rally of two thousand.

Even in Canada, Unitarian Universalists responded to Reeb's death. In Hamilton, Ontario, on Saturday, March 13, Bob Hemstreet called his nearest colleague, Arnold Thaw in Port Credit. They decided to go south to join the protestors. Hemstreet couldn't pay for a plane ticket, but "a parishioner, Stan Blonski, who had a store in downtown Hamilton, literally emptied his till" to give him $300. Thaw and Hemstreet flew to Atlanta and "were met by members of the Atlanta congregation and taken to Gene Pickett's home, where about twenty of us discussed strategy."[233]

In Boston, the UUA board recessed its meeting that day and eight of its members flew to Birmingham, where they were hosted by members of the congregation. Attending the Birmingham UU church on Sunday they heard its minister, Alabamian Larry McGinty, deliver a fiery, unsparing sermon:

> Another man died in Selma, within the same social context, shot by a state trooper in an atmosphere of violence. His name was Jimmie Lee Jackson, a Negro laborer, wounded in Marion, who lay in a Selma hospital in critical condition for eight days. Nobody really cared or got upset about Jimmie Lee Jackson. . . . He was a human being, as was James Reeb and as are you and I. But he was a Negro human being! And here's the tragedy. He was not a human to this nation, to Southerners or to non-Southerners, for implicit in the response of the government and of the people was just that "another nigger" was dead. This is a white man's country. Let's face it. And here is the evil lurking in all of us, all across this country, North, East, South and West.[234]

Following lunch, there was a briefing for the board, during which Orloff Miller told them, "Once you're inside the Negro compound, don't go out for any reason."[235] Then the board, members of the UUA staff, and a group of twenty-five people from California and Hawaii left for Selma "in two chartered buses, taking care not to let the drivers hear any 'subversive' talk."[236]

At 5 p.m. the board reconvened in the St. Elizabeth's Catholic Mission, with thirty-seven ministers and ten laity in attendance. Homer Jack gave a comprehensive report on the situation, then outlined the accommodations for the board and plans for Reeb's memorial service. Donald S. Harrington, the senior minister of the Community Church of New York, ended the meeting by reading from Howard Zinn's *SNCC: The New Abolitionists*: "Finally it all boils down to human relationships. It is the question of . . . whether I shall go on living in isolation or whether there shall be a we. . . . Love alone is radical. Political statements are not; programs are not; even going to jail is not."[237]

At that evening's rally at Brown Chapel AME, Dana McLean Greeley and eighty-four-year-old Judge Lawrence Brooks, vice moderator of the UUA's board of trustees, both spoke. Before they did, Richard Leonard, who had been in Selma since March 8, sidled up to Greeley and whispered, "never mention James Reeb without mentioning Jimmie Lee Jackson in the same breath—they are both martyrs in everyone's eyes, and only to talk of Reeb is to display our own racism."[238] Greeley understood and henceforth spoke of them as brothers. When Judge Brooks rose to speak, Chris Raible remembered, "He spoke simply and briefly, saying what he would say to a state trooper if he were asked 'What are you doing here?' He said, I would reply, 'I am here because I am a judge and I cannot stand injustice; I am here because I am an American and wherever there is injustice I am involved.' And he went on to say that his father-in-law had been a white colonel of a Negro regiment for the North in the Civil War."[239]

In Memoriam

There were many memorial services for James Reeb. On Tuesday, March 16, at All Souls (Unitarian) in Washington, D.C., Duncan Howlett and Dana McLean Greeley conducted a service, with Vice President Hubert Humphrey and Senator Edward Kennedy in attendance. Marie Reeb and Jim's father were there, as they would be on Thursday at a service held at Arlington Street Church in Boston. But before these, a service was held in Selma on Monday, to which people flocked from across the country.

A throng of dignitaries planned to appear. In preparation, Dana Greeley assigned his assistant, Irene K. Murdock, to work with SCLC leader C. T. Vivian to organize seating on the platform for the VIPs. Among them were Walter Reuther, head of the United Auto Workers; Right Rev. John Hines, the presiding bishop of the Episcopal Church; and, perhaps most impressive, the colorfully robed Archbishop Iakovos, primate of the Greek Orthodox Archdiocese of North and South America. Leon C. Fay, director of the UUA Department of Ministry, counted 109 UU ministers in attendance.

Peter Weller, who was serving a UU congregation in Seattle, Washington, remembers that the service began with a "magic moment of transition. The wildly exuberant rally that had erupted with the appearance of MLK Jr. abruptly ended when the minister of Brown Memorial Chapel stepped to the pulpit and raised his arm, in signal that the memorial service was about to begin. Heeding that signal, the entire assembly became silent, and the service proceeded."[240] The number of speakers preceding King seemed endless, but eventually King stepped into the pulpit to eulogize James Reeb:

> "And if he should die,
> Take his body, and cut it into little stars.
> He will make the face of heaven so fine
> That all the world will be in love with night."

> These beautiful words from Shakespeare's *Romeo and Juliet* so eloquently describe the radiant life of James Reeb. . . . His death was a result of a sensitive religious spirit. His crime was that he dared to live his faith; he placed himself alongside the disinherited black brethren of this community. . . .
>
> James Reeb could not be accused of being only concerned about justice for Negroes away from home. He and his family live in Roxbury, Massachusetts, a predominantly Negro community. [They] devoted their lives to aiding families in low-income housing areas. James, we must ask the question: Why must good men die for doing good?

King went on to ask, "Who killed Jim Reeb?" "A few sick, demented, and misguided men," he responded. Then he asked, "What killed Jim Reeb?" And he answered that it was an indifferent ministry, an irrelevant church, irresponsible politicians, a law enforcement establishment embracing lawlessness in the name of law, a timid federal government, and cowardly Negroes who stood on the sidelines. Toward the end of his eulogy he returned to a refrain that was familiar to everyone present:

> We will be able—right here in Alabama, right here in the deep South, right here in the United States—to transform the jangling discords of our nation into a beautiful symphony of brotherhood. We will be able to speed up that day when all of God's children—as expressed so beautifully in this marvel-ous ecumenical service—all of God's children, black men and white men, Jews and Gentiles, Protestants and Catholics, [will] be able to join hands in unity and brotherhood to bring about the bright day of the brotherhood of man under the guidance of the fatherhood of God.
>
> So we thank God for the life of James Reeb. We thank God for his witness. We thank God that he was willing to lay down his life in order to redeem the soul of our nation.[241]

Following King, Dana McLean Greeley offered a prayer that began "God of our Fathers and of our future" and ended with the Lord's Prayer. Then everyone rose and sang "We Shall Overcome." Christopher Raible remembered, "When we had sung four stanzas, we hummed, and a rabbi, [Eugene Weiner] who had been asked to give the benediction, stepped to the pulpit. He repeated in Hebrew the great Kaddish, the memorial prayer for the dead, over our humming. As he completed it, we sang again, and from nowhere there came two little Negro girls who began to sing a high piercing descant above our singing. The rabbi leaned down, picked up the four-year-old, and held her in his arms. And the tears flowed down my face." And all around him, people were crying.[242]

Summing up the experience at Brown Chapel AME, seventy-one-year-old Lewis McGee, one of only five African-American UU ministers and the only one present, said, "James Reeb lost his life and Dr. King, a Baptist minister, delivered the eulogy at a memo-rial service for Rev. Reeb, a Unitarian minister, in the local A.M.E.

Church. There was not the slightest feeling of denominational or racial difference."[243]

At the very end of the service a leader announced that the federal court had upheld the protestors' right to march to the courthouse and hold a service there. They had tried that morning and been stopped; now, with Greeley, C. T. Vivian, a nun, Rabbi Eugene Weiner, and two others in the front row, they marched again. At the Selma Wall, they were once again stopped by Wilson Baker. When Baker stated that he was upholding the Constitution of the State of Alabama, a provoked Greeley shot back, "And what of the Constitution of the United States of America?" Three thousand strong, they headed toward the courthouse.

Jack Mendelsohn, the Reeb family's minister, lined up next to Farley Wheelwright. They had been on opposite sides of the 1963 General Assembly debate over whether to amend the UUA's bylaws to require member congregations to have "maintained a policy of admitting persons to membership without discrimination of race, color, or national origin." Mendelsohn had asked how the UUA could treat "congregational polity as something over here and segregation and integration as something over there" and voted for the amendment. Wheelwright had said, "A vote against it appears to be a vote in favor of sin [but] it sets up some kind of a creedal policy . . . and runs contrary to the great tradition of free religion" and voted against. Now they were marching together, and since one was six feet three inches tall and the other six foot four, they towered above the crowd. "I didn't know Farley all that well," Mendelsohn recalled, and "had no idea what a rambunctious son of a bitch he could be. Boy was I scared, because Farley was just taunting these rednecks who were lining the sidewalks with hate in their eyes, and he was just taunting them every step of the way. He was literally challenging them to do something. Oh, he was calling them all sorts of names. Finally, I said, 'For Chrissake, Farley. Will you shut up!' "[244]

That evening President Johnson addressed a joint session of Congress, and uttered the now famous words with which he introduced the Voting Rights Bill:

At times history and fate meet at a single time in a single place to shape a turning point in man's unending search for freedom. So it was at Lexington and Concord. So it was a century ago at Appomattox. So it was last week in Selma, Alabama. There, long suffering men and women peacefully protested the denial of their rights as Americans. Many were brutally assaulted, one good man, a man of God, was killed.

In Selma John Wells, a minister and lawyer, watched the news coverage of the speech with Rudi Gelsey, minister of the UU Church of the Restoration in Philadelphia. The previous Friday, while several thousand clergy protested in front of the White House, Wells, Duncan Howlett, and Joseph Ellwanger, the organizer of the Concerned White Citizens of Alabama, had been part of a delegation that met with the president for two hours. As Gelsey listened to the address, Wells kept interjecting to tell him which of the members of the delegation (including Wells himself) had originally said the words Johnson was now offering. And as the president echoed the anthem of the civil rights movement, "And we shall overcome," residents in the George Washington Carver Homes which surround Brown Chapel AME—as well as people all across the nation—said hallelujah and cried.

Purim

Tuesday arrived, but there was still no court order allowing the assembled masses in Selma to march to Montgomery. They waited. Ministers came and went. Gerry Bailey, a clinical psychologist and a member of David Cole's Rockville church, also came to Selma. Having just submitted a report to the government on controlling "the escalation of violence," he felt called to protest this "abrogation of human rights." He joined the vigil at the Selma Wall, but found that he could only stand there for so long. One morning he and Rudy Nemser, the minister in Fairfax, Virginia, took a walk through the black area on the edge of town. What they saw, Bailey said, was a vast sea of shacks extending as far as you could see over a flat, poorly drained area. The March rains had turned the unpaved streets into a quagmire. There were no curbs or sidewalks, and muddy ruts moved in and out among the homes in a crazy fashion. Crooked porch railings and roof supports and wobbly fences. . . . Occasionally there would be a chimney standing alone. Residents called the Selma firemen chimney-savers, because that was all that was left by the time they arrived when one of their homes was ablaze.[245]

The rally continued at the Selma Wall and each day saw mass meetings. UU minister Jim Hobart remembers the offering being collected in a very Baptist style: "Individuals came forth, placed their money or check in the basket held by a tall and large Black preacher." At one memorable rally a man came up and "explained, almost defiantly, that he and other atheists had taken up a collection totaling $5,000." Hobart recalled that, "without any change of expression, the preacher looked out across the congregation and inquired, 'Are there any other atheists here with $5,000?' "[246] In Selma, ecumenism knew no bounds.

While the standoff with the police at the Selma Wall continued, other forms of protest evolved. The SCLC's strategies were met by strategies from the city, which were met by counter-strategies, and so on. Gerry Bailey took part in an SCLC action that was kept secret even from other protesters. For two days they laid plans. The SCLC composed a letter to Mayor Smitherman asking for improved services for the black community. Bailey and others tried to see him to deliver the letter, and when that failed about forty people implemented a new strategy on Wednesday: picketing the mayor's house. "The tension," Bailey said, "was unbelievable. People were crying and hugging good-byes as if there were no tomorrows. There had been talk of guns on the porches of the houses in the neighborhood where we were going. We felt that we were going into a trap in which we would surely die. I wet myself," he confessed. "Not a mere trickle, but an explosive flood that soaked all of my right pants leg."

Drivers appeared, and we sorted ourselves into groups for transport closer to the Mayor's house. . . . We disembarked a few blocks from our destination and fell into a file, two by two. Then a weird thing happened. The dozen or so people in front of us just melted away one or two at a time and reformed at the end of the file, until suddenly there were David [Cole, my minister] and I at the head of the picket. We looked at each other and stood still. . . . As we started to walk I figured we would be first to be shot.

We hardly moved a block or so before they came down on us from every direction, screaming and hollering murderous threats. It could have been bad news, but the town Safety Commissioner, Wilson Baker, held things in check and in a few minutes we were on a school bus, being whisked off to jail.[247]

The group of about forty was held in the courtroom. That Wednesday was Purim, the Jewish spring festival which celebrates Esther's intervention with the king of Persia that saved the Jews from annihilation and brought about the downfall of Haman, who had planned to have them slaughtered. Among those incarcerated were rabbis. Members of the local synagogue brought them robes and the Scroll of Esther, and so they celebrated Purim, which laughs at the pretensions of all tyrants. It was "an observance," Cole said, "that had special meaning for all of us that night."[248]

Late Wednesday afternoon, March 17, word spread that Federal District Judge Frank Johnson would permit the march and ordered that it be protected by both the state and federal governments. It would take place on Sunday.

On Thursday, the SCLC pressed on with a new action: small groups of four to six people—too few to count as a march and thus need a permit—were sent out. Jim Hobart remembers,

Each group was given instructions of where to begin our walk and the direction we were to walk, but we were not given our destination. I was one of a group of four, as it turned out all young and white UU ministers. We walked into the white neighborhood, all dressed professionally wearing coats and ties. I was very nervous. I wondered silently, "Are we being watched? If so, are we being watched by people with guns and itchy trigger-fingers?" After only a couple of blocks we came upon a police cruiser, its lights flashing. As we approached an older police sergeant opened the car door, got out and said to us, "Boys, don't you understand that the people of this neighborhood don't want you here? Some of them are really mad about it. We don't want you to get hurt. Get into this police car!" We agreed with his logic, so we crawled into the back seat. He returned to the front passenger seat, picked up the radio microphone, and spoke to headquarters, "We've got these four preachers in the cruiser. What are we holding them for?" There was a pause. . . . Then came the response, "Temporary insanity." Both the front seat and the back seat broke up with peals of laughter. Yes, it was funny, and we on the back seat were relieved to be off the street. Off we drove to an uncertain future at the police station. Now, as the police soon discovered, there were numerous groups of four to six people taking walks in the white neighborhood. We knew not where we were going. However, the SCLC strategists knew we were all walking from different directions toward Mayor Smitherman's house.

Hobart's group was only the first. Eventually over three hundred people were arrested. He continues,

We were escorted into the police court room and took seats. Soon others joined us. Before long it became apparent there were too many to fit into the court room [and] the police had to decide what to do with all of us. Not only were there too many to fit in the court room, there were too many to fit into jail cells. Their answer was to march us all several blocks to a Black community center, where we were held while the authorities decided our fate. We crowded into the room, some standing, some sitting on the floor. Soon there was singing. Singing was as necessary as breathing in the Civil Rights movement! From time-to-time there were discussions between the authorities and our designated leaders. They talked together. We got reports back. No decisions were made about what would be the next step. Food was brought in. We settled in for a long and uncomfortable night. Then, after dark the word came. The police said we were free to leave without any charges. The response? "No!" It would not do for several hundred people to walk without escort in the dark the several blocks back to Brown Chapel. Our leaders demanded a police escort. It did not occur that night. However, it did occur the next morning. The police escorted several hundred sleep-deprived and disheveled people through a taunting and threatening crowd of white people back to the relative safety of "the compound" around Brown Chapel.[249]

On to Montgomery

The order from Judge Johnson was clear: the march was to be allowed and the marchers protected. President Johnson was equally clear in a meeting with Governor Wallace, but after returning to Alabama the governor reneged, and the Alabama state legislature asked the president to convince the SCLC to call off the march. President Johnson, in turn, federalized 1,800 Alabama National Guardsmen and sent two thousand additional troops and a hundred FBI agents. The judge's ruling stipulated that as many as wished could walk on the first and last days of the march, when they would be on a four-lane highway; but on the middle days, when they would be on the two-lane Route 80, the march would be limited to three hundred.

In Selma and Montgomery, and across the country, people began to prepare. Jane Boyajian, the director of religious education at the UU congregation in Fairfax, Virginia, had been attending local SCLC meetings. She had wanted to go to Selma, but hadn't been able to: the minister had gone, and she was asked to remain and tend to the congregation. At an SCLC meeting Rev. Walter Fauntroy, who would later become D.C.'s first representative to Congress, approached her to say that King and the SCLC leadership wanted her to organize the national mobilization. She was to get as many people as possible, representing as many organizations as possible, to Montgomery, where they would welcome the Selma marchers on the final day and then march together with them to the capitol building. Fearing what might happen, King and the SCLC did not want people flocking down in private cars.

Knowing she would have to take time off, Boyajian consulted with the minister, the board chair, and the chair of the Religious Education Committee. They were supportive but concerned: She was a single mother with five- and eight-year-old daughters, and she was a white woman. Leaving the SCLC office in inner-city D.C. late at night was perilous. "I did think about it," she said, "but I felt compelled."[250] As the situation unfolded, she was escorted to and from the office by SCLC staff; she was also tailed by the FBI (which was concerned about her activities, rather than for her well-being), and she moved her daughters to a parishioner's home in the country. Working for the SCLC made her realize that the security she had long taken for granted was no longer a given.

Boyajian set about recruiting support from the leadership of every major denomination, as well as from unions and interest groups. She issued press releases and promoted the use of charters and public transport. Uniformly, those she contacted were "responsive and collaborative"; the one exception was the UUA. Calls to Homer Jack went unanswered. She turned to Jack Mendelsohn, hoping he would intercede, but when that effort failed she gave up.[251]

As Sunday approached in Selma, organizers scrambled to assemble the necessities for a five-day march of three hundred people. They needed generators for the campsites, ground tarps, air mattresses, blankets, food, and water. In Atlanta, UU minister

Eugene Pickett put out the call for members of the United Liberal Congregation in Atlanta to go if they could, or to send blankets if they couldn't. The church telephone tree sprung into action, and in a single Sunday church members supplied 250 blankets.[252] Liz McMaster, a member of the Atlanta congregation, wanted to go but her husband counseled her not to, so instead she "scoured the house for blankets."[253]

On Sunday afternoon, March 21, the march to Montgomery set out, led by Martin and Coretta King, Ralph and Juanita Abernathy, Ralph Bunche, Rabbi Abraham Heschel, Dick Gregory, and other notables. Behind them came 3,200 more. Overhead flew a single-engine Piper Cub dropping KKK leaflets.

Joseph Nerad, minister of the First Universalist Unitarian Church of Wausau, Wisconsin, arrived on Monday morning for Reeb's memorial and stayed on with a local black family (Lonzo and Alice West) until the conclusion of the march two weeks later. Father Morris Samuel of East Los Angeles, who had also been assigned to the West family, was asked to form a night security group and invited Nerad to join. This invitation created a dilemma for Nerad since he wanted to march the entire way. But, wrote Nerad, "the march was limited for most of the way . . . to 300—chosen from those beaten, jailed, gassed, or otherwise brutalized and there were enough [of those] to limit UUA representation to only one man—and I was second on the list. Dick Leonard was determined to go!" So Nerad accepted the offer to be on the security team "and was told absolutely no more participating in demonstrations!"[254]

Leonard was, indeed, determined to go. In his diary he wrote, "I [made] a . . . resolution to myself—that if I failed to make the final list the next day, I would make the march myself, . . . and if necessary, following the three hundred marchers but without the protection of the federalized National Guard. It would be a dangerous thing to do, offering oneself almost as a target to an angry crowd."[255]

Leonard told the committee that because of James Reeb they needed someone representing Unitarian Universalism. But the organizers responded that they already had a UU—James Bell, an

African-American young adult who was a member of the Germantown Unitarian Church in Philadelphia. Bell would serve as one of the marshals to guide the marchers. When Leonard persisted, one of the committee members replied, "That sounds like you're putting yourself and your wishes ahead of everyone else's. Would you do it if it jeopardized everybody else?" This thought gave Leonard pause, but still he "resolved to march as far as [he] could on the four-lane road, and then see if [he] could find some way to go on with the march."[256]

Steve Graves, a Meadville Lombard student, was no less determined to march the entire fifty miles. Graves was on his own and "couldn't tell how the winnowing process worked." Setting out, he steadily moved toward the front of the march where, to his surprise, he was "designated a 'line marshal' to help keep an orderly line of marchers."[257] Later, when he was replaced by an official marshal, Graves kept right on marching with the three hundred, as did Leonard. So it came to pass that the two Unitarian Universalists who marched the entire distance were uninvited guests.

Nerad describes the five-day march in his diary:

On Sunday, we left Selma shortly after 10 a.m. and arrived at the first campsite before noon. Our group of men under Father Grant Muse went out to inspect a high cliff about ¼ mile away, overlooking the camp. Pete Flint and I took lookout for a road crew leveling a country lane. One of the workers was TV star Gary Merrill! The marchers arrived about 5 p.m. and after supper, we began to get cold, and shortly after dark, we moved our camp from outside to the Press tent which was little used by press-men. Fires began to appear shortly after dark, and people were up most of that first night. The temperature dropped in the swampy pasture to about 25 degrees! It was good to see the dawn and feel the sun's warmth in the morning. . . .

We were at the second camp, however, before noon, and had begun setting up security and looking over the lay of the land. After lunch I tried to get some rest—too much confu-

sion for sleep. . . . It was there we began to have troubles with
some of the young men dropping out because we insisted on
segregation—women from men! It was not nearly as cold on
Monday night. . . . King was supposed to speak, but someone
reported seeing a man who looked like a clergyman, carrying
a pistol! We were dispersed through the crowd to watch for an
assassination attempt, but apparently the leadership decided
to cancel the talk and get to bed early.

On Tuesday morning, I had a watch ending at 6 a.m.
Between 6 and 6:30, I got some breakfast, then went back to
awaken the rest of the doctors, only to find them up and quite
excited. One of the ministers from the camp had undergone a
nervous breakdown and they were getting him into an ambulance. . . . [Tuesday's] campsite was the worst as far as mud was
concerned. The others had been pastures—this was a plowed
field with no cover! Bales and bales of hay had been laid down,
but still feet sank in to the ankle and more! It was at this camp,
on Tuesday night that I met Pete Seeger and his wife.

[Wednesday evening,] before I could get to eat, I was
posted at the front gate for a 6–9 stretch. It was tough with
people coming at me from both sides! The big show—Peter,
Paul and Mary, Harry Belafonte, Dick Gregory, Sammy Davis
Jr., et. al.—was late getting started. Several people fainted—
hundreds were leaving. . . . This was the second muddiest
camp! I got some rest from 9 to 1: the loudspeakers were too
loud for sleep, and I was again at the post from midnight on
until after 3:30. I got two hours sleep and was reassigned at
about 6:10.

I got in the line of the march for the final 4 miles at about
10 a.m. Through the Negro neighborhood, people cheered us
and we waved at each other. At the schools, pupils and teachers
crowded windows. One group of tots lined an intersection and
were shouting "Freedom! Freedom!" as we passed. Things got
quieter as we passed into the transition neighborhood. Along
the streets downtown we began to meet vilification and spit-

ting! We saw no American flags except our own—on helmets, uniforms, being waved at by sidewalk spectators, on official state cars—only the flag of the Confederacy!—even atop the statehouse![258]

Meanwhile, Ernie Pipes and a member of his congregation, Leon Papernow, had arrived in Montgomery. In the days preceding the climax of the march, they did organizational work. Through Papernow, who had business interests in the area, Pipes had access to a car, so he was assigned to meet people flying in to join the final leg of the march and bring them to the housing that had been arranged, mainly in the black community. He said,

My pickups were, naturally, both black and white—and a car with racially mixed passengers on the streets of Montgomery, Alabama in 1965 was, to the locals, provocative. There were hostile reactions and we drove only during the day, never at night. Every evening small groups of us were schooled in the methods of non-violent action. . . . During the days we would pass out flyers as a final effort to recruit marchers. We would work in the black neighborhoods for the obvious reasons of safety and where we imagined marchers could be found. But the local blacks, while polite, courteous and grateful for our efforts, would rarely agree to join the march. They were employed, nearly altogether by the white community and, with their livelihoods at jeopardy, there was too much at stake.[259]

In Bloomington, Indiana, an anonymous member of the UU church put up the money to charter a DC3 to fly a group down for the end of the march. The congregation invited the leading black pastor in town and some members of his congregation to join them.[260]

In Mount Vernon, Virginia, after the congregational telephone tree was activated, Judy Street and another member volunteered to go. They would travel on a train chartered by the SCLC. "Her thunderstruck husband found his objections unavailing. She was going and that was that. To his astonishment, he found this gentle creature, who abhorred camping even under a tent, moving off down the train platform with nothing more than a rolled-up blanket, leaving [him] and two teenage boys staring forlornly through the bars as all they held most dear in the world moved determinedly toward an unknown and possibly terminal fate."[261] The train was called the Freedom Train, and it also carried a group of six from Cedar Lane Unitarian Church in Bethesda, Maryland. The train was crowded and its occupants advised to remain low in their seats or on the floor, as trains and buses going to Alabama had been fired upon. Indeed, so was theirs.[262]

In Denver, when the call came to join the final day of the march, Dick Henry, minister of the First Unitarian Society, felt "torn between going and helping as many as possible add their presence to the cause." He had moved to Denver in 1957 from Knoxville, Tennessee, where he had been involved in race relations, and in Denver he was elected president of the Religious Council on Human Relations. In the end, he decided, "rightly or wrongly," to help facilitate the participation of others. Ninety flew from Denver, and Henry spent the evening "checking them in at the airport."[263]

In Birmingham the UU congregation prepared for a second onslaught, larger than the first. Coming to participate in the final day of the march were two buses from Rochester, New York, carrying 150, and a plane Dana Greeley had chartered from Boston carrying 75. They needed to be fed, given home hospitality, and returned to the church by 5 a.m. to be put on five buses and driven a hundred miles to Montgomery.[264] Charles Gaines, the UU minister in Milford, New Hampshire, was among those on the charter from Boston. After a warm welcome, he went with a group of ten to spend the night on his host's living room floor. As he was falling asleep there was a knock at the front door. "One of the northerners from our party got up and went to open it, as the host came from the bedroom whispering, 'Don't open the door until you know who is outside.'"[265]

When Chicago alderman Leon Despres arrived in Montgomery, the group on his chartered plane was met by Rev. Aron
Gilmartin, the UUA point man. Gilmartin warned them, "As soon
as the afternoon program is concluded, you are asked to proceed
immediately to the area where special buses will pick you up for
the airport. It is absolutely essential that all demonstrators leave
Montgomery immediately after the program, because we expect
the troopers and National Guard to be withdrawn this evening.
Since policing will fall into the hands of the local authorities, we
consider the situation unsafe and advise against any of you remaining."[266] Bussed to St. Jude Catholic Church, they assembled for the
four-mile walk to the capitol.

As the end of the march drew near, Jane Boyajian felt she
needed to be there too. She wanted to see all those she had worked
with arrive at their goal. The SCLC promised to get her there, but
asked her to keep working in D.C. as long as possible. On the final
morning of the march, she flew to Montgomery on a plane chartered by Americans for Democratic Action.[267]

On the next-to-last day, when others were allowed to join the
three hundred, stately, independent Alison Murphy Mathews,
mother of five—one of whom was still at home—joined the march.
She came as the regional director of the Unitarians for Social
Action in Olympia, Washington. The group had "raised enough
money for her plane ticket to Selma." How she "will get home is
another question," reported the *Daily Olympian*.[268] On the final
day, among the 30,000 who marched were about 500 UU lay people, including Connie Burgess, the executive director of the UU
Women's Federation; and about 250 UU ministers and, of course,
Dana McLean Greeley was one of them.[269]

Waving well-wishers greeted the marchers at the outset of the
march's final leg as, singing freedom songs, they moved through
African-American neighborhoods. Then the well-wishers vanished. As they passed through the white areas, they were spat upon,
cursed, and called "white niggers" and "Commies." "This invisible
line of demarcation was sharply etched in my consciousness," said

Howard Matson, associate minister of the First Unitarian Church of San Francisco, "by an incident that happened to Ray Manker (the minister in Phoenix). As we went through the Negro areas he would dart off the line now and then to attempt to purchase film for his camera. They were all sold out. As he began to enter another store, he was suddenly tackled by a Negro march marshal almost as though he were a blocker in a football game. 'Are you out of your mind!' the marshal shouted. 'That's a *white* store!' "[270]

Marchers felt they were reliving the Civil War. The statehouse flew the flag of Alabama and beneath it the Confederate flag; nearby were the statue of Jefferson Davis and the spot where, in 1861, he took the oath of office that made him president of the Confederacy. "And down on the lawn the flag of the United States draped from a short staff," Ray Manker explained to his congregation a week later. "I resented it terribly. . . . The ideals of the Confederacy, which in our naiveté we had thought was long dead, still reigned over Alabama, high over the ideals symbolized by Old Glory."[271]

A block from the statehouse sat the Dexter Avenue Baptist Church, where King had been pastor during the bus boycott. Federal troops guarded every corner and watched from rooftops. The rally began with a warm welcome from Ralph Abernathy, who chided Governor Wallace for his refusal to come out and receive their petition. King then introduced Rosa Parks as "the First Lady of the movement," and Dr. Ralph Bunche, the UN undersecretary for special political affairs, called the civil rights workers "the contemporary Minute Men of American freedom."[272] Speaker after speaker and singer after singer called for freedom. Finally, when King spoke, he said, "So I stand before you this afternoon with the conviction that segregation is on its deathbed in Alabama and the only thing uncertain about it is how costly the segregationists and Wallace will make the funeral."[273]

The march to Montgomery was a milestone, but it was not an end to the work or the losses. Change was imminent, but it would be expensive—and the next payment came due that evening. Unitarian Universalist Viola Liuzzo, a part-time student at Wayne State University and wife and mother of five, had driven from Detroit to join the march, coming alone and despite her family's protest. On her arrival in Selma, she had been assigned to staff the welcoming table, greeting new arrivals. After the march, she ferried marchers back from Montgomery to Selma, along Route 80. Earlier that day she had a sense of foreboding, but had shrugged it off and gone about her business. She was heading back to Montgomery to do another shuttle run when a car pulled up beside hers and a gunman shot her in the head, killing her instantly.

Mary White Ovington

Jenkin Lloyd Jones

Celia Parker Woolley

John Haynes Holmes

Members of the Commission on Unitarian Intergroup Relations (1952–54). *Standing, left to right:* Albert D'Orlando, Errold D. Collymore, Frederick May Eliot, Charles N. Mason Jr., Arthur Foote. *Seated:* Howard Thurman, Alfred McClung Lee (chairperson), Raymond M. Wheeler. Lillian Smith, a member of the Commission, was not present for the photo.

At the March on Washington for Jobs and Freedom. *Left to right:* Robert West, Arthur Graham, Robert Palmer, O. Eugene Pickett, Alfred Hobart, on August 28, 1963.

Homer Jack

Facing the camera, Royal Cloyd and Orloff Miller in Montgomery on March 25, 1965, participating in the final day of the march from Selma to Montgomery.

Activist in Selma, 1965

James Reeb

Left to right: Jack Kent, Clark Olsen,
Clifton Hoffman in Selma, 1965

Cornelius McDougald and Richard Leonard
in Montgomery on March 25, 1965

Viola Liuzzo

Child with clergy at demonstration in Selma, 1965

Kenneth Marshall orienting group in Selma, 1965. Unitarian Universalist ministers shown, *left to right:* Christopher G. Raible, Richard Leonard, Kenneth K. Marshall, Sid Peterman, Gene Bridges, Sam Beecher (layperson, UUA Board member), Joseph A. Schneiders, John Evans, Howard Matson (center foreground, back to the camera).

UUA President Dana MacLean Greeley (center, looking toward camera) and C.T. Vivian (right of Greeley), at the front of a procession halted at the Selma Wall by Public Safety Director Wilson Baker

Marching in Selma on March 15, 1965, the day of James Reeb's memorial service. *Front row, left to right:* Henry Hampton, G. Robert Hohler, Wilson Piper, Paul Vogel.

Martin Luther King Jr., as photographed by Orloff Miller in Selma, 1965

Orloff Miller, at the Unitarian Universalist Church in Birmingham, preparing the UUA Board and others for the memorial service for James Reeb in Selma

At the memorial service for James Reeb, March 15, 1965, in Selma. *Left to right:* Dana McLean Greeley, Eugene Weiner, Martin Luther King Jr., Ralph Abernathy.

THE BROADER STORY

The Second World War had a catalytic effect on race relations. The Allies framed the war as an epic battle between the forces of freedom and the despotism of the Axis, a struggle to make the world safe for democracy, and in its aftermath they had no way to retreat from their own propaganda. Everyone made sacrifices for that victory; in America, not the least of those sacrifices were made by women and African Americans.

Selma continued and extended this fight for freedom. It, too, catalyzed the struggle for civil rights in the United States, yet its impact went beyond that. The world was watching. The message it sent about human dignity and freedom, about courage in the face of oppression, crossed national borders and caused those in Canada, England, and elsewhere to wonder about themselves; it inspired an emerging women's movement; and it facilitated a previously unheard-of level of collaboration between religious groups.

Selma was about change, and more change was coming. *Amos and Andy* was on its way out, while the bugle-blowing black soldier Gabe Jones integrated *Sgt. Fury and His Howling Commandos* from the comic's first issue in 1963. The kind, judicious father that Robert Young had played on *Father Knows Best* until it ended in 1960 gave way to the goofy, human, well-intentioned father portrayed on the *Dick Van Dyke Show*. Some women were breaking free of implicit conventions; many more were restive. Selma represented a milestone on the journey to human rights that continues to this day. The vision of equality and justice it symbolized led to more change. Change led to anxiety, and anxiety awakened resistance. That broader story can be seen within the drama of Selma.

British and Canadian Unitarians

Five Unitarians from the First Unitarian Congregation of Toronto—a teenage girl enrolled at the University of Toronto, a longshoreman, a middle-aged housewife, the minister, and Arthur Hughes, the young man who had instigated the trip—drove in Hughes's Chevy convertible to Montgomery. On the day of the march they arrived at St. Jude's at dawn. Arriving early placed them right up front, behind the SCLC leadership. They noticed that all the men were dressed alike, wearing dark blue suits and sunglasses; only later did they learn that they had dressed this way to make it more difficult for a sniper to pick out King. Welcome to America.

The Canadians had stopped in Selma the day before, where they had met Dr. Sullivan Jackson, a dentist. He told them that Dr. and Mrs. King would be dropping by his home after the march and invited them to come. When the rally ended they rushed back to Jackson's house. "As we were the first ones to arrive back, the people there were anxious to hear about the final stage of the march," Hughes said. "Dr. Jackson explained that few *local* Negro folks would have participated, for fear of retribution. . . . It was beginning to get dark as we enjoyed tea, coffee, sandwiches and southern treats, while everyone was looking forward with anticipation to the visit of Martin Luther and Coretta King. Then someone dashed in to say there had been a shooting back on Highway 80. Everyone fell silent." The elation of the day disappeared. Later they would learn that the victim was Viola Liuzzo, but at that moment their host focused on getting the guests safely out of Selma right away. A man affixed an Alabama license plate to their Chevy and sent them north on Rural Route 22, avoiding Highway 80.[274]

The world watched, and Unitarians paid especially close attention. In England, the April 4 headline in the *Inquirer*, the Unitar-

ian and Free Christian weekly, read "Civil Rights: The Struggle
Continues—The American Scene." In France the Unitarian Fellowship of Paris sent a contribution to the UUA Freedom Fund.[275]
In Budapest, Hungarian Unitarians held a memorial service for
Reeb.[276] The British General Assembly passed an emergency resolution of solidarity with the UUA, "well aware that these British
Islands are not free from some of the dark problems of racial prejudice."[277] Greeley, who attended the meeting, was amazed by the
degree to which Reeb's death had affected people of all religions
around the world. "But religious liberals in particular," he said, "in
England, Romania, and India, for example, seemed to feel that it
meant also a light upon the horizon."[278]

In 1933 and 1943 the British General Assembly of Unitarian
and Free Christian Churches had passed resolutions on minority rights. Like those passed by the AUA in those decades, they
focused on the persecution of the Jewish people. Then, as it did
in the United States, the emphasis shifted. In 1952 and 1955,
after South Africa instituted the Population Registration Act, the
British Unitarians passed resolutions decrying apartheid. Resolutions also began calling "the attention of our own people to
the need to consider the colour problem in Great Britain and
to establish understanding and goodwill toward the coloured
people in our midst."[279] In 1963, while the civil rights movement
gathered steam in the United States, in Great Britain Bill no. 57,
the Racial Discrimination and Incitement Act, was submitted
to the House of Commons and the British Unitarian General
Assembly passed a resolution urging the bill's passage. Articles
about racial issues appeared periodically in the *Inquirer*, but they
were more often concerned with apartheid than with the U.S.
civil rights movement.

The situation in Canada differs from that in both the United
States and Britain. Canadian congregations, though part of the
AUA and later the UUA, are not simply extensions of an American
association. Canadian culture has French and British roots, and
Canada is part of the Commonwealth. Nonetheless, its proxim-

ity to the United States and its special role as the primary trading partner of the United States makes Canada unavoidably engaged with its neighbor. The difference in worldview between the two countries constitutes part of the relationship.

When the UUA Commission on Religion and Race conducted its survey in fall 1963, only nine of the forty-six Canadian member congregations responded. The commission's report noted, "Many of the Canadian churches that did reply mentioned that the form of the questions did not readily apply to the kinds of situations they face in their communities."[280] Dana Greeley mused, "Our Canadian brethren think that we are preoccupied with national problems, and wonder what their share can be in the North American Unitarian Universalist Association."[281] It was an apt question.

By the 1960s, with race relations on the U.S. agenda, the issue rose in the consciousness of many Canadian Unitarians. On September 24, 1963, in response to the bombing of the Sixteenth Street Baptist Church in Birmingham, the Unitarian Congregation of South Peel (now the Unitarian Congregation of Mississauga) sent $222.45 to the new Unitarian Universalist Civil Rights Disaster Fund. When King called for clergy to go to Selma, Canadians went too—Christians, Jews, and UUs. Bob Hemstreet, who was serving Hamilton, called Arnold Thaw, the minister in South Peel; they decided to fly down together. Once he got there, Thaw immediately joined a picket line, and by that night he was in jail. After his release he remained in Selma; he also stayed in touch with the Metro Unitarian Council in Toronto, relaying information about what was happening and what Toronto-area UUs might do. On the other hand, after watching the "terrible bludgeoning" on CBC television, David Pohl, an American minister serving in Ottawa, called his two nearest colleagues, Leonard Mason in Montreal and Charles Eddis in Pointe Claire, Quebec. They said they weren't going, so neither did he.[282]

In Vancouver, the memorial service the Unitarian church held for Reeb drew so many people it had to be moved outdoors. They collected $1,300 and sent it to the James Reeb Memorial Fund.

In Montreal, Leonard Mason began the March 14 service with a memorial to Reeb; three hundred attended. In Ottawa on that same Sunday four thousand people (including seventy-five Unitarian Universalists) marched from Parliament Hill to the U.S. embassy. A few days later Mason participated in a protest march of seven hundred up Montreal's Mount Royal. In Toronto, a student demonstration in front of the U.S. consulate led to arrests, and a later rally drew two thousand.

After the five members of the First Unitarian Congregation of Toronto returned from Selma, the congregation's minister, John Morgan, wrote to Homer Jack, "There is tremendous interest and concern here, and there is much that we can do as Canadians, but we do not want to go off on some tangent of our own, but rather under proper direction and supervision."[283]

Canadian Unitarians remained engaged. Toward the end of April, Elder William Greer, an African-American leader from Selma, toured New York and Michigan and also came to London, Ontario, visiting Unitarian churches along the way.[284] David Pohl invited Bob Jones, the director of the UUA's Washington social responsibility office, to come to Ottawa and preach about Selma; Jones brought two SNCC workers along, and the collection of $320 was split between the UUA Freedom Fund and SNCC. At the beginning of the summer Arnold Thaw wrote to Homer Jack, "There are three and possibly five laymen here who would like very much to do some work in Selma."[285]

The three ministers of Canadian Unitarian congregations who traveled to Selma—Bob Hemstreet (Hamilton), Arnold Thaw (South Peel), and John H. Morgan (Toronto)—were Americans; the one birthright Canadian there, V. Emil Gudmundson, the district executive for the UUA's midwestern Prairie Star District, had given up his Canadian citizenship to become an American. Of the fourteen UU ministers serving in Canada, ten were American. Leonard Mason in Montreal and Phillip Hewett in Vancouver were British; and Charles Eddis in Pointe Claire and Philip Petursson in Arborg, Manitoba, were Canadian. They all had to consider key questions: What did the events of Selma mean for an American minister settled in Canada? And if not an American but concerned nevertheless, how should one relate to these events? Should they go or not, and if they didn't go, what should they say or do? Behind these lay other questions: Where did their commitments lie? Where should they direct their energy? What about the situation in Canada? Later Phillip Hewett, who had been minister of the Unitarian Church of Vancouver in 1965, asked whether being "vicariously involved in someone else's problem [was] a neat way of avoiding" one's own.[286]

Another Canadian, Angus Cameron, formerly the minister in Montreal, was serving the First Unitarian Church of Philadelphia and sitting on the UUA board of trustees in 1965. He was in Boston when word of Reeb's death came. Rather than travel with the board to Selma to attend Reeb's memorial service, Cameron returned to Philadelphia, where he preached that Sunday. "A long battle is ahead," he said. "A few dramatic incidents, the blood of martyrs will not end the war—nor make the crooked straight. What is needed is courage, yes—but also, a quiet, continual persistence, and unremitting, relentless pressure." Building to the climax of his sermon, he brought the issue home to Philadelphia. "Here in the North we have not solved the underlying problem in our cities and towns. . . . Here, in Philadelphia, they worry and do much worse if a Negro moves next door! Our sickness is an American tragedy. The Rev. James Reeb saw through the sickness. Selma was just a place he went in order to protest it."[287]

Those ministers settled in Canada likewise faced the challenge of bringing Selma home. In Winnipeg on that Sunday, Bill Jenkins preached a memorial to James Reeb in which he asked whether any Canadian issue might spur the kind of idealism that Reeb acted upon. "In the years that I worked in Toronto with the Civil Liberties Association to establish human rights for negroes I don't remember any protest marches like this. It seems to me there should have been. . . . Do we have no cause that is significant to fight? Is there nothing in Canada that is worth dying for?"[288]

Bob Hemstreet in Hamilton thought action was called for. Upon his return from Selma, the March 20 edition of the *Hamilton Spectator* reported that he "planned to investigate the problems of the Canadian Indian and the Eskimo, and those of recent immigrants."

After reflecting on the events, on June 6 Phillip Hewett preached the sermon "What Unitarians Did at Selma." As Henry Nelson Wieman had done in eulogizing Reeb three months earlier, Hewett stepped back and set Selma in a larger context: the international "struggle between the 'haves' and the 'have-nots,'" which he said was often, but not always, a struggle between "the so-called 'white race'—and those of non-European ancestry." Then he told the story of Selma, ending with words from the sermon Lawrence E. McGinty, the minister in Birmingham, had preached: "Nobody really cared or got upset about Jimmie Lee Jackson . . . for implicit in the response of the government and of the people was just that 'another nigger' was dead. This is a white man's country. Let's face it. And here is the evil lurking in all of us, all across this country, North, East, South and West." Echoing McGinty, Hewett asked hard questions of himself and the congregation: "Did you react differently to the death of James Reeb from the way you reacted to others in the tragic succession of deaths in the American South? I did. Was it because [Reeb] was a white man and a Unitarian? . . . Was it of no influence that he was like us?" Hewett concluded with a challenge:

> Intellectually, we may be ready for the new age into which we are called upon to enter. But at heart we still have some fundamental adjustments to make. Some Unitarians made that adjustment overnight in Selma. All of them came away saying they would never be the same persons again. And somehow or other we have to let this tragedy of our time enter into our hearts until we can say that too.[289]

Women and the March

In May 1964, 386 UU ministers signed a petition encouraging the U.S. Senate to pass the Civil Rights Act; among the signers were seven women. At the beginning of 1965, fourteen women held full or associate fellowship in the UUA[290] and, judging from two major reports released in the preceding years, it sees no one considered this figure low. "A Plan of Education for the Unitarian Universalist Ministry" had been issued in 1962. In discussing recruitment and selection, it did not mention gender; it did, however, contain an entire section on "The Married Student." This section focused on the wives of theological students and how to integrate them into the seminary environment, because "the education of the married theological student is the education of the student and his wife together." It ended with a warning: "Above all, any separation of the wives into their own 'wives of students' group should be avoided."[291] (Meadville Lombard, however, did have a group called the Meadville Wives that put on an annual dance and skit.) In 1963, *The Free Church in a Changing World* duly cited "A Plan of Education" and added, "We could extend our recruiting to Negroes and women." Nonetheless, in the section concerning ethics and social action, which bore the title "The Great Issues of the 1960s," it made no mention of women.[292]

Betty Friedan published *The Feminine Mystique* in February 1963. Feminism was stirring but it had not yet broken into UU consciousness. In their attitudes, Unitarian Universalist men paralleled the male leadership in the civil rights movement. Fred Cappuccino, minister of the UU Church of Silver Spring, Maryland, held a gathering in his home, packed with fifty-five members of his congregation eager to hear Stokeley Carmichael. Asked about the position of women in the civil rights movement, he responded, "Prone."[293] When Dorothy Cotton, the SCLC educational director, was asked what it was like to be the only woman in its inner circle, she said, without bitterness, "Oh, in the beginning they were a bunch of chauvinists." They expected her to make the coffee and serve as secretary, even though she had as many other responsibilities as anyone else.[294] In 1964, two female SNCC staff members co-authored a "position paper" on the treatment of women in the movement. It began with a list of grievances and described "the unequal treatment [of women] that resulted because of the patriarchal system." Not surprisingly, the paper was written by Euro-American women ten years younger than Cotton.[295]

When Dana Greeley received the telegram from Martin Luther King Jr. in the wee hours of March 8, he wrote in its right-hand margin, "See if Homer would alert some of our men to go." His instruction seems to have been taken to mean exactly that: men, not women. Among the list of 177 UU ministers and seminarians known to have gone to Selma or Montgomery, no woman appears, but it is not certain that none were there. The only one known to have been present, Vilma Harrington, was there prior to Bloody Sunday. Some 45 UU ministers marched on March 9; 109 attended Reeb's memorial service on March 15; and an estimated 250 came to Montgomery on March 25. If any female UU clergy were present, it seems that no one took notice.

Among the fifteen UU laypeople who made the trek across the Pettus Bridge on March 9 were two prominent laywomen: Emily Taft Douglas and Lillian Crompton Tobey. Every contemporaneous reference identified them by their husbands' first names rather than their own: Mrs. Paul Douglas and Mrs. Charles Tobey.

In 1952, in the AUA's first deliberate effort to examine its own attitudes to race, Lillian Smith was the one woman on the Commission on Intergroup Relations. In 1963 Rev. Greta Crosby, who had been outspoken during the debate over requiring congregations to have open membership, was the sole woman appointed to the Commission on Religion and Race. When the SCLC asked Jane Boyajian to mobilize people for the culmination of the march to Montgomery, men in the UUA hierarchy discounted and ignored her. When it came to Selma, patriarchal assumptions held sway.

Richard Leonard wrestled with whether or not to tell his wife that he was going to Selma. "When I reached home," he said, "Barbara was just heading out to meet her first patient for the day. To open a discussion of my plans at that moment would precipitate a first-class argument."[296] He chose evasion and called her from the airport. On the other hand, James Reeb and his wife, Marie, talked about their differences. She was worried and didn't want him to go, while he talked of wanting to go, indeed of *having* to go. Finally ceding, she said, "If you must, you must."[297] How many different ways did this conversation play out in those days? Rollene S. Wells, who had taken her husband John out of the segregated Methodist church in Arlington, Virginia, and to the Unitarian church, said that never for an instant did she doubt that he had to go. She would have gone herself, except that they had four daughters. She accepted her part. Like her husband, she'd grown up in the South and understood the power of evil and the capacity of people, even people she loved, to be hateful. That knowledge "generated a lot of fear about what might happen."[298]

Gretchen Manker in Phoenix supported her husband's trip to Montgomery, despite her own hectic life as minister's spouse, student at Arizona State University, and mother of five. "What about the children?" was an oft-repeated refrain. Nancy Doughty (née Wynkoop), the minister of religious education at the First Unitarian Universalist Church of Detroit, said, "My first impulse was to go to Selma. But with a commitment to preach and a family to think about, I reluctantly did not go."[299] Likewise Greta Crosby, minister in Roanoke, Virginia, wanted to go but was nursing a three-month-old. In Atlanta, Liz McMaster, who would become a minister in 1988, was married and had three small children and "very badly" wanted to go. But, she said, "My husband (probably wisely, but not to my liking then) said he didn't think I should go because of the children." So she contributed as many blankets as she could "and rued staying home."[300] But many men—Ray Manker and John Wells, Orloff Miller and Clark Olsen, Charles Blackburn and James Reeb—had young children and nonetheless left for Selma, assuming it was their wives' duty to take care of their offspring. That was the implicit social contract in 1965, governing the behavior of both men and women and held in place by law, economics, and mores. Social convention deemed that women were responsible for the children; indeed, concern for children is mentioned often when women recount the events of those weeks. Men, in turn, write over and over about calling home to their wives.

Wives, caring for both husband and cause, lived with the anxiety of an unknown future. "They also serve who only stand and wait," John Milton wrote. Doing what had to be done on the home front took its own kind of courage and deserved to be honored. It never was.

Some women wanted to go but didn't; others outwardly supported their husbands in going but quietly resented it. When interviewed about her husband's participation in the march after the attack upon him, Orloff Miller's "attractive wife," as the *Register Leader* referred to her, said, "I feel very proud—and very lucky." But looking back, Orloff Miller could see how his wife's resentment had built up. While he repeatedly placed his family's future at risk, Mary Jane was left behind to deal with anonymous, hateful phone calls. In the end, Miller maintains that his going, without a doubt, contributed to the dissolution of their marriage.

Typically, the women who did manage to go remained in the background doing the unglamorous but necessary tasks. Irene Murdock, Dana Greeley's assistant, helped C. T. Vivian arrange the seating of the dignitaries at the memorial service. Ethel M. Gorman, president of the Birmingham Church, agreed to serve an additional year to give the congregation stability while it dealt with both the civil rights turmoil and a new minister. Jane Boyajian coordinated the mobilization of multiple organizations for the final day of the march to Montgomery.

Signs of change, however, were multiplying. In the summer of 1964, students from the North poured into Mississippi to work on the Mississippi Summer Project. Of the thirty-five UU students known to have participated, twelve were female. There were many more UU women at the conclusion of the march in Montgomery than had been in Selma, among them a cadre from the Unitarian

Universalist Women's Federation. Ruth Steiner, from the Unitarian congregation in Denver, preached a sermon after spending three months with the Summer Project. She went back to march in Montgomery. Viola Liuzzo and Judy Street went despite the protest of their families. A few weeks after the march Margaret Mosley, a UU from Barnstable, Massachusetts, went to Selma with a group of women from the Women's International League for Peace and Freedom to help support voter registration.

Years after the events of Selma, Orloff Miller said that "the nation (even UUs) soon forgot the death of Viola Liuzzo—after all, she was just a housewife!"[301] An archival search of the Andover-Harvard Theological Library that houses the records of the AUA and UUA reveals nineteen results for the name James Reeb; there are *no* results for the name Viola Liuzzo. One of Viola Liuzzo's sons, in a sermon he delivered at the First Unitarian Universalist Church of Detroit, told the congregation that his mother was never properly honored because she was a woman, and people thought she should have stayed home with her children.[302] Indeed, many believed she belonged at home and were angry at her for going. In July 1965, in a poll taken for the *Ladies' Home Journal*, 55 percent of the women interviewed said Liuzzo had no business being there. Only 26 percent approved of her decision.[303] Perhaps Liuzzo's violation of gender roles is the reason she is rarely mentioned in the reminiscences of those who were there, and why she is treated like a footnote rather than a civil rights martyr.

In "After Selma—What Can Women Do?" Connie Burgess, the executive director of the Unitarian Universalist Women's Federation, observed,

> In Selma some of us came to realize how important a factor in the solution of racial problems is the Negro woman. Negro women labor under unbelievable handicaps, enduring discrimination for both their sex and their color. We must . . . overcome any sentimental notions that [the problem] can be solved easily. I believe we are almost totally ignorant of life in

our inner cities, of the unbelievable conditions of many slums, schools and homes, and of the efforts needed to cope with conditions of poverty before there is any real progress made toward civil rights.

She then put forth a challenge which, because of white trepidation and emerging black nationalism, turned out to be insurmountable:

Let those of us who have been isolated from contact with minority problems try to establish truly friendly relationships with Negro women from disadvantaged areas, through discussion of our common problems and concerns, and work to make our communities places of opportunities for all. This will not be easy, for quite naturally many Negroes are suspicious about our intentions and staying power.[304]

It was not to be. Inspired by the civil rights movement, women moved to liberate themselves. Yet, in a way that is typical of those who have been victimized, middle-class Euro-American women became enthralled by their own suffering and could not see beyond their own needs. White sisters simply didn't get it. That is to say, Euro-American women did not acknowledge that, despite their second-class status, they benefited from white privilege and they, too, participated in maintaining systemic racism. Seeing this, African-American women abandoned an alliance that was not about to blossom.

Ecumenism

In 1960, when John Wolf arrived in Tulsa to become the minister of All Souls Unitarian Church, he was not welcomed into membership in the Tulsa Council of Churches because he did not accept Jesus Christ as lord and savior. But that did not keep an indefatigable Methodist laywoman, Beth Macklin, from asking him to chair the council's Social Action Committee. When, in 1965, Selma

demanded America's attention, Wolf and a group of clergy suggested to Ben Hill, minister of Vernon Avenue AME Church, that
they organize a city-wide service and march.[305] And so the first
truly ecumenical service ever held in Tulsa took place at All Souls.

"Most Catholics and Protestant Christians, until fairly recently
anyway, would have said that we are not Christians," Dana Greeley wrote in 1971.[306] Although Greeley engaged in interfaith work
(and had attended the Second Vatican Council, which commenced
in 1962), in general the relationship between Christianity and Unitarian Universalism was ambivalent. The UUA was not a member
of the National Council of Churches, nor did it then have observer
status. (It gained that later.) A 1967 survey by the UUA Committee
on Goals showed that 43.1 percent of respondents defined their
religion as Christian; by 1989 only 15 percent of Unitarian Universalists identified as Christian.[307] The UU move away from Christianity was still gaining speed and ferocity when Selma happened.
Suddenly, UUs found themselves deeply involved in a movement
that was not just saturated with Christianity, but founded in and
nurtured by it. At one point during a mass meeting at Brown Chapel
AME, when the congregation had been singing "nothing but
amens for ten or fifteen minutes," Dana McLean Greeley watched
more than one hundred Unitarian Universalist ministers and laity
clapping and singing "with as much lustiness as anyone else" and
thought how ironic it was that in the new UU hymnal, *Hymns for
the Celebration of Life*, all the *amens* had been eliminated.[308]

The irony went beyond the *amens*. The impassioned, soulful
singing that was the lifeblood of the civil rights movement was
far from the UU norm; indeed, the Commission on Religion and
the Arts had ruefully admitted that "many, possibly most, of our
people do not sing lustily."[309] Nor were Unitarian Universalists
comfortable with traditional religious language, and they increasingly held Christianity in disdain. When asked in 1967 how religiously close they felt to various other religious groups, 79 percent
said they felt "very distant" from Roman Catholics, more than any
other group; 56.7 percent felt "very distant" from Lutherans and

49.1 percent from Episcopalians. Yet these were exactly the people who rushed to Selma in response to King's call and whom UUs stood next to at the Selma Wall. These were the people UUs ate with, slept beside, and sang, prayed, and marched with. The God Squad, they called themselves.

The irony went deeper. Compared to the Roman Catholics, Unitarian Universalists were Johnny-come-lately in Selma. Ira Blalock and Gordon Gibson had arrived in February 1965, as representatives of the UUA. By then the Society of St. Edmund and the Sisters of St. Joseph had been doing pioneering work in Selma for thirty years. They operated a school and the rebuilt Good Samaritan Hospital, where Jimmie Lee Jackson and then many of those wounded on Bloody Sunday received care. Not just the local black community turned to the Catholics; when the UUA board reconvened in Selma, it met at St. Elizabeth's Catholic Mission. The presence of nuns in the march comforted some and was a revelation to others. UU minister Clarke Dewey Wells recalled wanting to avoid being on the flanks of a march, where the danger was greatest. So he moved into the center of the line, spotted "a sturdy, maternal looking and wimpled nun," locked his arm around hers and said, "Mother . . . I mean, Sister, I'm marching with you."[310] Another colleague confessed, "For the first time in my life . . . I had an intense conversation with a nun (from Detroit), coming away knowing her as a human being with feelings and concerns. 'I never felt so cloistered in all my life,' she said. 'But one day in Selma is worth five years of maturity.' She was not that remote figure in a strange 'penguin suit' that was all I had previously known of nuns."[311]

When UUs engaged with devout Christians and saw them as real people sharing a common cause, they stopped using caricatures of them as sermon fodder. In Selma, and indeed across America, mindsets changed in a way that allowed doors and hearts to open wide to ecumenism. As Ray Manker saw it, "Creedal differences and ancient ecclesiastic bitterness and distrust melted as people became just people—people at their best—striving for the beloved community."[312]

Above all, the memorial service for James Reeb symbolized a conjunction of faiths for a just cause, and showed that a commitment to justice could be more compelling than ecclesiastic doctrine. In an AME church, in the presence of the presiding bishop of the Episcopal Church in the United States and the archbishop of the Greek Orthodox Archdiocese of North and South America, the eulogy was delivered by a Baptist, the prayer by a Unitarian Universalist, and the Kaddish by a Jew. All this was done for a person who was raised Presbyterian, became a Unitarian Universalist, and worked for the Quakers. A Catholic newspaper even suggested that he be nominated for sainthood. The service for James Reeb was a sublime religious collaboration. Rampant ecumenism! Sister Mary Paul wrote afterward that the mass meetings at Brown Chapel AME were "the most ecumenical experience I've ever had." "There was a tremendous sense of unity with each other—Protestant, Catholic, and Jew. The camaraderie was a magnificent experience in itself."[313] Her words were echoed by Sister Joseph Gertrude: "The most wonderful thing . . . occurred. The power of life had melded us into one family, into a unity that was strong and indomitable. The downtrodden had reached out to us, and opened their arms, and in the response, a great ecumenical community had been formed. In committing ourselves and becoming fully involved, we found that we loved each other also. The usual barriers that separated us were gone and we entered into a tremendously rewarding dialogue with one another."[314]

Farley Wheelwright was bedding down one night on a bench in Brown Chapel AME. A nun sat in the next pew. "Well, sister," he said, "I understand we may have to stay here all night in the church. At least it's good to know that you and I are both happily married." Offering a demure smile, she replied, "But knowing the reputation of you Unitarians, I suspect that my marriage is a good deal more secure than yours is."[315]

What people experienced in Selma transcended provincialism. Yet their collaboration was built on religious particularity. Each invited others into the faith tradition she or he held dear. When groups experienced divisions, they were not between those who gathered in Selma. Rather, difficulties tended to erupt within the communions to which they belonged. The Catholic archbishop of Mobile gave orders not to participate in the march; the local superior, Father Crowley, obeyed but published an advertisement stating his mission's support for the struggle. Activists embedded in religious communities were not necessarily supported by those communities. On Saturday, March 20, the day before the marchers set out for Montgomery, nearly two hundred Episcopal priests convened to hold a Communion service at St Paul's Episcopal Church. They were turned back by Wilson Baker, the public safety director, at the request of the Episcopal bishop of Alabama. The clerics simply returned to Brown Chapel AME and held their service there.

Among the leadership of the UUA, no such resistance to activism could be found. The call went out at Dana Greeley's behest. Given the minuscule size of Unitarian Universalism compared to Catholicism, Episcopalianism, Lutheranism, Congregationalism, Methodism, and Judaism, it was well represented. Although UUs were not the most numerous religious group in Selma and were not among the leadership there, although Unitarian Universalism had had no presence there before February 1965 and had few outposts anywhere in the South, two of Selma's martyrs, Reeb and Liuzzo, were Unitarian Universalists. The leadership of the movement knew that the Unitarian Universalists had shown up, and in later years remembered, praised, and thanked them.[316]

Resistance

"Your job might not be here when you get back," a board member told Frederick Lipp on Monday, March 9, after Lipp shared with him his need to respond to King's call. Lipp clarified: This was not about his job. It was imperative that he stand with his brothers and sisters who were being denied their basic rights. Lipp had only graduated from Meadville Lombard the previous June and found a settlement in Beverly, Massachusetts, and now he was about to risk his ministry. When he set out for Selma, the only blessing he received was from his supportive, but frightened, wife. In the end, however, the congregation did more than merely tolerate his passion. It supported him when, upon returning, he began working for fair housing in Beverly and even when he arranged for Ralph Abernathy to address the local high school.[317]

As Harry Hoehler, the UU minister at First Parish in Weston, Massachusetts, prepared to go to Selma for Reeb's memorial service, he began receiving visits and phone calls from concerned congregants urging him not to go. Some reminded him that he had not yet been their minister for a full year. Meanwhile, however (and without his knowledge), the Standing Committee met and "unanimously voted to reaffirm the right of the Minister to act in this, as in all matters, in accordance with the dictates of his conscience." The affirmation was signed by over two hundred members, and Hoehler went on to enjoy a thirty-year ministry in Weston.[318]

In 1963 Hoehler had driven with Ernest A. Brown to the March on Washington. The following year, at the annual meeting of Brown's congregation in North Andover, Brown made a special request for an "affirmation of our open membership policy" regarding race and color, which was enthusiastically passed.[319] Now, as Brown prepared to go to Selma, he too felt pressure from church members not to go. In the privacy of the parsonage kitchen, Brown and his colleagues raged at the stealthy nature of the resistance, expressed disappointment with their parishioners, and bemoaned the trials of ministry.

At least one minister experienced outright intimidation. Robert Storer, the minister in Winchester, Massachusetts, had been among the 386 signatories of the petition supporting the passage of the Civil Rights Act the Unitarian Universalist Ministers Association had submitted to the U.S. Senate in May 1964. He, too, wanted to go to Selma. But as he prepared to depart he was privately told by some congregational leaders, "If you go to Selma,

take your boyfriend and don't come back." Storer was gay and clos-
eted in an era in which only one UU minister was out and no one
spoke about homosexuality. He didn't go, but did go on to have a
long and successful ministry in Winchester.[320]

In New England, provincialism always hovered in the background. These instances of intimidation and ambivalence in the
Northeast corroborate the findings of the 1953 survey done by the
AUA Commission on Unitarian Intergroup Relations and the 1964
survey by the UUA Commission on Religion and Race. In the 1953
survey, New England congregations made up 60 percent of the
respondents, yet of the twelve congregations that reported five or
more African-American members, only one was in New England:
Arlington Street Church in Boston. In 1964, only 34.5 percent of
New England respondents said they would consider calling a minister who was a member of a minority group, the lowest percentage
of any region; even in the Southeast the percentage was higher, at
37.5. Moreover, New England's overall response rate to the survey
was also the lowest of all regions outside Canada, at 37 percent.
When the Commission on Religion and Race analyzed race relations within the UUA, it concluded that evasive and indifferent
answers to both the 1953 and 1964 surveys most commonly came
from New England.[321] This is corroborated by the experience of
Kenneth C. Hawkes, who, as the district executive for the Northeast District during the Greeley administration (1958–69), was in
a position to know. He went to Selma for Reeb's memorial service
and later said he was "proud that he was one of a very few people
from Maine who supported the Civil Rights movement of Martin
Luther King."[322]

New England was not entirely alone in its resistance to becoming more racially inclusive. Three of the four congregations in the
1953 survey that were opposed to racial integration were in the
South. Indeed, part of the mandate of the UUA Commission on
Religion and Race when it was established in 1963 was to work
with such congregations. Commission members visited Kinston,
North Carolina, and Columbia and Charleston, South Carolina.

All Souls Unitarian Universalist Church of Shreveport, Louisiana, was founded in 1950 and, like other congregations, was divided in its support. On May 9, 1965, Helen Pease, the vice chair of its board, sent a note with her response to a Commission questionnaire inquiring about the congregational response to Selma. "I am enclosing [a] copy of the article I 'dared' to write for our newsletter. I felt, with a few others, that more tribute should have been given to James Reeb than we did. . . . [While I was away, the newsletter's] editor preached one of the all-time hateful sermons from our pulpit including running down James Reeb. I find the general feeling or rather lack of feeling for humanity in our fellowship so disturbing . . . that I expect to become inactive next year. I hope to find other outlets where I can live my beliefs."[323] And Helen and Alvah Pease did leave.[324]

The Huntsville, Alabama, congregation, organized in 1958, was also divided. Some of its leaders were active in civil rights from the beginning, but after its first minister, Charles Blackburn, was arrested in McComb and then marched in Selma, a dozen members resigned. That took place during his first year as their minister; during his second year, seventy-five joined.

"Parish needs trump social action," wrote Farley Wheelwright, every inch an activist, "[so] I returned from Selma without continuing the march to Montgomery . . . to attend to a congregation which was not civil rights minded." But despite this responsibility, Wheelwright returned to Selma for Reeb's memorial service and again in the summer to spend his vacation registering voters in Mississippi, Alabama, and Georgia. "I became more politically radical, getting into and out of jail and justifying a new Farley to a mostly indifferent congregation."[325] On the other hand, a church history records that "a statement of our appreciation for his representing us in this March for Social Justice was read before a packed church and there was much applause and friendliness abounding."[326] Did Wheelwright misread his congregation? Or was Nassau, like other congregations, divided, sending a double message: strong support from some, and eye-rolling indifference from others?

How many ministers chafed at questions like "But why did you go?" or "Why would you break the law?" How many received a confused letter, as did Bob and Helen Dick, asking them to explain? Since Helen had marched in Montgomery, the letter-writer asked her what had actually happened in Selma and enclosed a copy of the March 30 *Congressional Record*, which had left its recipient "dumbfounded."[327] Speaking in the House of Representatives, Alabama congressman Bill Dickinson had described a pamphlet reporting that "drunkenness and sex orgies were the order of the day in Selma, on the road to Montgomery, and in Montgomery. There were many—not just a few—instances of sexual intercourse in public between Negro and white." Dickinson went on to charge "that Martin Luther King has been virtually surrounded by Communist or Communist-fronters since 1955."[328]

Ministers murmured of colleagues who found they needed to leave their positions after marching in Selma. But whereas later, in the Vietnam War era, resignations were sometimes formally negotiated in such circumstances, no such separations can be identified in the mid-1960s. More often, some ministers and seminarians felt such a compelling call to social action in the aftermath of Selma that the vagaries of congregational life and the tepidness of their congregations' commitment to social justice became unbearable.

In 1954 the report of the AUA Commission on Intergroup Relations said, "Almost no one will admit he denies the concept of equality of all men even though in practice he may deny it with every breath."[329] Activists experienced resistance from congregation members and most of it was passive. Indeed, there are few examples of active resistance. Researchers today find it difficult to document resistance because neither congregations nor ministers will admit they opposed civil rights. Yet there can be no doubt there was division, if not about the goal, then about the means and pace of getting there. Today it is a matter of shame, but already, in the 1950s and '60s, the resolutions passed by the AUA and UUA were crystal clear on the issues of discrimination and integration. Given these espoused values, which by then were regarded as tenets of liberalism, any resistance had to be subtle, masquerading at some times as indifference or denial, at others as caution or skepticism.

Flight was another response. In 1948, following Homer Jack's first sermon at the Unitarian Church of Evanston, a member approached Jack and told him that he was too radical, and that the member would quietly leave. That was W. Clement Stone, the billionaire insurance magnate.[330] It is impossible to document how many others quietly slipped away.

Rev. James Madison Barr III represented an exception; he was not quiet, did not slip away, ardently opposed the demonstrations in Selma, and regularly received letters from his colleagues castigating his position. The Sunday following James Reeb's death Barr—who, like his UU colleagues elsewhere, served on the board of his local Urban League—preached a sermon declaring that we must "remove every trace of racial prejudice from the marrow of our bones. There is no place for this in our midst." Afterward the congregation sent $125 to the Reeb Fund. But the main thrust of his sermon was that King shared the guilt of Reeb's death because he created the conditions that led to it. A local paper headlined his argument: "Both King, Killers Blamed in Death." Barr opposed the demonstration in Selma, even though nine months earlier he had mounted a one-man demonstration supporting California's Proposition 14, which allowed homeowners and landlords to sell or rent to whomever they wished, ergo to discriminate. In his sermon he cautioned, "Let us not unwittingly help destroy the very supports necessary to keep us a free people—respect for the courts of our land." To say this he had to ignore the fact that King did obey the court injunction against the march.[331]

A week after Barr preached against the march in Selma he went on the *Roundtable Forum*, a television talk show, where he debated Rev. James Lawson, who had studied non-violent resistance while in India in the 1950s and gone on to train many civil rights leaders. When Lawson differentiated between violent revolt and civil disobedience, describing the latter as "passive, loving and nonviolent," Barr disagreed, saying that "demonstration stirs hatred in the hearts of men."[332] As a self-proclaimed Jeffersonian, he considered limiting the power of the federal government to be of paramount importance, and protested whenever he thought it violated the rights of the individual or the state. And while free speech was essential, he was "'offended' by civil rights demonstrations."[333] Indeed, in a letter to the *Register-Leader* in 1964 he wrote, "[I] abhor the Civil Rights Bill—those extreamist [*sic*] demonstrations—and the all too powerful conformity of such things in the denomination."[334] He seemed not to consider the right to assemble and protest to be a matter of free speech—at least when exercised by those with whom he disagreed. He represents a strain of exaggerated individualism to which Unitarian Universalism is prone. While his position lacked consistency, this may be because, as a contrarian, he was more comfortable being at odds with his colleagues than following the stampede of what he derided as "misplaced loyalties."[335]

A new Unitarian Universalist fellowship was founded in Memphis, primarily by those who could no longer stomach Barr. One of its members wrote to the press decrying Barr's position: "As a Unitarian, I am disturbed when Babbitry overwhelms humanitarian idealism and when 'don't rock the boat' becomes the rally cry of the pious, the smug, and the complacent."[336] But *babbitry* means an unthinking conformity with middle-class standards, and this does not characterize Barr. This polemicist was no conformist. Rather, the word described the quietism of the post–Second World War era: America under the Eisenhower administration.

That era had come to an end, and in Selma the SCLC and SNCC were rocking the boat. Reeb, in throwing in his lot with the disinherited, working and living alongside them, was rocking the boat. Viola Liuzzo, in being unfettered by social convention, steadfastly independent, and passionate in her concern for others, was rocking the boat. And Robert Storer—who, as a gay man, would have found few allies to rally around him in 1965—was reluctant to rock the boat too much. Indeed, gay men went to Selma, but it would be years before any of them came out.

Women, homosexuals, and other oppressed groups could not help but intuit the implications of the civil rights movement. People were awakening to human liberation. Black Power, feminism, and the gay rights movement would all assert themselves before the end of the decade.

THE AFTERMATH

The march from Selma to Montgomery culminated on Thursday, March 25, and by the following Tuesday Homer Jack had sent a memo to the Commission on Religion and Race urging the UUA not to lose "the marvelous dynamic of Selma/Montgomery." Likewise, upon his return to Boston Orloff Miller began looking forward:

> I go back to the college project with a tremendously broadened sense of what our college students feel about the civil-rights movement. Now I know personally the tremendous sense of frustration felt by those students who have been in the civil-rights projects in the South. I know why they believe their academic work is so utterly irrelevant. For a long time, we at the UUA headquarters have been part of the Liberal Establishment in the eyes of our own students. Hell, we're just now catching up to *them*.[337]

This passage appeared in the *Register-Leader* under the headline "A New Direction for the Denomination?" In the aftermath of the march, what would catching up mean, and how would the UUA build on "the marvelous dynamic"?

The UUA was not the only organization looking to the future. So was the SCLC. The battleground was about to shift.

After Montgomery

Two days before the march from Selma to Montgomery was to begin, Richard Leonard and a small group of others met with King's SCLC aide, Jim Bevel, over breakfast. Bevel told them that as far as the SCLC was concerned, "the battle for voting rights for blacks in the South was, to all intents and purposes, over." Ahead lay the march to Montgomery, the vote in Congress, and the work of getting people to register, vote, and to run for office. He also predicted that there would be more violence, but what had begun could not be stopped. Change was coming to the deep South; the SCLC would focus next on the North.[338]

The shift in focus came quickly. On April 4, only a few days after the march ended, Bevel was in the north at the Unitarian Church of Evanston, delivering the sermon "Next Steps for the Civil Rights Movement." By the end of the summer Chicago had been chosen over Boston, Harlem, Rochester, and Los Angeles as the next site to concentrate SCLC's effort. Soon King would lead marches in the Windy City that would be met with seething white hatred and political recalcitrance rivaling that of the South.

During breakfast that March morning in Selma, Bevel had described the future. On August 6, President Johnson signed the Voting Rights Act into law, and in the ensuing years African Americans in the South registered in increasing numbers. Then they began to be elected to public office. In Selma, five were elected to the city council in 1972. In nearby Uniontown the breakthrough came even earlier. Andrew Hayden, a black building contractor, was elected to the city council in 1968, and in 1972 he became mayor. The advancement of black elected officials would continue, and across Alabama the numbers would swell.

On March 26, the morning after the march to Montgomery ended, Ray Manker and three colleagues rented a car and set out for Quitman, Mississippi, to meet with Gregory Kaslo. Kaslo, who had grown up in the congregation Manker was serving in Phoenix, had been working with the Freedom Schools and the voter registration drive since the previous summer. After his colleagues departed, Manker accompanied Kaslo as they visited some of the families he had been working alongside. Then they went to a meeting of the Mississippi Freedom Democratic Party. Finally, they ended up at the Council of Federated Organizations (COFO) headquarters in Meridian. COFO had been formed by SNCC, CORE, the NAACP, and the SCLC in 1962 to coordinate and unite voter registration efforts. Manker spent a morning with Rev. J. C. Killingsworth, who had just returned from three weeks in Selma. Manker later reported,"He said it was the greatest experience of his life, and he was anxious that I, a white Unitarian, could go with him, a Negro A.M.E. to visit his people and by example as well as by word share with them this wonderful experience of interracial, inter-religious brotherhood."[339]

On the same day that Manker and his colleagues set out for Quitman, a *New York Times* headline read "Woman Is Shot to Death on Lowndes County Road." The triumph of the march was marred by the murder of Viola Liuzzo. On Saturday the governor of Michigan, George Romney, declared the upcoming Monday and Tuesday official days of mourning for her. That evening he visited the Liuzzo family. Viola Liuzzo had joined the First Unitarian Universalist Church of Detroit a year earlier, and Rev. Tracy Pullman, its senior minister, went to offer Anthony Liuzzo his condolences. Mr. Liuzzo, a devout Catholic who objected to his wife's attending the UU church, refused to allow Pullman into the house. Pullman assumed that Mr. Liuzzo blamed the church and its activism —of which there was plenty—for his wife's death. Homer Jack also attempted to contact Liuzzo, and he, too, was rebuffed. But it may have meant nothing at all beyond the reaction of a grief-stricken man overwhelmed by calls and visits from friends, officials, and reporters.

The funeral took place on Tuesday at the Immaculate Heart of Mary Parish in Detroit. Seven hundred and fifty attended, including Governor Romney and the Teamster leader Jimmy Hoffa, as well as Walter Reuther, Martin Luther King Jr., and other civil rights leaders. Pullman did not attend the funeral and, in fact, there seems to have been no UU presence at the service. Whatever Anthony Liuzzo was feeling right after his wife's death, later that year he worked with Jack Mendelsohn on the chapter about Viola Liuzzo in Mendelsohn's book *The Martyrs: Sixteen Who Gave Their Lives for Racial Justice.*

A few days after the culmination of the march, sixty-three-year-old Margaret Mosley, an African-American UU from Barnstable, Massachusetts, and a lifelong activist, arrived in Selma with a group of six women from the Women's International League for Peace and Freedom (WILPF). With Liuzzo on her mind, she went to the home in which Viola had stayed and listened to the family, who were still in shock, as they talked about her.

WILPF was in Selma to support people in registering to vote. All its members there, except for Moseley, were white. While they were well received by the black citizens, local whites reviled them. Moseley was followed; she was harassed; she stared down Sheriff Clark on the courthouse stairs. But she feared for the other WILPF members more than for herself because she could see they were viewed with a special hatred.

Viola Liuzzo came to mind again when Moseley and another WILPF member departed. On the way to the airport their van was tailed. Two cars tried to box them in and force them off the road, and Moseley worried that she was about to share Liuzzo's fate. As the black man driving their van sped down the highway, Moseley and her friend "held on for dear life" until the van screeched into the airport parking lot. The two passengers bolted out the door and sprinted into the terminal.[340]

Grace Linquist, another UU who marched in Montgomery, also thought of Viola Liuzzo. Because of the danger, Grace and her husband Carl had decided that only one of them should go. She said that "Mrs. Liuzzo was most courageous, and we all grieved for her," and Carl expressed their sentiments in a letter to Anthony Liuzzo:

Dear Mr. Liuzzo,

We are grief-stricken for you and your children. Our eyes are wet with tears. But beneath our grief is pride. . . . She did something for us. We are determined it shall not be in vain.

She had gone with others who have died for humanity—Medgar Evers, Rev. James Reeb, James Lee Jackson, the three Civil Rights workers, the four girls in Sunday School, and many more. All these, and Viola Liuzzo, died for humanity—for human rights, for justice, for love of their fellow men.

What can we do? We can and must do what your wife did. We can take action and not sit idly by. We can go and do something.[341]

With the letter Carl Linquist included a contribution for the Liuzzo family.

In response to Selma, and particularly to Reeb's death, money poured in. The American Friends Service Committee (which had employed Reeb), the SCLC, and the UUA jointly created the James Reeb Memorial Fund, and by May 3, contributions had reached $46,565. In addition, the UUA received over $50,000 to be spent specifically to aid Marie Reeb and her four children. In that same month the Freedom Fund—established as the Disaster Fund following the bombing of the Sixteenth Street Baptist Church that took the lives of four girls in September 1963—grew from $6,426 to $62,584.[342]

Volunteers abounded. In Canada, Arnold Thaw had been designated by the Unitarian Council of Metropolitan Toronto to screen Canadian Unitarians interested in volunteering in the South and to direct them to appropriate agencies. And Homer Jack's office received nearly a hundred letters from people eager to go to Selma or elsewhere in the South. In response to the many requests, Jack prepared a list of programs and agencies for which Unitarian Universalists might volunteer. It included the Council of Federated Organizations (COFO), the Mississippi Freedom Democratic Party (MFDP), the Delta Ministry of the National Council of Churches, the Congress of Racial Equality (CORE), the Medical Committee for Human Rights (MCHR), and the Lawyers' Constitutional Defense Committee (LCDC).

Una and John Williams, members of the Huntington Unitarian Fellowship on Long Island, felt they "had to go to Selma," and so they went south as volunteers with Social Workers for Civil Rights Action. For Una, the trip to Selma represented a homecoming of sorts. Six years earlier she had been employed as a social worker in a Selma child care agency. But, living and working in white Selma, she had known nothing about the African-American community. "This 'going home' was not what I might have been expecting," she said. "Participants in the Selma Civil Rights activity were unwelcome in the white community and members of our group who attempted to walk through the community were arrested and jailed. Visiting a former place of employment was considered unacceptable. This 'going home' was to a changing world. This home became a place of discovery for me." People went to help change the world and usually found that they were the ones who were changed.[343]

A Unitarian Universalist Presence in Selma

Homer Jack sent a memo to the Commission on Religion and Race on March 30 titled "Next Steps after Selma/Montgomery," proposing that the Commission employ a "James Reeb Traveling Fellow." This person would serve as the UUA "field worker in civil rights representing the Commission and the denomination to settle 'where the action is.'" He advised, "In the future this could mean Harlem or Roxbury as much as Selma or McComb." Although deliberation over the proposal continued into June, Jack had already dispatched the first volunteer in a program sponsored by the UUA Department of Social Responsibility.[344]

This program, "A Unitarian Universalist Presence in Selma," began on March 26 with the arrival of Rev. Robert Lawson and ran until September 16. The second volunteer, Eugene Luening, arrived in Selma on April 1 and remained until the 20th. During his stay, he developed a guide for volunteers. It described the current situation in Selma as relatively quiet and delved into what had changed since the march, what organizations were doing, and how volunteers should behave, especially regarding safety. Lawson and Luening were followed by thirteen others, each of whom stayed for fifteen days.[345]

While the volunteers rotated in and out of Selma, the momentum that Jack tried to capture was evident when the UUA General Assembly met in Boston during the last week of May. Early in the second session of the plenary meeting, the Commission on Religion and Race delivered its report and the Assembly affirmed the continuation of the Commission. Then a contingent submitted a resolution protesting segregation in the Boston public schools, recognizing the issue as one of James Reeb's major concerns. After lengthy debate, it passed 531 to 256. The next motion asked the Assembly to send a message of sympathy and support to the UU congregation in New Orleans, where both the parsonage and the church had been bombed. At the session's conclusion, some delegates marched to the Boston School Committee office for a silent vigil. The next plenary saw a resolution calling for federal registrars for voting and another titled "Mississippi Challenge" that supported the MFDP's challenge of the seating of the congressmen from the five Congressional districts in Mississippi because of discrimination against black voters. All these resolutions passed by more than two-thirds majorities.

Viola Liuzzo was not mentioned either in a resolution or in the report of the Commission on Religion and Race. There are several reasons. She was a woman and layperson, and while many knew of her death it seems few knew that she was a Unitarian Universalist. Following the march, the coverage in the *Register-Leader* offered no indication that she belonged to a UU congregation, nor did anyone at the UUA compile a folder of articles, correspondence, and background materials about her as they did about James Reeb. Liuzzo had joined the First Unitarian Universalist Church of Detroit about a year before she was murdered. In the Spring of 1964 she had driven to New York City with her friend Sarah Evans, with whom she attended NAACP meetings, to attend a UUA-sponsored United Nations seminar. Her twelve-year-old son accompanied her to church on Sundays, but he chose to wait for her in the social hall rather than participate in the religious educa-tion program. She brought her college-age daughter to a Student Religious Liberals dinner, but the minister of religious education, Nancy Doughty (née Wynkoop), had the impression that the daughter attended because her mother had insisted. Liuzzo was a seeker. Exploring liberal religion was consistent with her com-mitment to justice and her willingness to disregard the status quo. Yet, in March 1965, her connection to the congregation in Detroit was still developing in the midst of her husband's disapproval and her children's ambivalence, and was tenuous enough that only a few church members remembered her at the time of her death. Perhaps all that can be drawn from these fragments is that Viola Liuzzo's life—as a wife and mother of five, student, and activist—was a whirlwind.[346]

From mid-June to mid-July, Ben Kjelshus and Theodore Webb served as the UU presence in Selma. By then the limitations of the two-week visitations in the program Homer Jack had set up were becoming obvious. Projects begun by one volunteer were not followed up on by the next; relationships with local people estab-lished by one person could not simply be transferred to the next volunteer. Nonetheless, the black community appreciated the UU presence and show of concern, and perhaps the volunteers made a little difference. Once the march ended, more than two hundred African Americans lost their jobs in reprisal. The SCLC reorga-nized its personnel, and some committee members jockeyed for position. One local black leader was charged with financial mal-feasance, another banished by the SCLC for misrepresenting him-self. UUs witnessed this chaos but could not influence it; what they could do was respond to the personal needs of a few. Leon Hopper, the minister in Golden, Colorado, wrote in a letter home that he would try to "fit in and do those unspecific things which are the demands of the moment. I only hope that I will be able to fulfill the needs of the unspecific of the next two weeks." He ended up helping Mrs. Ella Mae Moton, the mother of Leroy Moton, the young man who had been in the car with Viola Liuzzo the night she was shot. Hopper and the UUA helped Mrs. Moton "clean up some debts and legal problems" when Leroy lost his job and had to leave the city.[347]

While it is difficult to assess how the UU presence served Selma, it is clear that being there deeply affected those who participated. Kjelshus said that "it was a tremendous experience for me," and Webb observed that "the Selma experience taught me . . . instead of I having taught them."[348]

The minister of the First Unitarian Church of San Diego, John Ruskin Clark, arrived in Selma on August 9. He soon connected with Jonathan M. Daniels, a student from the Episcopal Theological School in Cambridge, Massachusetts, and Richard Morrisroe, a Catholic priest from Chicago, and went with them as they delivered SNCC workers to their assignments. On Saturday, August 14, Daniels, Morrisroe, and twenty-six teenagers were arrested at Fort Deposit in nearby Lowndes County for protesting discrimination at a drive-in. On Monday and Tuesday Clark and two doctors from the Medical Committee for Human Rights visited them in the Hayneville jail. On Wednesday Clark returned again, accompanied by two Episcopal priests, but was told he couldn't visit them again until Sunday. On Friday, however, they were suddenly released. Once out of the jail, Daniels and Morrisroe and two black teenage girls headed down the street to buy soft drinks. In front of the store a volunteer Lowndes County deputy sheriff pointed a shotgun at them. Daniels pushed one of the girls out of the way as the deputy fired and Daniels, taking the full blast, died instantly. Morrisroe was critically wounded while protecting the other girl. "I was called into Wilson Baker's office on Saturday afternoon, the twenty-first," Clark wrote, "with a group of Negroes and whites to help warn the Negro community of the danger and tension following Daniels's murder and the arming and deputizing of three hundred 'rednecks' by Sheriff Jim Clark in anticipation of a 'riot.' "[349]

On Sunday, August 22, Richard Boeke preached the evening service at Our Home Universalist Church in Ellisville, Mississippi, where Donald Thompson, the UU minister in Jackson, served part time. Boeke was the minister of the Flushing, New York, church and had spent the summer serving a congregation in Gulfport, Mississippi. Now he and his wife, Johanna, were heading home. During supper he asked the woman seated next to him, "Where's a good place to spend the night?" She whispered back, "Get out of town." Richard and Johanna took her advice and drove through the night.[350] The next evening, eighty-five miles away in Jackson, Don Thompson was shot.

Thompson had settled in Jackson in 1963, shortly before the assassination of Medgar Evers. Afterward Thompson volunteered to fill Evers's position on the Mississippi Human Relations Council and this work demanded much of his time. On that Sunday he was returning home from an evening meeting, and as he walked toward his apartment buckshot tore into his back, severely wounding him. He survived by mere chance.

At its October meeting the UUA board of trustees passed a resolution commending Donald Thompson for his work, courage, and spirit. It also voted for the resolution "Protection against Racial Assault," urging the U.S. Department of Justice to vigorously prosecute such assaults under existing laws. Updates on and responses to unfolding events in the civil rights movement now occupied part of every UUA board meeting. In June the board established the position of the James J. Reeb Memorial Field Worker; in August its Executive Committee accepted into the UUA the James Reeb Fellowship in Sacramento, California, and received a report that Homer Jack had visited Jimmie Lee Jackson's mother. Meanwhile, across the country, ministers and congregations redoubled their efforts in their own communities.

The three defendants in the murder of James Reeb went to trial on December 6, 1965. Despite the testimony of Orloff Miller and

Clark Olsen, who identified one of the defendants as leading the gang that attacked them, the jury swiftly acquitted all three. The *Boston Globe* headed its December 11 report "What Else Could We Expect?" Other all-white Alabama juries later acquitted the murderers of Viola Liuzzo and Jonathan Daniels, and in the Donald Thompson case, no arrest was ever made.

The After Selma Committee

At Homer Jack's behest, before leaving for Europe that April, Dana Greeley wrote to seven people asking them to participate in at least one meeting of a committee to "draw any lessons that it can from both the crisis and context of Selma."[351] Eight days later, the After Selma Committee met, comprising Homer Jack; Royal Cloyd, the director of the UUA Department of Adult Programs; Joseph Barth, the new director of the Department of Ministry; Joseph Ulman Jr., editor of the *Register-Leader*; Roscoe Trueblood, a parish minister; and Raymond C. Hopkins, the UUA vice president, as chair. Jack Mendelsohn had been invited but was unable to attend.

The major questions before the committee were what the Selma experience meant and how Unitarian Universalism might take advantage of it as a denomination. Revealingly, no women or African Americans sat at the table. Nonetheless, the minutes of that meeting's musings and analysis reflect an honest, insightful, and remarkable gathering. Some moments in the conversation are almost prescient.[352]

The committee members took note of the newly initiated UU presence in Selma, the existence of the Reeb and Freedom Funds, and the intensification of work in local communities. Then they asked, "Are there other things we should recognize before it is too late?"

Trueblood talked about the need for UUs in his suburban setting to hear a "dynamic statement" of "the new fusion in our movement" between individual concerns and a commitment to addressing social needs both nationally and worldwide. Jack reported that "discussions regarding the theological and philo-sophical presuppositions for social action" had already begun with the faculties of several UU theological schools.

Hopkins pointed out that Unitarian Universalists had to work in conjunction with, and to cooperate with, black leaders, "or we will only be doing the same old thing." How could this be done? Barth responded that "our essential concern is the quality of rela-tionships." Such relationships had to be built locally, but doing so was difficult because "both the Negro and white communities feel relatively isolated" from one another. Moreover, UUs had to admit that their churches were, in practice, largely segregated, and their members generally held privileged class positions. "We do not act," he admitted, "and it is very difficult to get Negroes, as such, to feel essentially part of the community." He found that blacks were withdrawing from interracial activities and often resented "offers of help." Building on this, Jack added "that whites were not invited to strategy meetings of the SCLC."

Barth responded that UU churches had to improve their level of integration, but Cloyd warned that this would be difficult. "Our people are willing to live with 'brotherhood' as an idea and give money[, but] when it comes to living or sharing briefly as we did in Selma, it is another thing." When projects like Selma ended, whites went back to their "comfortable communities," while blacks returned to troubled ones in which they owned no significant businesses; instead, they were "exploited by chain stores [which] sell inferior products at higher prices." If they tried to move to the white suburbs, they were refused loans.

While Unitarian Universalists could not "remain aloof," they could also not presume to dictate the terms of their engagement. "All we can do here is to help open doors when the Negroes want them to open. They want help for what they want to do and when they want to do it." A warning was offered: "Hypocrisy is easily discovered. A lot of Negroes really do hate whites."

Jack raised the possibility of a "brainstorming session" involv-ing "Unitarians and Universalists of both races." Hopkins "pointed out that if a Negro joins a predominantly white church, he is often cut off from his own community."

Joe Barth then introduced the issue of class:

Obviously as long as our churches remain "class structured," we have a problem. Unless we have an integrated society, we will not have integrated churches. We do not do ourselves any good as an association of churches if we disassociate ourselves from people on the lowest level of the class structure. We must do this in joining with other people and churches and other classes in doing things.

Hopkins wasn't sure how to break through the "hard shells which exist even among" white religious liberals, and the conversation returned to the issue of privilege. "Whites have many privileges which are denied to Negroes and have power to maintain this privileged position and in no really significant way have we shown we are willing to relinquish this status." Indeed, as Trueblood then pointed out, mostly-white communities often assumed that they had no racial problems.

As the meeting drew to a close, its members reiterated that while "Selma gave us a chance to do something physically and it was appreciated," they could not do the same sort of thing in the North. Hopkins returned to an earlier suggestion that the UUA restate its "theology and philosophy of the dignity of man." Jack suggested that the UUA think about the creative use of its investment portfolio. Finally, and briefly, they recognized the "lack of Negroes in ministry." At that moment, there was but one settled African-American minister, two African-American seminarians, and one PhD candidate.

They set a date for a second meeting of the After Selma Committee; however, if it took place, there are no minutes of its deliberations.

As time went on, the ideas in this conversation received differing amounts of attention. Some were acted on by Homer Jack in his work as director of social responsibility and as staff support to the Commission on Religion and Race. Some of them presage what would come to pass before his position was eliminated in 1969, when the UUA budget and staff were cut by 40 percent. And some would not be addressed for another two decades.

Five months earlier, in November 1964, Jack had begun trying to address the lack of African-American ministers. He organized a meeting to discuss how to integrate the UU ministry. The meeting took place on February 3, 1965. James Reeb attended, representing the Commission on Religion and Race. Following the events in Selma, Reeb's death, and the April 14 meeting of the Beyond Selma Committee, the Intra-denominational Committee for an Integrated Ministry (formed after the February 3 meeting) met. On June 10, in preparation for that meeting, a study paper circulated. "Negroes in the Unitarian Universalist Ministry" detailed the African-American ministers and prospects and described their experiences; it was accompanied by an outline of recommendations for committee members to consider.[353]

On September 24, 1965, the Committee for an Integrated Ministry issued its report, "Toward Integrating the UU Ministry." It called on the denomination to prioritize integration and made recommendations about the recruitment, training, and settlement of African-American ministers.[354] They made little headway. Lamenting that "organized baseball in America is more integrated than organized religion, including our own Unitarian Universalist family," Homer Jack outlined the denomination's failings in May 1967 in his article "A Flaw Within: Toward Integrating Our Liberal Ministry."[355] Not until 1987 would the Department of Ministry Task Force on Affirmative Action for African American Ministers develop and implement a plan that successfully began to address these issues.[356]

In the meeting of the After Selma Committee, Trueblood had said that Unitarian Universalists needed to hear a "dynamic statement" of "the new fusion in our movement." In May 1966, the UUA General Assembly adopted a six-page statement called "Consensus on Racial Justice" that touched on every facet of the issue, outlining the responsibilities of member congregations, the UUA administration, and individual UUs, and offering a clear theological grounding in UU values. And Homer Jack had wondered if a "real brainstorming session" involving UUs of both races would be helpful. Triggered by the many riots that took place during the summer of 1967, that meeting came to pass. In October 1967, the Emergency Conference on the UU Response to the Black Rebellion was held at the Biltmore Hotel in New York City. At this gathering people became aware, some for the first time, of the cultural fissure that the Beyond Selma Committee had intuited in its discussion of power, class, privilege, and race.

In 1968, the Black UU Caucus, born at the Emergency Conference, demanded a million-dollar commitment to black empowerment. The following year, it unveiled "a plan for reparation *investments* rather than reparation *grants*."[357] This, too, echoed Jack's suggestion at the April 14, 1965 meeting that the UUA consider using its investment portfolio creatively, including investing in loans.

The After Selma Committee, as it processed what it had learned from the UUA's involvement in Selma, correctly read the emerging attitude among African Americans. Blacks had grown increasingly suspicious of whites and interracial undertakings, and now demanded black community control and independence. An even more amazing aspect of that meeting was the discussion of white privilege. In 1965 this terminology had not yet entered into the social justice vernacular; indeed, the most widely known essay on the topic, Peggy McIntosh's "White Privilege: Unpacking the Invisible Knapsack," was not published until 1989. Exploring that idea and then linking it to class oppression was farsighted—even if the committee had little idea of how to approach the issue beyond the necessity of fostering collaborative relationships.

The After Selma Committee missed many things. Its members tended to portray problems and challenges as extrinsic to Unitarian Universalism; they leaned toward making prejudice and segregation the culprits. They saw these as the causes of discrimination in employment, housing, and educational opportunity. Convincing

Unitarian Universalists to take action against such practices was a challenge, yet many rose to it. The greater challenge was helping religious liberals understand that they themselves harbored racial prejudice. Moreover, persuading many UUs outside that meeting that they benefited from race and class privilege would have been nearly impossible. It is also revealing that, although they discussed "the lack of Negroes in ministry" and the geographic separation of UU congregations from black residential areas, they were scarcely aware of the myriad other ways in which Unitarian Universalist congregations were inhospitable to African Americans: hymnals devoid of worship materials that reflected the African-American experience, and religious education materials that were silent about black life, culture, and achievements. The committee could not recognize the institutional racism embedded within the fact that there was only one African-American professional staff member at the UUA and none on the UUA board or on any denominationally elected committees, and that no African Americans had been appointed by the UUA board to positions on any committees other than the Commission on Religion and Race. The fact that this conversation occurred without an African American present reveals the depth of the blindness that left these well-intentioned men groping as they tried to see beyond Selma.

In the aftermath of Selma many UUs, scrambling to live out the lessons they had learned, recommitted themselves to the cause of freedom and equality. Unitarian Universalists came at it the only way they could. They expected to be able to live where they wanted, to go to school where they wished, to vote, to be employed in an occupation commensurate with their education, and saw the injustice that African Americans could not do likewise. However, buffered as they were from prejudice and social stigma—the things which Kenneth Patton wrote about after his experience with crossing the color line—they did not understand that their earnest yearning, fair-mindedness, and good deeds would not suffice, or foresee that changing laws would not be sufficient.

WHY DID THEY GO?

There are hundreds of stories of lives forever changed by the events of Selma and thousands of reasons why people went there. But behind them all lies a shared context.

America was going through a major shift in attitudes; Selma represented a seismic event in that shift. The Second World War accelerated a change in race relations. The executive branch of the federal government exerted pressure when it ordered the end of discrimination in all federal services in 1948. The Supreme Court increased that pressure in 1954 when it ruled that school segregation was unconstitutional. Congress increased it further still in 1958 and 1964, when it passed civil rights bills. Three hundred eighty-six UU ministers signed a petition in support of the 1964 legislation, and the UUA lobbied for it. During the years leading up to, and following, the Second World War, Unitarians and Universalists had slowly woven their lives into a web of values, relationships, efforts, and institutions in ways that connected them to the African-American struggle for human rights. Religious liberals strove to guarantee equal access, fair housing, and integration; and the more they acted, the more they became invested in the cause. The more contact they had with African Americans, the more aware UUs became of racial issues and the more they became convinced that discrimination was wrong and the responsibility to promote equal opportunity theirs.

Support was not universal, or even overwhelming. But having reached a critical mass, when the time came, Unitarian Universalists responded.

The Tipping Point

Hundreds went to Selma and Montgomery. No matter their ratio-nalizations for going, emotion, not reason, underlay their decision. "Why did I go?" reflected Richard Gilbert. "The immediate reason was an urgent request from denominational president Dana McLean Greeley. But more than that, like Reeb, I could not stay home."[358] James Reeb said it differently, but expressed the same sentiment, in responding to Marie's plea. "There are others to go. You belong here," she had said. "No," he replied, "I belong there. It's the kind of fight I believe in. I want to be part of it. Every man who can go is needed."[359]

Selma was the tipping point. The injustice was so obvious, and the righteousness of the cause so evident, that for some an inner moral calculus instantly provided an answer. Others did not choose to go so much as they were sent: Ernie Pipes and David Johnson were literally drafted by their congregations and dis-patched to represent them. But both those who went and those who did not go had to engage in a moral reckoning with them-selves. When Neal W. Ferris heard of Martin Luther King Jr.'s call on March 8, 1965, for clergy to come to Selma he wrestled with what to do. He had been called to the Unitarian Church of Mead-ville, Pennsylvania, in 1962. He and his wife had one infant and she was pregnant with their second. It was clear to him that going to Alabama would be risky. As he struggled with how to balance his responsibilities to family and congregation with his urge to go to Selma he called his mentor, Irving Murray, whom he had served under as assistant minister in Pittsburgh. He outlined his thinking and asked whether Murray was going. He was not. Ferris decided against going, but then had a different opportunity thrust upon him. He was the vice-president of the local NAACP while the pres-ident was a member of an African-American congregation. After Reeb's death that congregation invited Ferris to come speak. In his eulogy, Ferris lamented that it had taken the murder of a white man to get the nation to focus on the troubles in Alabama; the congregation's response told him they agreed.[360]

Sometimes staying home was the morally compelling decision. For John Wolf in Tulsa, going would have meant missing an opportunity to begin to address, and heal, the rarely acknowledged 1921 race riot in which white Oklahomans burned the African-American community in Tulsa to the ground, leaving as many as three hundred dead. "To tell the truth," Wolf said, "though I envy the experience of [those] who went to Selma, if I had to do it over again there would not be the least reticence about doing what we did, and my part in it. . . . It had a salutary effect upon this community."[361]

Others responded in a way that grew out of their relation ships to African Americans. For them, Selma was an attack on a people they held dear. While at Harvard Divinity School, William R. Jones and Clark Olsen worked together as student ministers at the Unitarian Society of Wellesley Hills, and in the process they became close. Toward the end of their years together, Jones gave Olsen a compliment he would never forget. "Clark," he said "you're a damn good nigger!"[362] When Orloff Miller arrived at the Boston University School of Theology (BUST) in 1953 he was asked if he was willing to have an African-American roommate. He said yes. So it was that he and Philip R. Cousins, who was preparing for the African Methodist Episcopal ministry, became friends.[363] Likewise, Gene Reeves came to know Martin Luther King Jr. at BUST and when his friend called, Reeves went.

Fred Lipp began building relationships with African Americans in college. Enrolled at Wooster College in Ohio, he spent his sophomore year in Nashville as an exchange student at Fisk University, where he was one of only two white students on campus. He found Fisk to be full of beer and dancing, black literature and love. He requested a transfer, but was denied. He returned to Wooster "bored and lost," "missing the eager joy of learning" he had discovered among his black friends. The scales had fallen from his eyes, and he saw the "innocent entitlement engendered in a totally white community."[364]

Steve Graves, the Meadville Lombard seminarian who walked the entire way from Selma to Montgomery, knew Coretta King from Antioch College, where they had chaired its United Way drive together. Spying him among the marchers, Coretta shouted, "What are you doing here?" "The same thing you're doing, Coretta," Graves replied.[365]

Ministers were led south by their children, sometimes literally. In December 1964 Alex Jack, the son of Homer Jack, participated in Carpenters for Christmas. College students rebuilt Antioch Missionary Baptist Church in Blue Mountain, Mississippi, which had been burned to the ground in reprisal after civil rights leader Fannie Lou Hamer had spoken there. Alex's undertaking preceded his father's visit to the South with the denominational team. Ray Manker went to Quitman, Mississippi, to visit Greg Kaslo, who belonged to his congregation and had been working for the Delta Ministry program since the summer of 1964.

Another UU student, Cathy Cade, had been among the first wave to go south. On June 21, 1963, nine days after Medgar Evers was assassinated and two weeks following her graduation from Carleton College, Cade arrived in Albany, Georgia, to participate in the first summer civil rights program attempting to use a significant number of white volunteers. SNCC planned to concentrate on direct action in Albany, as opposed to its earlier emphasis on voter registration. By her second day Cade was in jail, which did not discourage her; she would continue as a SNCC activist in Georgia, Mississippi, and New Orleans until 1967.[366]

The fact that so many young UUs went south stood as a model, and a challenge, to their elders. Musing about why he had gone to Selma, Orloff Miller said, "I had always assumed it was mostly due to my experiences as a Unitarian Universalist—the experience of working with UU students involved in sit-ins and other demonstrations, joining with other UUs in the 1963 March on Washington for Jobs and Freedom [where he had marched with the Student Religious Liberals contingent], and my participation in the UU staff team that went to Mississippi in January 1965."[367]

UUs had responded to the call of conscience before. Over half the ministry had signed the petition to the Senate supporting the 1964 Civil Rights Act; over and over again the UUA General Assembly passed resolutions calling for racial justice; sixteen hundred UUs participated in the March on Washington; many UUs were active members of the NAACP, the Urban League, or CORE; many worked for fair housing in their local communities. In addition, many knew ministers and young people who volunteered in the South. The crisis in Selma lit up the UU network as ministers of congregations across the country called one another and said, "I'm going. How about you?"

"There was a place I had to go," said Jack Taylor. "I had never been in Selma before. I'd never been in the deep South before. I didn't want to go," but his classmate, Orloff Miller, had called.[368] Taylor wasn't alone in feeling trepidation. Even the irrepressible Farley Wheelwright was reluctant. In a letter to his congregation, Wheelwright wrote,

> I didn't want to go. I didn't want to go so badly I called half a dozen friends whom I knew could not go and told them I'd go if they would, thus hoping to salve my conscience. In the end my conscience was not that easily salved, and with a little prodding from Harry Purvis I flew to Selma Monday night.
>
> On Tuesday, following the successful and historic protest, exultant I returned home only to be greeted with the news of the assault on three Unitarian Universalist ministers, and I am once again moved to turn around and return to Selma, Alabama. How many of us must the forces of hate mug, mob, humiliate and murder before they learn the liberal religious proclamation of the supreme worth of every human personality?
>
> I go back to Selma to be part of the answer to this question. I go back to Selma to replace Jim Reeb. I go back to Selma because at least for the next week I cannot live with myself anywhere else in the world.[369]

Before six-foot, four-inch John Collins and three other graduate students from Northwestern University wedged themselves into a VW Beetle to head off to Montgomery for the final day of the march, they had wrestled with the decision. Three were married and had young children. Their wives would have liked to go, "but felt constrained by their maternal duties." As members of the Unitarian Church of Evanston, John and his wife had demonstrated against redlining. But "in the back of our minds, in making the decision to go, was that sense that we had a duty to the future that our children would grow up in, to help make ours a more just society."[370]

Collins's perspective was a reversal of conventional wisdom. Most often, the significance of family and one's responsibility to one's children represented an argument not to go. "As far as his responsibility to his family," Carl Ulrich wrote to one of his siblings who was vexed by Reeb's decision, "it seems this is always the question that each person has to answer. But if one is to use this type of reasoning one can never stand up for anything. This is the reason that Germans did not stand up against Hitler . . . there was too much danger to their jobs, their families, and their lives."[371]

Many said they went to stand up for human dignity and to protest the abrogation of human rights. But this was never the only reason. "I felt," Helen Dick wrote after going to Montgomery, "that if other American citizens did not protest this, that it would be like the German people who were silent under Hitler and did not protest—and look what that did to that country and to the world."[372] The trauma of a war that caused many to say "Never again."

A portion of the credit for the strong response must go to Homer Jack. His long tenure in the civil rights movement gave the UUA credibility and the breadth and depth of his connections meant he could stay on top of rapidly unfolding events, while his decisiveness and clarity of vision gave the UUA direction. His effort was backed by the UUA leadership, and Dana McLean Greeley stepped forward when Jack called him to do so.

While Greeley, himself, had not been quick to champion the cause of racial justice, he nonetheless had inherited a legacy that could be built upon. The clergy was primed, because since the 1940s theological education had emphasized the centrality of social engagement to ministry. The espoused values were clear because in nine of the ten years leading up to Selma, the AUA and, later, UUA General Assembly had passed one or more resolutions supporting desegregation, civil rights, integration, and African independence. Indeed, the 1963 General Assembly had agonized over whether or not to require congregations to be racially inclusive. Unable to amass the required two-thirds majority to change the bylaw, instead the Assembly urged congregations to voluntarily drop segregationist rules and it established the Commission on Religion and Race. The words of the "Resolution on Admission of Members without Discrimination," and of many other resolutions, would have turned to ash in their mouths and become a symbol of monumental hypocrisy if they had not acted.

The number of UUs who went to Selma may also reflect gender, age, and idealism. The gender factor is straightforward: across all the faiths represented in Selma, nearly all the clerical participants, aside from the nuns, were men. As for the age distribution among UUs, the first to go, Ira Blalock and Gordon Gibson, were 31 and 25. Among the initial responders to King's telegram were Orloff Miller, who was 33; James Reeb, 38; Clark Olsen, 32; Charles Blackburn, 32; John Wells, 37; Farley Wheelwright, 37; Richard Leonard, 37; Fred Lipp, 27; John A. Taylor, 33; Ralph Mero, 29; Brad Greeley, 26; and Dave Johnson, 28. David H. Cole, at 43, was a bit older; even Homer Jack was only 48. The eldest was probably Alfred Hobart, the associate director of the UUA's regional office in Atlanta, who was 65. Donald and Vilma Harrington were 50 and 52, and they were an anomaly, coming on their own initiative, unconnected to the UUA. But they came from a congregation that had held racial justice as a core value since 1910.

The age range of those who came to Reeb's memorial service was broader. Steve Graves was 36, Richard Gilbert 29, Jim Hobart 30, Donald Harrington 50, Jack Mendelsohn 46, Dana Greeley 56, and Donald Thompson 58. Lewis McGee, age 72, and Judge Lawrence Brooks, age 84, would have been the most venerable of the

UUs gathered to honor Reeb. In general, those not in their youth were entering their prime.

The idealism of participants suggests a twentieth-century crusade: a collective struggle against injustice. Telling her husband why she had to go, Viola Liuzzo said, "It's everybody's fight. There are just too many people just standing around talking."[373] Reeb used similar words: "It's the kind of fight I believe in. I want to be part of it." And Gerald Krick, who had marched beside Reeb, said that "the Selma marchers have been using spiritual swords."[374] Given the moral fury that fueled them, the metaphors of fighting and weapons came naturally. To borrow William James's phrase, Selma was "the moral equivalent of war." The fight in Selma built upon what James claimed is an innate human martial nature which cultivates the "surrender of private interest," promotes "obedience to command," and encourages "strenuous honor."[375] The civil rights movement relied on all of these. And, as UU theologian William R. Jones pointed out, "The alleged rift among civil rights leaders is not a conflict over the desirability or necessity of force but a difference of opinion as regards what *types* of force are legitimate and *effective* expressions of *non-violent* coercion."[376] Activists took aggressive action, but with morality as a shield, sacrifice as a weapon, and camaraderie bolstering their morale. Selma was that generation's war.

That is how Alan Deale saw it. Leading a memorial service for Reeb in Rockford, Illinois, Deale said, "James Reeb was a soldier in the struggle for justice. He died on the field of battle—a battle in which we all are involved." Deale used Archibald MacLeish's 1940 poem "The Young Dead Soldiers" to give voice to that martial spirit.

The young dead soldiers do not speak.

Nevertheless, they are heard in the still houses:
who has not heard them?

They have a silence that speaks for them at night
and when the clock counts.

They say: We were young. We have died.
Remember us.

They say: We have done what we could
but until it is finished it is not done.

They say: We have given our lives but until it is finished
no one can know what our lives gave.

They say: Our deaths are not ours: they are yours,
they will mean what you make them.

They say: Whether our lives and our deaths were for peace
and a new hope or for nothing we cannot say,
it is you who must say this.

We leave you our deaths. Give them their meaning.
We were young, they say. We have died; remember us.

The evolution of UU engagement with the civil rights movement during the mid-twentieth century was akin to the development of Universalist and Unitarian involvement with the
abolitionist movement a century earlier. In both cases, they met
broad resistance at the beginning, but a few radicals kept raising the issue and nudging their denominations toward taking a
stand. At the same time, social attitudes were shifting. Finally, after
decades, an event—the Dred Scott decision in the one case and
Selma in the other—galvanized Northern and Unitarian and Universalist opinion. Between 177 and 250 UU ministers and hundreds of laypeople journeyed to Selma and Montgomery. Others
led demonstrations in their local communities. The ministers who
went to Selma represented a quarter to a third of all UU ministers
in full fellowship. Add to that the dozens who spent time with the
Mississippi Summer Project, the Delta Ministry Project, and other
efforts in the South afterward; Gene Navias, the UUA's religious

education consultant who worked with the congregation in Savannah the weekend after Reeb's death; those who, like John Wolf and Dick Henry, led their communities' response; and the dozen ministers who participated in the UU presence in Selma through the summer of 1965. It isn't a stretch to estimate that half of the 710 UU ministers in full fellowship were actively engaged in this struggle. For many, the experience changed their lives. And it brought to the UUA a sea change in attitudes.

Unitarian Universalists Reach Consensus

An attitudinal shift that went beyond civil rights was at work in Selma. The political landscape in the UUA and across America was changing. During the first half of the twentieth century, prior to the rise of McCarthyism, Unitarianism had included outspoken Socialists like John Haynes Holmes on the one hand, and on the other a strong contingent of Republicans, including President William Howard Taft and Senator Leverett Saltonstall. On the Universalist side, Clarence Skinner represented the progressive wing, while several congressmen who attended National Memorial in Washington, D.C., were Dixiecrats.

The 1967 report of the Committee on Goals offers clues to the nature and magnitude of the shift taking place. Consider three questions about political affiliation that the committee asked in its survey: "What political party did your parents generally support?" "Which political party do you generally support?" and "For whom did you vote in the last presidential election?" Regarding their parents, 37 percent of respondents answered Democrat; 48.6 percent Republican; and 14.4 percent Other, Politically divided, or None. But when asked which party they themselves supported, 56.3 percent said Democrat; 33.8 percent Republican; 3.7 percent Other; and 6.2 percent None. In the 1964 presidential election, 18 percent had voted for Barry Goldwater, 73.2 percent for Lyndon Johnson, 1.3 percent for someone else, and 7.5 percent had not voted at all.[377] The continuation of these trends can be seen in the

American Religious Identity Surveys of 1990 and 2008. In 1990, 18 percent of UUs were Republican, 42 percent Democrat, 37 percent Independent, and 3 percent Other. In 2008, 6 percent were Republican, 64 percent Democrat, and 30 percent Independent[378]

These numbers suggest a fracture between generations. In 1967 half the parents of the American respondents were Republican, while over half the American respondents themselves were Democrats, and nearly three-quarters of them had voted for Lyndon Johnson in 1964. That was the year in which Southern Democrats began voting Republican, the beginning of a political shift that carried the South into the Republican Party. The mirror image of this shift transpired within Unitarian Universalism. The percentage of UUs who identified themselves as Democrat increased, while the percentage of those who identified as Republican dropped precipitously.

The espoused values of Unitarian Universalists paralleled emerging progressive political trends. Civil rights was the first in a series of issues that grew to include Vietnam War resistance, Black Power, women's liberation, gay rights, environmental concerns, and, most recently, immigration reform. These movements reshaped, and polarized, the American political landscape.

When the UUA board met on March 12–13, 1965, feminism was just beginning to stir in America. The release two years earlier of Friedan's *The Feminine Mystique* had given the movement voice, but its institutionalization in the National Organization for Women was still a year away. Opposition to the war in Vietnam had begun to mount, but the Stonewall Riots were four years in the future—and remained unimaginable. For the UUA board, gathering the day after James Reeb's death, civil rights was front and center. The agenda for Saturday included considering whether or not to add "without regard to race, color or national origin" to Article II, Section 2(3) of the Association's constitution. Those against the motion argued that the existing wording, "To affirm, defend and promote the supreme worth of every human personality," left no room for doubt, and that changing it would "encourage 'Constitutional tinkering,'" which might lead to someone wanting to add "without regard to sex." Additionally, changing the constitution would make it appear that only now, "after 'segregation is on its death bed'—the UUA had decided to get on the bandwagon." With three female members in attendance, the board ultimately recommended against the amendment.[379] The board then recessed, flew to Birmingham, and reconvened the next day in Selma.

The board's experience in Selma seems to have prompted change. At the General Assembly of 1966 the delegates took a different course of action. Citing Article II and the resolutions on segregation and discrimination passed in 1962, the Assembly adopted the resolution "Consensus on Racial Justice," pledging Unitarian Universalists to "work to eliminate all vestiges of discrimination and segregation in their churches and fellowships and to encourage the integration of congregations and of the Unitarian Universalist ministry, and work for integration in all phases of life in the community." The six-page resolution included sections titled "Segregation and Discrimination," "Racial Violence and the Administration of Justice," "The Franchise," "Education," "Housing," "Employment," "Public Accommodations and Facilities," "Federal-Aid Programs," "Demonstrations and Civil Disobedience," "Inter-racial Marriage and Adoption," "Personal Associations," and "Integration of the Churches and Ministry." However, while its preamble called on the UUA to pledge "to eliminate all vestiges of discrimination" from its congregations, ironically the document focused largely on the government and other non-UU institutions. The words *should* and *urge* appear more than sixty-five times. Once again, UUs found it convenient to locate the problem elsewhere, rather than look at how racism was endemic within the UUA and its congregations.

The Committee on Goals released its report in spring 1967, two years after Selma. One of the questions on its survey explored attitudes toward liberal religion's involvement in education and action in various social problems, and 69.7 percent of respondents indicated that it was "very important" that the church get involved in the issue of "racial integration." No other issue was rated so highly. Another 24.7 percent rated it "somewhat important." Altogether, 94.4 percent of the respondents affirmed that their church or fellowship should be involved in integration. When asked how they felt about the denomination's involvement in "areas of social controversy," 46.6 percent "strongly approved" of involvement in "Civil Rights (i.e. race relations)" and 44 percent "approved." And 62.3 percent approved of "non-violent civil disobedience" "when laws are unjust."[380]

Following Selma, UUs reached a strong consensus about civil rights. However, when we examine that consensus closely, four problems emerge:

- The dichotomy between Unitarian Universalism's espoused values and values in practice remained entrenched, and the association remained largely unaware of the lack of congruence.
- Racial integration, to which Unitarian Universalists were more strongly committed than ever, was becoming irrelevant.
- Since he embodied New England Unitarian culture, Dana McLean Greeley was ill prepared to provide the leadership that the UUA needed as it tried to meet the challenges of race relations in the post-Selma era.
- There was a significant gap between the Unitarian Universalist laity's understanding of the UU consensus about race and what a radicalized ministry thought it meant and implied for the future.

The Dichotomy Lives On

While Selma came to symbolize Unitarian Universalism's commitment to racial justice, it did not end the dichotomy between UU values and practice. In and of themselves, noble aspirations and heroic deeds cannot undo systematically embedded patterns. Following Selma, the values UUs espoused were articulated in the

1966 "Consensus on Racial Justice" and confirmed in the 1967 report of the Committee on Goals. But when we turn from them to examine UU values in practice, we see limited results:

- "Toward Integrating the UU Ministry" was issued on September 24, 1965. By May 1966 the only follow-up amounted to "some correspondence with the departments and groups involved."[381] In 1967 four African Americans were in training to become UU ministers, and the only settled black minister served in a part-time position.

- In 1965 one African American was elected to the UUA board. None served on the UUA Nominating Committee or Commission on Appraisal, nor would any until 1969— the year Greeley left office. Meanwhile, in May 1966, only one African American, Cornelius McDougald, sat on the Commission on Religion and Race, and no women served.

- Except for four chapters about George Washington Carver in the 1965 *Worshiping Together with Questioning Minds,* no improvement had been made on the religious education front.

- *Hymns for the Celebration of Life,* which included nothing by or about African Americans, was published in 1964. A revision did not appear until 1979, when, in response to the demands of feminists, a booklet of gender-neutral hymns titled *25 Familiar Hymns in New Forms* was published.

- In "Did Selma Make a Difference in Your Town?" a *Register-Leader* article published in the summer of 1965, ministers repeatedly cited the issues of housing and employment and the need to work together. Indeed, congregations across the United States stepped up their work for fair housing, equal access, school desegregation, tutoring, and Head Start programs. Nevertheless, many of the congregations, and all the newly founded ones, were located away from urban centers.

- Dana McLean Greeley's opening remarks at the October 1967 Emergency Conference on the Unitarian Universalist

Response to the Black Rebellion laid bare the dichotomy. What people truly value is better revealed by what they support financially than by what they profess. At that pivotal gathering Greeley reported, "Our Unitarian Universalist Freedom Fund is four years old. While we raised in several months more than $100,000 for the James Reeb Memorial Fund, in four years we have raised less than this amount for our more inclusive Freedom Fund. In an affluent denomination in an affluent society, this is embarrassingly small."[382] In 1964–65 the Freedom Fund raised $72,400; in 1965–66, $19,300; and in the first seven months of 1966–67, just $4,405. In March 1968 it was dissolved and folded into the new UU Fund for Racial Justice Now.[383]

This final example has much to teach us. The generous giving of Unitarian Universalists to the one fund and not the other revealed their priorities. The Freedom Fund had been initially called the Disaster Fund, and was established in the wake of the bombing in Birmingham in which four black girls died. The James Reeb Memorial Fund was started in response to Reeb's death. The UU Fund for Racial Justice Now was dedicated to the ongoing work for racial justice. Why the outpouring of support for Reeb's family? Why more for the Reebs than for the families and church of four African-American girls? And why give to the families of the individuals killed by racists (e.g., a home for Jimmie Lee Jackson's mother and funeral expenses for Jonathan Daniels), but not to remedy the social situation that had taken their lives? This prioritizing reflected whom Unitarian Universalists identified with. Moreover, compared to the full-hearted engagement and sacrifice in Selma, the financial resources Unitarian Universalists directed to the cause of civil rights was, as Greeley lamented, "embarrassingly small." Why was this so? Abstract principles such as racial justice awaken the mind, but it is the plight of people perceived as one's neighbors that touches the soul. All people, not just UUs, give more generously when they feel an emotional connection in addition to an ethical commitment.

Taken together, these examples highlight the continuing disparity between Unitarian Universalism's espoused values and its values in practice. Certainly, UUs preached more sermons about human rights, sang more freedom songs on Sunday mornings, and devoted more Sunday School classes to the situation of African Americans. But they sang the songs and preached the messages, by and large, in lily-white settings. Without a doubt, UUs participated in more protest marches and community action. But how much attention would the cause receive in the years ahead when issues that affected Euro-American UUs directly—such as the war in Vietnam and Women's Liberation—became urgent? For how long would the cause of African Americans—people who were not their peers nor part of their lives—remain paramount? What would summon UU attention when African-American songs and stories appeared in neither the hymnal nor the curricula and African Americans represented perhaps 1 percent of the UU population[384] and had no voice on UU governing bodies? Unitarian Universalism in practice, structure, and complexion remained out of sync with its values.

The Eclipse of Racial Integration

In the context of Black Power, the hard-won UU consensus in favor of integration was beside the point. On February 12, shortly after the escalation of the voting registration drive in Selma but before Jimmie Lee Jackson was shot, SNCC staff met in Atlanta. During that meeting the SNCC chairman, John Lewis, read a passage from Thomas Merton that proposed that whites would have to "let Negroes run their own revolution." Amplifying this, Lewis said, "If the Movement and SNCC are going to be effective in attempting to liberate the black masses, then the civil rights movement must be black controlled, dominated, and led."[385]

Few UU leaders were attuned to this shift in mood and practice. At the meeting of the After Selma Committee, both Joe Barth and Homer Jack had noted that African Americans were pulling away from interracial activities, especially regarding decision making. The phrase *Black Power* had been around for a while, but during the summer of 1966 the crowds at rallies responded to it ever more strongly, and Stokely Carmichael started peppering his speeches with it.

In 1967 Beacon Press published *The Coming of the Black Man*. Written by longtime UU Benjamin Scott, one of the leaders of the Black UU Caucus, it moved quickly to the point and the problem:

> In actual practice integration has not been understood by whites to mean loss of "whiteness." There has been the assumption that everyone would finally merge into the majority culture when he was "ready" and if the majority could be induced to allow it. Whites who advocate integration do not expect a serious dislocation of their own identity.[386]

Unitarian Universalists liked to emphasize integration. And yet it is difficult to find a passage of their writings or speeches in which *integration* does not really mean *assimilation*. There is no evidence that white UUs grasped that integration meant genuine change rather than assimilation; the hymnal *Hymns for the Celebration of Life* is a prime indication of this. They understood that their ultimate goal was to honor the worth and dignity of every person and to give each person an equal opportunity. But the UU emphasis on integration led most to confuse the means with the ends. The goal was never integration for integration's sake. The goal was racial justice.

One cannot address the difference between integration and assimilation without delving into the question of identity. Some African-American UUs began to ask, Can I be *black* and UU? What does this faith have to say to that indelible aspect of my identity? In 1967, Jack Mendelsohn, who was both Ben Scott's and James Reeb's minister, welcomed the formation of the Black Caucus. He recognized that its founding was a matter of identity for both black and white. And he hoped it "might make it possible for more of us who are white to be able genuinely to get some feeling of the world as it's seen through black eyes . . . and not always filtered through the way we do things."[387]

Dana McLean Greeley

On June 18, 1965, the UUA board of trustees unanimously passed a resolution commending Dana Greeley for leadership in civil rights.

> [The Trustees] express their admiration for the leadership shown by Dr. Dana McLean Greeley during the dramatic days of Selma. He has shown wise judgment and has acted discreetly and modestly, combining tactful moderation with firm determination. He has avoided the pitfalls of sensationalism and self-seeking publicity for himself and the denomination.[388]

He deserved the commendation, both for what he had done and for what he would do. In 1963 he had led the sixteen hundred UUs who participated in the March on Washington and later met with UUs in Kinston, North Carolina; Charleston, South Carolina, and elsewhere in his effort to move congregations toward being truly inclusive.[389] In 1964 he had lobbied for the Civil Rights Act; he'd gone to Selma and to Montgomery; at the meeting at which the commendation was voted he brought forward a recommendation from the Commission on Religion and Race to hire a James J. Reeb Memorial Civil Rights Worker; in August 1965 he returned to Alabama and met with Jimmie Lee Jackson's mother and then visited striking plantation workers in Mississippi; a month later he traveled to Mississippi again to visit Donald Thompson after Thompson was shot by the Ku Klux Klan.

The commendation was appropriately given. And yet Dana McLean Greeley was part of the problem. *For the crux of the matter was the waning New England-centric Unitarian culture he embodied.*

Greeley was not prejudiced nor lacking commitment, and he was not unconcerned. The problem springs from his upbringing and acculturation, which left him suffering from cultural myopia. Where Greeley grew up there were few, if any, African Americans. Lexington, Massachusetts, situated twenty miles northwest of Boston, was a well-to-do community of 6,000 in 1920 when he was a boy. In 2010, a little more than one hundred years after Greeley's birth, its population was still affluent and had grown to 31,394. And while there had been a significant influx of Asian citizens, the African-American population in Lexington was a scant 1.5 percent (473 people). Regarding black people, Lexington's cultural milieu—like New England's generally—was, and remains, particularly insular.[390] Greeley would have had few African-American contacts either in his home town or at Harvard University, and those he met would almost certainly have been in service roles. Nothing in what has been written by or about him suggests anything different in his early years, nor do his memoirs of his ministry from 1935 to 1958 at Arlington Street Church.

In *25 Beacon Street and Other Reflections* Greeley writes that in 1935, in his early days at Arlington Street, the executive secretaries of both the Boston NAACP and the Urban League were members of the congregation, as was "the publisher of the major black newspaper in the city." He says nothing more about them. And despite the presence of three pillars of the African-American community in his congregation, he was "only moderately active in early days in the Boston Urban League."[391] It is hard to understand how this could be.

His sermons do little to demonstrate that race relations was of special concern to him. For Brotherhood Week in 1943, he preached "Christianity and the Brotherhood of Man,"[392] in which he said, "Socially it is not wise for black and white or Occidental and Oriental to marry each other, but intrinsically they are the same. . . . But the brotherhood of man, we repeat, doesn't mean intermarriage; it means the recognition of human rights; it means the acknowledgment of the divine heritage of the whole family." Here he offers up the conventional liberal wisdom of the era (i.e., no miscegenation) alongside sweeping, high-minded principles.

He goes on to quote Abraham Lincoln before mentioning, in passing, "great spirits" such as Booker T. Washington, Roland Hayes, and George Washington Carver. In his first book, the sermon collection *Toward Larger Living: Sermons on Personal Religion* published in 1944, he mentions neither race nor civil rights. The closest he comes is in another sermon delivered during Brotherhood Week. In "Religion and Social Passion" he again praises Lincoln, but does not mention African Americans.[393] In 1947, prior to a local election, he preached on "What Boston Needs." He listed Boston's "minorities" as Canadians, Italians, Russians, and Irish, and once again quoted Lincoln—once again without mentioning "Negroes." Strangely, he discussed the declining quality of public schools and the need for metropolitan government without mentioning the racial subtext of either. Nor did he address the dire housing situation of African Americans in Boston. Two-thirds of the African-American population of Massachusetts lived in Boston, and the majority of those were crowded into three neighborhoods. Indeed, during his tenure at Arlington Street Church the number of African Americans living in Boston nearly tripled, while the overall population peaked and began to decline; it is not possible that he was unaware of this. During his entire ministry there, he sat on the board of the Benevolent Fraternity of Unitarian Churches (now The UU Urban Ministry), and from 1945 to 1950 he served as its president. The Benevolent Fraternity's mandate was to work with the disinherited and downtrodden in Boston, yet, whatever he accomplished, he does not volunteer.[394]

Greeley's legacy regarding racial justice pales compared to that of his contemporaries: Donald Harrington in New York, who founded and co-chaired the Americans for South African Resistance; A. Powell Davies in Washington, D.C., whose last sermon before he died suddenly in September 1957 addressed the crisis in Little Rock over school desegregation; Leslie Pennington in Chicago, who founded the interracial Hyde Park-Kenwood Community Conference; or Stephen Fritchman in Los Angeles, who wrote, "I understood the anger, the torment, and the commitment to a cause that whiplashed old John Brown at Harper's Ferry. . . . I only regret that no day was long enough and no human body strong enough to finish the task."[395]

Greeley's most in-depth discussion of race among his published works is the chapter "Race Relations" in *25 Beacon Street*. In twenty-six pages, he touches on its place in his ministry at Arlington Street Church, the establishment of the Commission on Religion and Race, and the events in Selma. Then he uses the bulk of the chapter to offer his position on the controversy over the UUA response to Black Power, which dominated the final years of his administration. Beyond this there is little. In the first chapter of *25 Beacon Street* he discusses his personal beliefs, and it is clear that the intellectual history that inspired him is largely Anglo-American. There and in his other two books Greeley demonstrates his knowledge about world religions, but nowhere in his writings is there any but the slightest indication that he was familiar with African-American literature or history.

Greeley had a patrician background and a Harvard education, and the realities of Negro life were outside his Boston-bound purview. He was optimistic, buoyant, friendly, and well liked. A globe-trotter with a gleaming smile and a hail-fellow-well-met handshake, he strode confidently through the world. Yet to some things he seemed oblivious. For example, he didn't notice that Coretta Scott and Martin Luther King Jr. attended Arlington Street Church "many times" while they were studying in Boston. Greeley didn't realize this until King's roommate told him so later.[396] Such myopia is startling.

Greeley's limitations did not serve the denomination well. With two exceptions, until late in his administration he neither nominated nor appointed any African Americans except to the Commission on Religion and Race. This failure contributed to the crisis that would overtake, and nearly destroy, the UUA by the end of his administration.

Greeley put the force of his formidable will to work for the causes of world peace, interfaith collaboration, college ministry, the merger of Universalism and Unitarianism, and the growth of the UUA, but not for race relations. He took the initiative in working for peace, but admitted that his engagement in civil rights was a response to circumstances rather than an achievement.[397] Because human dignity was of paramount importance to him, he rose to the occasion in Selma. Yet because civil rights, in and of itself, hadn't been an ongoing and urgent interest for him, he lacked the depth of experience and insight that would have helped him to understand and adapt to the exigencies of the developing situation. He did not sense the undercurrents at work in Selma, as those who participated in the After Selma Committee did, or understand that the civil rights movement was undergoing fundamental change.

When it was required, Greeley responded commendably. But he never truly asserted leadership, because although he agreed that it was important, civil rights was not his passion; peace was. When it came to transforming the UUA by aligning its espoused values on racial issues with its practices, he was at a loss. Therefore, when black UU anger erupted at the 1967 Emergency Conference, Greeley—along with the vast majority of Unitarian Universalists—had no understanding of how integration had been recognized as assimilation in disguise and vehemently rejected, and he was unprepared to engage with a new, confrontational black militancy. Greeley, and most of his constituency, did not understand what was at stake. Blinkered by the patrician self-confidence that was his birthright, he could not see why his goodwill was insufficient and his approach unacceptable.

The Spirit of Selma

Leon Hopper, minister of the Jefferson Unitarian Church in Colorado, had neither rushed to Selma nor marched in Montgomery. Nor had he gone to McComb, Mississippi. Nonetheless, he felt called to participate in the UU presence in Selma. Before embarking on that project, he attended the UUA General Assembly and saw that his colleagues had been transformed by their experience in the South. After he returned home, but before he left for Selma, he preached about what he had heard:

> In Boston there was an essence described as the "Spirit of Selma" which pervaded the meetings. A quarter of the active Unitarian Universalist ministry journeyed to Selma or Montgomery last March. The catch phrases "civil rights"—"human freedom"—"personal dignity"—"equality," words which have so easily flowed from the lips of religious liberals, have now taken on a feeling tone as well as possessing their rational, logical meaning of old. It seemed as if the intellectualism of the pulpit and discussion group had broken through a great barrier to the reality in life, and thus, as a religious movement, uncovered a greater contact with life where most people live it—in pain in struggle—in ignorance—and yet in hope. In participating in Selma we, as a denomination, have found a new lease on life. What is really at issue is much more than the involvement in the civil rights movement—it is a recognition that we are indeed emotional beings, and logic and reason alone do not bring trust or involvement. That we had fallen prey to all the stereotypes of the privileged educated who no longer knows how to communicate with someone of less privileged background. Our religious pronouncements prior to Selma possessed the character of being *for* or *about* the problem. Now they are *with*.
>
> For the first time at a denominational meeting I heard discussion of the problems of our core cities and our responsibility. Since the end of World War II we have been predominantly a movement of expansive retreat to the suburbs. Church after church has moved from the faltering heart of the metropolis to its frenetic periphery. City center churches have died and suburban institutions thrived, prospered and grown complacent on the fat of the privileged class. . . . Can we afford to avoid the core city and its problems? Can we continue to be separate from the concerns and programs of our downtown sisters and they from us?[398]

Transformed by the experience in Selma, ministers found that their worldview had changed, and they now faced a conundrum they couldn't solve. Looking back on Selma in *Long Challenge: The Empowerment Controversy, 1967–1977*, UU minister Victor H. Carpenter reflected,

> My being in South Africa during most of the 1960s had pre-vented my involvement in the American Civil Rights move-ment, thus curtailing the deep emotional attachment which many of my UU colleagues developed for the ideal of integra-tion. Without that emotional attachment to racial integration, my eyes were open to the revolutionary re-direction of liberal religion's social witness being demanded by black UUs at the Biltmore Hotel.[399]

Certainly some saw Selma as a victory for integration. John Ruskin Clark came away from his time serving as a UU presence there with a "renewed determination to help promote dialogue between Negroes and whites."[400] Selma did become an icon of interracial solidarity and collaboration. But explaining its impact on UU ministers requires a more nuanced explanation than Car-penter offers. Most of the 177 ministers known to have gone to Selma or Montgomery became, like Carpenter, supporters of the Black Affairs Council (BAC).[401]

"Probably, the reality of my experience in Selma," wrote Harry A. Thor in 1999, "made me a supporter of [BAC] and [its] unpopu-lar financial agenda for our denomination." Farley Wheelwright, another BAC supporter, claimed Selma made him "more politi-cally radical." Theodore Webb, a "UU presence," said it taught him about poverty and sent him back north a more "confirmed progressive and a committed Democratic Socialist." Another, Stewart E. Hild, having glimpsed the shift to come, said that Afri-can Americans in Selma were "becoming more conscious of the fact that they themselves are the real key to eventual victory."[402] And Harry Hoehler, who journeyed to Selma and Montgomery and later attended the meeting at the Biltmore Hotel at which the Black Affairs Council was formed, said, "I supported BAC because I believed firmly in the black empowerment movement."[403] Such testimonies point to the possibility that, rather than confirming UU ministers' faith in integration, Selma radicalized them. Those who went realized the issue was not integration; it was poverty, prejudice, and an asymmetry of power.

Those who went also learned to trust black leadership; they had little choice other than to do so. Reporting to his congregation after his return, Howard Matson said, "There were times when action happened so fast that one needed to follow instructions the way one follows instructions in battle. It took our Unitarian ministers but a short time to become aware they were but students in the hands of a most gifted Negro leadership. These men with a minimum of sleep and a constantly changing battlefield made the difficult decisions that touched the weal and woe of millions."[404] Selma prepared many of the ministers in the UUA to engage with Black Power by giving them experience in following African-American leadership.

The impact on those who responded to King's call was enduring. William C. Rau, who spent nine months working for the SCLC, explained, "Andy Young told us that we would eventually leave the movement, but the movement would never leave us. Andy Young was right. I left the South with a heightened sensitivity to injustice and a clear understanding of the need to fight injustice whenever and wherever it occurs."[405]

A story Irene K. Murdock, Dana McLean Greeley's administrative assistant, told years later about marching to the Dallas County courthouse following the memorial service for James Reeb captures some of the power of the experience:

> I was toward the end of the procession, and found myself walking beside a black woman with a little girl. . . . We each held the child's hand and swung her between us from time to time, the way you do with small children. As we walked

through the streets, we saw the sidewalks lined with men and women, with ugly faces and angry expressions. They shouted obscenities at us. At one point someone singled me out to say: "If you love that nigger baby so much, why don't you take her home witcha?" I held the little girl's hand a little tighter and I held my head a little higher, and I walked.

We approached the Court House and stood quietly near the back of the crowd, waiting for the program to begin. Suddenly a car behind us backfired. In a flash the little girl was up in the woman's arms. "Oh, Momma," she cried. "They're gonna git us!" "No, they ain't gonna git us!" said the woman reassuringly. "And, anyway, they'd have to git me first."

. . . I never knew [the little girl's] name, but I shall never forget her. For she taught me a very important lesson. It was she who made me understand who I was and what I was doing. Now I knew all along that my trip to Selma placed me in some danger, but never was it so clear to me as at that moment. I could have been shot, or beaten, or killed. It was quite possible, but it was more likely that I would spend a few days there and I would sing freedom songs and join protest marches. And I would be proud to stand up and be counted and offer my presence to bear witness. And then I would leave that terrible scene with its frightening atmosphere and go home safely. But those people who lived there had to endure this awful struggle day after day after day, and little children like *my* little girl were growing up in constant fear and terror![406]

Describing the founding of CORE in his memoir, Homer Jack quotes Gandhi: "The conviction has been growing upon me that things of fundamental importance to the people are not secured by reason alone, but have to be purchased with their suffering."[407] Most of the middle-class Unitarian Universalists who went to Selma had never witnessed such poverty and prejudice, nor experienced such hardships and discomfort, nor faced such hostility, nor known fear so intensely, nor suffered loss so acutely. The Unitarian Universalists who were led to Selma by moral reasoning were wedded to the cause of racial justice by suffering and comradeship.

Taking It Home

Those who went were changed. But how were they to take this transformational experience back to congregations full of the religiously wounded, many of whom—to varying degrees—were hostile to Christianity and enamored of intellectualism? The intellect was not suited to convey the intensity or truth of the emotions Selma had evoked. Yet congregants expected reasoned discourse. The Committee on Goals found that UUs said they attended church services first and foremost for "intellectual stimulation"; 74.4 percent of those surveyed ranked it "very important." Next highest was "personal reflection" at 49.3 percent; then "fellowship" and "motivation to serve others" at 45.2 percent and 32.7 percent.[408] The intellect requires us to step back in order to reason about and analyze what we have experienced. It is a reflective process and, like a mirror, it turns the immediate experience of life into a flat, cold facsimile of itself.

Reason has a place. The intellect aids in building, assessing, and articulating the beliefs that guide our lives. But what kind of faith community makes intellectual stimulation preeminent? One that is afraid of the spirit and uses the intellect as a way to hold emotion at bay. This emphasis on the intellect safeguards religious liberals from feelings, from vulnerability, from the unexpected, from loss of control, and from any power beyond their control. Unitarian Universalism, as a faith tradition, was intellectually alive but emotionally impoverished. Selma's emotional intensity "broke through a great barrier to the reality in life," as Leon Hopper described it. This is why many UUs see their experience there as the high point in their lives. Their emotions were so intense, their feelings so powerful, that rationality had little to do with what the experience came to mean to them: rebirth and rededication, solidarity with the oppressed, camaraderie with colleagues, awareness of what was right, and of what they had been willing to lay down their lives for.

Robert Kilgore was among those who marched to the court-house the day after the memorial service for James Reeb. "The rain increased in intensity as we sang freedom songs and hymns," he said, "and a Negro minister gave a short talk of encouragement. This was, I am sure, the most emotional group experience of my life. As we joined arms by rows and swayed to the music of 'We Shall Overcome' and other songs of determination and compassion, the rain streaming down our faces was washing away many a tear—tears of sympathy, hope, and admiration for these courageous people."[409]

"How can a man ever forget what it meant to be in Selma the week of March 7th 1965?" asked Hunter Leggitt. "I tell you, behind that clothesline, we had community. If I could give each of you just one gift for a lifetime, it would be: to have spent that week in Selma."[410] "It has been the most significant, the most exciting, and the most thrilling event of my life so far," wrote Joseph Nerad at 12:30 a.m. on the day he returned home.[411] Over and over again, those who had been there recalled the intensity of the experience. "Maybe a lot of Unitarians and Universalists," wrote G. Robert Hohler, "have found something on these muddy Alabama streets that has been missing from their lives for too long a time. This Unitarian has anyway and I promise myself that I will bring it back."[412]

But to whom would they bring it back, and how? How could those who went to Selma take an experience that stood so far outside the norms of their liberal religious communities, and that ran counter to the rampant individualism in Unitarian Universalism, and offer it to their congregations without putting their ministries at risk?

Being in Selma taught them to step out of individualism and think about community first, to confront authority and yet, within the movement, to obey it. They participated in a black religious tradition which asserts that salvation, in its essence, is collective. Its leaders did not denigrate the intellect, but neither did they make an icon of it. They wielded it in the service of justice. Those who assembled in Selma—and especially the emotionally restrained, spiritually skeptical UUs—were swept up by a power and a cause greater than themselves.

Ralph Stutzman said,

> Fear? Yes, in the stomach, throat, knees, pulsating in the eyes; pounding in the head. It was frightening simply to be in Selma, it was also profound; for now we clergy were doing something more than simply speaking out. Our feet, our bodies were now involved, fear and all. At least, and at last, we now knew some of the terror Afro Americans had been living with all their lives. For many clergy, Selma, Alabama had become a turning point.[413]

Their experience was visceral, tactile, and deeply emotional: they were intimidated by hate-filled mobs, taught by the knot in their guts, reeducated to fear the police, called niggers and nigger-lovers; they were thrown in jail, their lives were threatened, their colleague was murdered, and they found both the justice system and the state now working against them, rather than for them. For a little while they became one with the oppressed and disinherited. The fear that gripped them taught them. Crowded together, they linked arms and stood shoulder to shoulder, remaining at the Wall despite the cold, comforted by an old woman's hand, singing and singing and singing, sharing beds, eating communally with poor black folks who had little but gave everything they had. Their fundamental values—a belief in human dignity, freedom, and fairness that was deeper than church doctrine—brought them together in common cause. They gave up control because they had none. Following orders saved their lives. They were the students. The black folks, young and old and poor, knew more than they about how to survive in the South while living with dignity and joy. The visitors knew who the teachers were.

For these ministers, the world had changed. But they had no way to bring this change to their congregations except with words.

How do you explain an experience that words cannot fully convey? Standing before their congregations, they tried to communicate this conversion experience, this epiphany. Having had their assumptions overthrown, they began intuiting that perhaps it was they, themselves, who were shackled. If they had dared to say what they had discovered, it might have gone something like this: *I have just gone through an experience that has shaken me to my core, and awakened me. I return to you feeling that we—as much as any white Southerner—need to reshape who we are and what we believe; what we do and how we relate to one another; how we determine what is important and how we express ourselves. An experience grabbed hold of me and lifted me toward rapture and that scared the hell out of me, but I never felt more alive, miserable, and grateful than in Selma.*

It would have felt risky to pull, cajole, beckon, or entice a congregation to go in such a direction. The ministers no longer stood arrayed together, arms linked; they were no longer uplifted by song. At home, alone, they tried to encourage privileged white intellectuals to feel more deeply, sing more soulfully, act more courageously; to drop the middle-class pretense of being in control and give up the exaggerated emphasis on autonomy that grows out of fear of the reality that we are totally dependent upon one another, upon Mother Earth, and upon the web of all existence. How could they explain the pervasive ecumenism of Selma, their solidarity with Christian sisters and brothers, to the cadres of flat-earth humanists who looked with disdain upon those whom the ministers had depended upon in Selma? How could they convince their members that the issue was not integration but rather love and justice? For many ministers, indeed all of them, the task of transforming a congregation was more difficult and challenging than marching for civil rights.

Integration triumphed in Selma in a way that transcended the word's customary—and spurious—meaning. Genuine integration happens when parts form a new whole; it is a melding rather than the subjugation of one by another. Some Unitarian Universalists achieved that melding during March 1965, when their values and practices meshed, when black and white stood together at the Selma Wall, sharing in struggle and song, discomfort and celebration —needing one another. For this group of Unitarian Universalists, Selma was memorable because there they experienced what it felt like to be whole, rather than experiencing the different aspects of the self as at odds with one another. The barriers of race and class, head and heart, were breached. Selma was about being in authentic relationship to one's values, promises, and hopes, and honoring them by committing one's life even unto death; it was about being in authentic relationship to African Americans and to one's own intelligence, emotions, spirit, and body. They knew they had bodies because those bodies not only ached but were threatened; they relied on their intelligence in order to act and survive; they couldn't escape their emotions; and they experienced the spirit because, in the midst of singing, it could not be denied. In giving their selves over to that time and its demands, to their conscience and sense of honor, to their faith and what it stood for, to the future and what they all hoped for, they found redemption. Together, in Selma, they found that their lives had purpose. And many, perhaps for the first time, felt whole. This was the "Spirit of Selma"; in the midst of turmoil, their values and their lives became congruent.

Before Selma this was not the case. This book began by comparing Unitarian Universalism's *espoused values* to its *values in practice,* and showing how stark the disparity had been regarding race. UU behavior had routinely run counter to the denomination's aspirations. What do we find if we reverse the exercise and ask: In the years leading up to Selma, what did UU behavior suggest about the true values of the denomination?

Beginning in the 1940s African Americans were offered "integration," but at the cost of assimilation; the location of the congregations announced that not everyone was welcomed in Unitarian Universalism; the unwillingness to call black ministers laid bare an underlying prejudice; neither Universalists nor Unitarians had much knowledge of, or interest in, African-American culture; humanism nurtured an exaggerated sense of self-sufficiency; and the ascendency of Euro-American men remained unchallenged. In the 1963 General Assembly debate over non-discrimination in admission to membership, congregational freedom trumped fairness, and the ethos of individualism triumphed over a communitarian spirit striving to create the Beloved Community. The emotive aspect of worship was rebuffed. Lack of money limited what could be done; and UUs, even when in a charitable mood, have preferred to aid individuals rather than empower the church to heal the world. All this suggests that fear, rather than freedom, reigned. These values belonged to a constricted culture, more prone to withhold than to provide, a restive community made up of individuals reluctant to accept authority or any arbiter of decisions besides the self. They represented a people seeking something that they ultimately cannot have: control.

The transformation of those who responded to the call to Selma hinged on their choice to participate in something wholly outside their previous experience and largely out of their control. Selma was the mortar and pestle. Many who were sympathetic to the cause remained trapped within their own perspectives, unable, on their own, to crush their false assumptions about African Americans and integration, about emotion, community, and God. Without a transformative experience, there was no emotional or existential wreckage upon which they could build an inner transformation and do as James Bevel urged those who had flocked to Selma to do: "Retire into your closet and rethink your entire philosophy of life. No less is necessary."[414]

Selma

I was raised on the South Side of Chicago. But in 1965, when the events described in this book took place, I was fifteen years old and attending a Swiss boarding school called Ecole d'Humanité, meaning "school of humanity." My schoolmates came from Switzerland, Nicaragua, Israel, Denmark—the world. We lived a simple lifestyle, almost spartan, and we had almost no access to television or radio. What I knew about Selma I garnered from reading the *International Herald Tribune*. I read it hungrily, despite the pain, anger, and confusion that the news reports inevitably stirred up. Because my African-American parents, a nuclear chemist and a social worker, were firmly entrenched in the upper-middle class, there was not much in my life experience to help me make sense of what I was reading. Something terrible was happening—terrible, yet heroic and important, something being done for me and all people with skin like mine. Some of those protesting in Selma were younger than I was. Others were Unitarian Universalists like me. It was painful to be cut off from the movement. Unable to share in the effort, I felt guilty about living a life so free.

Forty-three years later, for the first time, I ventured into the deep South. I participated in the Unitarian Universalist Living Legacy Civil Rights Pilgrimage bus tour. We were a diverse group, in an early-twenty-first-century Unitarian Universalist way: four families, more seniors than young adults, about equal numbers of female and male ministers, about a quarter of us identified as lesbian, gay, bisexual, or transgender, another quarter as people of color (including one Latina), and one Canadian. The tour also included Bill Sinkford, the first African-American president of the UUA, and three veterans of Selma: Charles Blackburn, Gordon Gibson, and Clark Olsen.

As we traversed Alabama and Mississippi, terror gripped me. I knew the feeling was old and understood that it was based in what I had read and imagined, and what I had seen on television in the 1950s and '60s. Before that trip my total experience in the South had amounted to a few days in Atlanta in 1969 and 1985. The South had changed; but it didn't matter. Fear ruled me. I felt it in my gut and in the shallowness of my breath. I was hypervigilant, no matter how firmly I told myself I was overreacting. What comfort I found, I found in the companionship of the others on the journey.

On the fourth day of the pilgrimage, we arrived in Selma, Alabama, the epicenter of events that, in addition to reshaping American history, had haunted me. The feelings I had experienced so long ago had faded, but they had not gone away or been forgotten. On the way, we stopped in Marion and visited the memorial to Jimmie Lee Jackson. Seeing the gravestone pockmarked with bullet holes only deepened my anxiety. Before moving on to the site on Route 80 where Viola Liuzzo was shot and where her Oldsmobile careened off the highway, we spent the night in Selma. We ate in Walker's Café, sitting at those same tiny tables. We strolled up the street with Clark Olsen to the place where James Reeb, Orloff Miller, and he had been bludgeoned.

The following day, I stood in front of Brown Chapel AME waiting for our bus. The Carver Homes, simple red-brick row houses, were across the street, and I tried to imagine what it had been like in March 1965. I saw clusters of people scattered around the projects, and others streaming in and out of the chapel: black folks guiding their comrades in arms into their homes, providing places to sleep, food to eat, and thanks. I imagined how out of the ordinary it was for all of them, black and white, to live and link arms together, to form lines and find in one another the courage to meet phalanxes of police with only prayers, songs, and faith. I imagined the Selma Wall, where the interminable standoff took place. For me that empty street was full.

A low rumble in the distance interrupted my musing. I turned, and, looking down the street, I saw a few motorcycles. The rumble grew as more motorcycles came around the corner. And more. And more. The rumble became a roar. As they drew nearer I could distinguish the three leaders. They were police officers—two white, one black. Behind them, the entire block was filled with motorcycles. The ground trembled. The roar was deafening, even with their power bridled. The riders cruised up to the chapel, cut their engines, and dismounted. What bikes! BMW Roadmasters. Honda Gold Wings. Harley-Davidsons. Chrome shiny as a mirror. A few with sidecars. The leather-clad riders headed into Brown

Chapel AME, now a shrine to the civil rights movement. As they tromped by I could see the insignia on the back of their leather jackets: "Buffalo Soldiers." Over two hundred of them, from all across America—all of them were black and, like us, they had come to pay homage. I understood Archibald MacLeish's poem:

They say: We have given our lives but until it is finished
no one can know what our lives gave.

In 1965 no one who lived in Selma and no one who went to Selma could have imagined this sight. The protesters thought the struggle was about gaining the right to vote. It was that, and much more. That moral battle was a continuation of the American Revolution, a yet unfinished revolution. The victory at Selma served as the catalyst of an economic and political revolution that led to an African American becoming president of the United States. King delivered many biblical phrases that held up a vision of freedom and justice. But even from the mountaintop, it was impossible to foretell that the vision would be fulfilled like this.

Unitarian Universalists did not know that Selma would become a pivotal moment in their own history. In the past, our religious forebears had stood on the brink of making a difference in racial justice, and had wavered. *But not this time.* Called, sent, drawn, or compelled, hundreds responded. When they left there were two UU martyrs in their hearts and there was conviction in their stride. They had been changed in ways their lives would reveal but which words could never quite capture.

It is not possible, nor necessary, to know the outcome of our actions; therefore we act in faith. Faith asks not that we succeed, but that we try. We try because we yearn to live out our values. Conscience urges us on, for we have dreamed of a better, more just tomorrow. We care; therefore, we act. In acting, we risk having our hearts broken a thousand times; therefore, we are sustained by hope. That is the price those who cleared the way for us accepted. It is what living fully, deeply, and with integrity demands.

The second half of the second verse of "Lift Every Voice and Sing," the African-American national anthem, begins, "We have come over a way that with tears has been watered." That is the way our spiritual ancestors came. The way we follow will be different, and its outcome undreamed of. But, just as it did for our forebears, the way will require of us courage, sacrifice, and tears.

Mark D. Morrison-Reed
December 2013
Toronto, Ontario, Canada

CHRONOLOGY
1867–1968

1867   William White, a white Unitarian, proposes to the AUA that it organize a "Unitarian Colored Church" in Washington, D.C. A regional AUA meeting endorses the suggestion, but nothing materializes.

1871   Meadville Theological School admits Alfred Amos Williams, the first of five students preparing for the AME or AMEZ ministry. (The last is James Thompson Simpson, in 1909.)

1883   Jenkin Lloyd Jones reorganizes the Fourth Unitarian Society of Chicago as the inclusive and interracial All Souls Church. S. Laing and Fannie Barrier Williams join in 1888.

1889   Joseph Jordan, who organized a Universalist church and school in Norfolk, Virginia, is the first African American ordained by the Universalist General Convention.

1897   William H. McGlauflin, the southern missionary of the Universalist General Convention, advises the annual meeting not to seek African-American involvement in its Sunday Schools or YPCU.

1903   Canton Theological School of St. Lawrence University admits Joseph Fletcher Jordan.

1904   Joseph F. Jordan and his wife, Mary J. Jordan, take over the Suffolk mission.

1905   The interracial Frederick Douglass Center is founded by Celia Parker Woolley and Fannie Barrier Williams.

1906   Meadville Theological School admits Don Speed Smith Goodloe.

1909   Mary White Ovington co-founds the National Association for the Advancement of Colored People (NAACP) with W. E. B. Du Bois, John Haynes Holmes (minister of the Community Church of New York), and others.

1910   John Haynes Holmes begins integrating the Community Church. Meadville Theological School admits Egbert Ethelred Brown.

1912   The NAACP asks Jenkin Lloyd Jones to speak at its fourth annual conference.

1914   W. E. B. Du Bois, director of publicity and research for the NAACP, delivers the talk "World Problem of the Color-line" at the Lowell Church Forum.

1915   Meadville Theological School holds a convocation on race and immigration at which Booker T. Washington, Jenkin Lloyd Jones, and Celia Parker Woolley speak.

1916   Celia Parker Woolley publishes "Democracy and the Race Problem."

1918   Celia Parker Woolley, the director of the Frederick Douglass Center, invites the Chicago Urban League to move its office to the Douglass Center, rent-free.

1920   Ethelred Brown founds the Harlem Community Church.

1927   The White Plains Community Church (Unitarian) is integrated by Errold D. Collymore, DDS, who later chairs its board.

1929   The Canton Theological School admits Jeffrey Worthington Campbell. John Dietrich, minister of the First Unitarian Society of Minneapolis and a leading humanist, delivers the sermon "The Myth of a Superior Race." The AUA removes Ethelred Brown from fellowship.

1930   The Community Church of White Plains supports Collymore when a cross is set ablaze on the front lawn of his home. The AUA Ministerial Fellowship Committee denies fellowship to Harry V. Richardson.

1936   Roy Wilkins, editor of *The Crisis,* delivers the talk "The Present Black-White Situation" at the Ridgewood Unitarian Church. W. E. B Du Bois speaks on "Italy and Ethiopia" at the First Universalist Church of Peoria, Illinois, at that time the largest Universalist congregation in America. *Unitarians Face a New Age,* a report by the AUA Commission on Appraisal that is meant to set the tone for the future, fails to mention race or diversity in the context of extension or ministry.

1938   AUA field staffer Lon Ray Call recommends against recognizing the Church of the Unitarian Brotherhood in Cincinnati or fellowshipping its minister, William H. G. Carter.

1942   The AUA General Assembly passes the "Resolution on Race Relations." Rev. William H. Floyd, with the support of Rev. Joe Barth, establishes an African-American congregation in Miami, and the AUA makes a contribution to cover its rent. Alvin Neeley Cannon enrolls at Meadville Lombard Theological School.

1943   Under the editorship of Stephen Fritchman, the *Christian Register* publishes a special issue focusing on race. At the AUA General Assembly Walter White, the executive secretary of the NAACP, delivers the Ware Lecture. Homer A. Jack co-founds the Congress on Racial Equality (CORE). The UCA adopts the Affirmation of Social Principles, which states, "We must recognize that today Americans of Negro, Indian, and Oriental descent . . . are suffering from unjust forms of discrimination."

1944   The board of the First Unitarian Church of Dallas votes to "welcome Negroes into membership." Cannon graduates from Starr King School for the Ministry.

1945   The AUA Fellowship Committee denies fellowship to Cannon. The Iowa Unitarian Association votes to investigate the possibility of organizing a "Negro Unitarian Church" in Des Moines. The Chicago Unitarian Council expresses interest in forming an interracial church in Chicago.

1946   Donald S. Harrington, John Haynes Holmes's successor at the Community Church of New York, preaches the sermon on race relations "The White Problem." Lewis A. McGee enrolls in Meadville Lombard Theological School.

1947   In a radio broadcast and later in his sermon "Declaring for Color," Kenneth Patton resigns from the white race.

1948   Maurice Dawkins is hired by the Community Church of New York as its minister of religious education. The First Unitarian Society of Chicago votes "to invite our friends of other races and colors" who are interested in Unitarianism to join. The board of the First Unitarian Church of Los Angeles votes to affirm the congregation's openness to all races. The predominantly African-American Free Religious Fellowship (FRF) is founded on the South Side of Chicago, with McGee serving as its first minister.

1950   The First Unitarian Church of Richmond, Virginia, votes to welcome Negroes. All Souls (Unitarian) in Washington, D.C., which had never restricted membership, welcomes its first African Americans into membership. The members of the Church of Our Father (later the First Unitarian Universalist Church) in Detroit vote against calling Eugene Sparrow as assistant minister.

1952   The AUA establishes the Commission on Unitarian Intergroup Relations to study "discrimination against Negroes within our churches."

1953   A. Powell Davies, minister of All Souls (Unitarian) in Washington, D.C., delivers the sermon "The Shelter of Good Intentions," in which he pledges not to patronize eating places and places of entertainment where Negroes are not admitted and distributes a list of non-segregated eating places. More than 40,000 copies are eventually distributed.

1954   The Commission on Unitarian Intergroup Relations issues its report. Errold Collymore becomes the first African-American member of the AUA's board. William Y. Bell is appointed as director of adult education and social relations for the Council of Liberal Churches.

1955   Beacon Press publishes James Baldwin's *Notes of a Native Son* and Kenneth Clark's *Prejudice and Your Child*.

1956   Rev. Howard Thurman delivers the Ware Lecture. Rev. Martin Luther King Jr., is the keynote speaker for the New York State Universalist Convention's annual meeting. Isaiah Jenkins is granted preliminary fellowship in the AUA.

1957   The members of the First Unitarian Church of Flint, Michigan, vote against calling McGee as minister. The UCA Declaration of Social Principles recognizes "the worth of the person regardless of race, creed or standing" and specifies support for civil rights and school integration. Jenkins resigns his AUA fellowship.

1958   The Unitarian Church of Arlington, Virginia, receives a bomb threat. First Unitarian of Providence hires William R. Jones as assistant minister. First Unitarian of Los Angeles hires Lewis McGee as associate minister.

1960   Eugene Sparrow is hired as director of field services for the Midwest Unitarian Universalist Conference.

1961   Lewis McGee is hired as senior minister of the Chico Unitarian Fellowship in California, becoming the first African

American not passing as white to lead a white Unitarian or Universalist congregation. The CORE annual training conference takes place at Mount Vernon Unitarian Church in Alexandria, Virginia.

1962   The Midwest Unitarian Universalist Conference eliminates Eugene Sparrow's position.

1963   The UUA hires Henry Hampton as associate director of information. A motion to amend the UUA's bylaws to require congregations to admit members without consideration of race fails, and instead the General Assembly creates the Commission on Religion and Race. Approximately sixteen hundred UUs participate in the March on Washington for Jobs and Freedom.

1964   Three hundred and eighty-six UU ministers petition the U.S. Senate to pass the 1964 Civil Rights Bill. At least thirty-five UU students and five ministers participate in the Mississippi Summer Project. That fall, nearly a dozen UU ministers volunteer for the Mississippi Delta Project.

1965   January 1–9: A four-member UUA Civil Rights Survey Team tours the deep South.

February 8: UU ministers Ira Blalock and Gordon Gibson are arrested while demonstrating for voting rights in Selma.

March 6: The Concerned White Citizens of Alabama march on the Dallas County courthouse in support of civil rights; of this seventy-two-member group, thirty-six are UUs.

March 9: Sixty UUs join Martin Luther King Jr. in a march to the Pettus Bridge. James Reeb, Orloff Miller, and Clark Olsen are attacked.

March 11: James Reeb dies.

March 13: The UUA board adjourns its meeting and reconvenes in Selma to attend a memorial service for James Reeb.

March 14: Memorial service for Reeb in Selma.

March 16: Memorial service for Reeb in Washington, D.C.

March 17: Memorial service for Reeb in Boston.

March 25: The March to Montgomery concludes, with over 30,000 people walking the last leg, including several hundred UUs. Viola Liuzzo is assassinated.

March 26–September 15: Fifteen volunteers serve two-week terms in the Unitarian Universalist Presence in Selma.

March 30: Funeral for Viola Liuzzo, held at Immaculate Heart of Mary Catholic Church in Detroit.

May 27: Judge Wade H. McCree is elected to the UUA board and the position of vice moderator.

August 20: Jonathan Daniels is murdered.

August 23: Donald Thompson is shot but survives.

October 20: Viola Liuzzo's killers are acquitted.

December 10: James Reeb's killers are acquitted.

1966   The UUA hires George Johnson as the James Reeb Civil Rights Worker. King delivers the Ware Lecture. The General Assembly adopts the resolution "Consensus on Racial Justice."

1967   The Emergency Conference on the Black Rebellion is held in New York City.

1968   The inaugural meeting of the Black Unitarian Universalist Caucus is held. King is assassinated on April 4.

UU MINISTERS AND SEMINARIANS WHO
PARTICIPATED IN SELMA OR MONTGOMERY

Lyman I. Achenbach
Eugene H. Adams
Tom Aldington
Francis C. Anderson Jr.
Khoren Arisian Jr.
John Baker
Paul Beattie
Lawrence E. Beebe
Carl Bierman
Charles B. Blackburn
Ira J. Blalock
Karel F. Botermans
Robert D. Botley
Robert M. Bowman
Gene Bridges
George G. Brooks
David W. Brown
Dwight Brown
Ernest A. Brown Jr.
William David Brown
Robert W. Brownlie
David E. Bumbaugh
Fred A. Cappuccino
Paul N. Carnes
David H. Cole

Henry Cooper
J. Raymond Cope
Joseph Ira Craig
Vernon L. Curry
Alan G. Deale
Robert M. Doss
Charles I. Doughty
John B. Evans
Leon C. Fay
Stephen H. Fritchman
Robert L. Fulghum
Erwin A. Gaede
Charles A. Gaines
Harmon M. Gehr
Rudolph C. Gelsey
Straughan L. Gettier
Richard B. Gibbs
Gordon D. Gibson
Randall L. Gibson
Richard S. Gilbert
Aron S. Gilmartin
Steve Graves (seminarian)
Dana McLean Greeley
W. Bradford Greeley
V. Emil Gudmundson

J. Harold Hadley
Donald S. Harrington
Kenneth C. Hawkes
John F. Hayward
Robert M. Hemstreet
Paul B. Henniges
Stewart E. Hild
Alfred W. Hobart
James A. Hobart
Harry H. Hoehler
Clifton G. Hoffman
Manuel R. Holland
Frank O. Holmes
Amos B. Horlacher
William H. Houff
Ernest L. Howard
George C. Howard
Duncan Howlett
John B. Isom
Homer A. Jack
Arthur B. Jellis
David A. Johnson
Walter Royal Jones Jr.
Walter B. Kellison
Jack A. Kent
Robert A. Kilgore
Robert C. Kimball
Webster L. Kitchell
Bjarne O. Kjelshus
John M. Kolbjornsen
Gerald R. Krick
Edwin A. Lane
Robert Lawson
Hugo P. Leaming
S. Hunter Leggitt Jr.

Robert S. Lehman
Richard D. Leonard
Fred A. LeShane
Ford Lewis
F. Danford Lion
Frederick Lipp
Jack C. Loadman
Russell Lockwood
Kenneth T. MacLean
Raymond G. Manker
Ronald D. Marcy
George W. Marshall
Kenneth K. Marshall
Robert F. Marshall
Howard G. Matson
Lewis A. McGee
Charles McGehee
Mason F. McGinness
Lawrence E. McGinty
Donald McKinney
Jack Mendelsohn
Ralph M. Mero (seminarian)
Roy Mersky
Orloff W. Miller
William R. Moors
John H. Morgan
Roland E. Morin
Raymond Russell Nasemann
Richard L. Nash
Carl J. Nelson
Rudolph W. Nemser
Joseph F. Nerad Sr.
Richard J. Norsworthy
Robert J. O'Brien
Clark B. Olsen

David P. Osborn
Thomas A. Owen-Towle
Robert C. Palmer
John Papandrew
Robert Payson
Tony Perrino
A. Q. Perry
Sidney A. Peterman
O. Eugene Pickett
Ernest D. Pipes
Christopher G. Raible
Edward Redman
James Joseph Reeb
Gene Reeves
Paul Winslow Sawyer
Harold B. Schmidt
Joseph A. Schneiders
Harry D. Scholefield
Carl Scovel
Ed Seiverts
Robert E. Senghas
Harold K. Shelley
Tom Sinclair
Philip A. Smith
Deane Starr
Charles S. Stephen Jr.
James L. Stoll
Ralph W. Stutzman
Charles M. Styron
Rexford Styzens
Malcolm R. Sutherland Jr.
John A. Taylor
Arnold Thaw
Donald A. Thompson
Harry A. Thor

Carl E. Ulrich
Vester L. Vanstrom
Brooks R. Walker
Donald L. Wassman
Theodore A. Webb
William M. Weir
Peter Weller Jr.
Clarke D. Wells
John M. Wells
Robert Nelson West
Richard Weston-Jones
Horace F. Westwood
Farley W. Wheelwright
George C. Whitney
James P. Wilkes
John Wilkinson
George H. Williams
Arthur D. Wilmot
John E. Wood
Richard M. Woodman
Robert Zoerheide
Jack Zylman III (seminarian)

ABBREVIATIONS

ACLU—American Civil Liberties Union

AME—African Methodist Episcopal

AUA—American Unitarian Association

BUST—Boston School of Theology

CLC—Council of Liberal Churches (Universalist Unitarian)

COFO—Council of Federated Organizations

CORE—Congress of Racial Equality

DRE   Director of Religious Education

FDP—Freedom Democratic Party

FRF—Free Religious Fellowship

GSSA—General Sunday School Association

HPKCC—Hyde Park Kenwood Community Conference

HRC—Human Relations Council

LRY—Liberal Religious Youth

MFDP—Mississippi Freedom Democratic Party

MUUC—Midwest Unitarian Universalist Conference

NAACP—National Association for the Advancement of Colored People

NCC—National Council of Churches

SCLC—Southern Christian Leadership Council

SNNC—Student Nonviolent Coordinating Committee

SRL—Student Religious Liberals

UCA—Universalist Church of America

USC—Unitarian Service Committee

UUA—Unitarian Universalist Association

WILPF—Women's International League for Peace and Freedom

YPCU—Young People's Christian Union

FURTHER READING

Taylor Branch, *At Canaan's Edge: America in the King Years, 1965–1968.* New York: Simon & Schuster, 2006.

Taylor Branch, *Pillar of Fire: America in the King Years, 1963–65.* New York: Simon & Schuster, 1998.

Charles E. Fager, *Selma, 1965: The March That Changed the South.* 2nd ed. Boston: Beacon, 1985.

W. Edward Harris, *Miracle in Birmingham: A Civil Rights Memoir, 1954–1965.* Indianapolis: Stonework, 2004.

Duncan Howlett, *No Greater Love: The James Reeb Story.* New York: Harper & Row, 1966.

Homer A. Jack, *Homer's Odyssey: My Quest for Peace and Justice.* Edited by Alex Jack. Becket, MA: One Peaceful World, 1996.

Richard D. Leonard, *Call to Selma: Eighteen Days of Witness.* Boston: Skinner House, 2002.

John Lewis with Michael D'Orso, *Walking with the Wind: A Memoir of the Movement.* New York: Simon & Schuster, 1998.

Jack Mendelsohn, *The Martyrs: Sixteen Who Gave Their Lives for Racial Justice.* New York: Harper & Row, 1966.

Leslie Takahashi Morris, Chip Rouch, and Leon Spencer, *The Arc of the Universe Is Long: Unitarian Universalists, Anti-Racism, and the Journey from Calgary.* Boston: Skinner House, 2009.

Mark D. Morrison-Reed, editor, *Darkening the Doorways: Black Trailblazers and Missed Opportunities in Unitarian Universalism.* Boston: Skinner House, 2011.

Mark D. Morrison-Reed, *Black Pioneers in a White Denomination.* 3rd ed. Boston: Skinner House, 1992.

Roberta M. Nelson, editor, *Claiming the Past, Shaping the Future: Four Eras in Liberal Religious Education, 1790–1999.* Providence, RI: Liberal Religious Educators Association, 2006.

Mary White Ovington, *Black and White Sat Down Together: The Reminiscences of an NAACP Founder.* Edited and with a foreword by Ralph E. Luker. New York: Feminist Press, 1995.

Harvard Sitkoff, *The Struggle for Black Equality, 1954–1980.* 3rd ed. New York: Hill and Wang, 2008.

Mary Stanton, *From Selma to Sorrow: The Life and Death of Viola Liuzzo.* Athens: University of Georgia Press, 1998.

Ronald Takaki, *A Different Mirror: A History of Multicultural America.* New York: Little Brown, 1993.

Sheyann Webb and Rachel Nelson West, *Selma, Lord, Selma: Girlhood Memories of the Civil-Rights Days.* As told to Frank Sikora. Tuscaloosa: University of Alabama Press, 1980.

ACKNOWLEDGMENTS

In April 1999, after Skinner House Books decided to publish the diary Rev. Richard Leonard kept while in Alabama in 1965, a letter was circulated which invited UUs who had participated in the events of Selma and Montgomery to share a brief reflection, anecdote, or learning for possible inclusion in *Call to Selma: Eighteen Days of Witness.* That letter, which had been sent by Jack Mendelsohn and Judith Frediani, received responses from: Francis C. Anderson, Gerry Bailey, Frederick S. Beckner, Charles B. Blackburn, Jane Boyjian, David H. Cole, Maria Cranna, Helen H. and Robert T. Dick, Rudi Gelsey, Gordon Gibson, Richard Gilbert, W. Bradford Greeley, Edward Harris, Robert M. Hemstreet, G. Robert Hohler, Arthur Jellis, David. A. Johnson, Walter Royal Jones, Jack Kent, Robert A. Kilgore, Gerald Krick, Edwin A. Lane, Hunter Leggitt, Ford Lewis, Felix Danforth Lion, Grace and Carl Linquist, Elizabeth McMaster, Orloff Miller, Irene K. Murdock, Joseph Nerad, Eugene Navias, Albert Niles, Brad Norris, Tom Owen-Towle, Nettie Radford, Ralph Stuztman, John A. Taylor, Arnold Thaw, Harry A. Thor, Vester L. Vanstorm, Clark Dewey Wells, Theodore A. Webb and Una Joyce Williams. Eighty excerpts, which also included passages written by Connie Burgess, Howard G. Matson, Lawrence McGinty, Greg Street (about his mother, Judy Street) and Richard Norsworthy, were thematically organized and included to add a range of perspectives to *Call to Selma.*

The book was released in 2002 and I had read it before I went on the Living Legacy Civil Rights Pilgrimage in February in 2009. During that trip my roommate was Clark Olsen, and as I heard his story and those of Charles Blackburn and Gordon Gibson, I realized how little I understood about Selma.

In 2009 and 2010, as my work on *Darkening the Doorways: Black Trailblazers and Missed Opportunities in Unitarian Universalism* drew to a close, I realized that there were two sides to the story of African-American involvement in Unitarian Universalism. In order to explain what had happened, I needed to take a deeper look at Euro-American UU attitudes, and wondered if unpacking the events in Selma might provide a focus. In October 2010, I visited Judith Frediani and Jack Mendelsohn in Maynard, Massachusetts. They lent me the collection they had amassed, and I promised to do something with it even though I was not completely sure what.

Meanwhile, I had begun building upon the materials I had already collected. To the best of my memory, those who provided me with reminiscences, background materials, or insights were: John Buehrens, Fred Cappucino, John Collins, Greta Crosby, Nancy Doughty, Charles Eddis, Natalie Fenimore, Neil W. Ferris, Charles Gaines, Steve Graves, Roger Greeley, Dick Henry, Phillip Hewett, Jim Hobart, Harry Hoehler, Leon and Dorothy Hopper, Arthur Hughes, Frederick Lipp, Gretchen Manker, Gordon McKeeman, Jack Mendelsohn, Ralph Mero, John H. Morgan, David Pettee, David Pohl, Christopher Raible, William Rau, Anne and Marie Reeb, Gene Reeves, Robert Schaibly, James A. Schmid, Carl Ulrich, Kate Walker, Barbara Wallace, Rollene Sumner Wells, and John Wolf. I also returned to eight of those who had shared materials with Mendelsohn and Frediani.

Additional materials came from congregational archivists and historians who preserved and wrote about their congregations. Archives were crucial. I am thankful to Fran O'Donnell, Jessica Sauve and Gloria Korman of the Andover-Harvard Theological School; Eric Biddy and John Leeker of the Meadville Lombard Theological School Wiggin Library; David Dwykes and Alice Ford-Smitt of Dr. Williams Library in London, England; and Roger Mason, who gave me access to Leonard Mason's diaries that are part of its collection. Arliss Ungar assisted me in using the Starr King School of Religion Archive and Bruce Southworth made Community Church of New York's archive available to me.

At Meadville Lombard I teach "African Americans and the Universalists, Unitarians, and Unitarian Universalists." The students who have taken the class have provided me with innumerable leads and two, Kathy Tew Rickey and James Jaeger, wrote essays that became the basis for two sections in this book. I was also aided by the research assistance of Colin Bossen and David Yano.

The support of the Unitarian Universalist Funding Panel gave me the financial backing I needed to complete this project. The editorial discernment of Mary Benard, the Skinner House editorial director, shaped this book, and its editor, Marshall Hawkins, refined it. The proofreading of Avivah Wargon was invaluable.

I turned to three people repeatedly over the last two years: Gordon Gibson, Orloff Miller, and Clark Olsen. In trying to understand what happened and when, the larger context in which it happened, or the details of a moment, I went to them, and their knowledge and wisdom rescued me from hundreds of mistakes. I also thank my wife, Donna. Once engaged in the story, she became a fount of helpful ideas, while at the same time putting up with my absences and obsessiveness. To those four, in particular, and to everyone, I am grateful.

NOTES

1   Martin Luther King Jr. to Dana McLean Greeley, telegram, March 8, 1965, in personal papers of Orloff Miller.

2   This methodology is adapted from categories outlined by William R. Jones in the essay "Towards a Definition of World View," unpublished teaching aid, p. 3, Jones file, box 2, Morrison-Reed Collection, Sankofa Archive, Meadville Lombard Theological School, Chicago [hereafter cited as Morrison-Reed Collection]. In that essay Jones cites "Theory in Practice: Increasing Professional Effectiveness," by C. Argyris and D. Schon. They write, "We determine one's world view by observing a person's actual behavior, rather than by simply reporting what they report . . . their espoused theory."

3   P. T. Barnum, *The Life of P. T. Barnum* (Buffalo, N.Y.: Courier, 1888), p. 237.

4   Thomas Whittemore, *The Plain Guide to Universalism* (Boston, 1840), p. 290.

5   Willard C. Frank, biography of Joseph Jordan, in the *Dictionary of Unitarian and Universalist Biography*, www25.uua.org/uuhs/duub.

6   Russell E. Miller, *The Larger Hope: The Second Century of the Universalist Church in America, 1870–1970* (Boston: Unitarian Universalist Association, 1985), p. 197.

7   "Declaration of Social Principles," *1959–60 Universalist Directory and Handbook* (Boston: Universalist Church of America), pp. 10–12.

8   "Universalist General Convention," *Universalist Biennial Reports and Directory, 1937–38* (Boston: Universalist Church of America), p. 38.

9   *Universalism in America: A Documentary History of a Liberal Faith*, ed. Ernest Cassara (Boston: Beacon, 1971), p. 269.

10 John Murray Atwood, "Universalists Urged to Aid All People," *Reading (Penn.) Eagle*, June 2, 1944.

11 "Illinois Universalist Convention 1956 Committee on Resolution and Recommendations Report," Illinois Convention Archives, Folder "1956," pp. 3–4, box 2, Meadville Lombard Theological School Library, Chicago. Also in Elmo Arnold Robinson, *American Universalism: Its Origins, Organization, and Heritage* (New York: Exposition Press, 1970), p. 186.

12   Martin Luther King Jr., "Non-violent Procedures to Inter-racial Harmony," *Empire State Universalist,* November 1956. He delivered the speech on October 16.

13   "Is Color Appearance or Reality?" editorial, *Christian Register,* August 31, 1939, p. 504. For more information on Campbell and Davis, see John Hurley, "Jeffrey W. Campbell and Marguerite Campbell Davis," in *Darkening the Doorways: Black Trailblazers and Missed Opportunities in Unitarian Universalism,* ed. Mark D. Morrison-Reed (Boston: Skinner House, 2011), pp. 128–39.

14   "Dean Atwood, Mr. Perry, et al.," *Christian Register,* May 16, 1942, p. 293.

15   Oscar Hoyt Perry, "The Universalist Church and the Negro," *Universalist Leader,* December 23, 1939, p. 1227.

16   Clarence R. Skinner, "A Religion for Greatness: VI Racial Universalism," *Christian Leader,* March 18, 1944, p. 174.

17   "First Year of Desegregation," *Universalist Leader,* June 1955, p. 143.

18   To be in fellowship is to have successfully completed the process of ministerial accreditation. At the time that the UCA and AUA consolidated to form the UUA full fellowship was the designation used for ministers serving congregations, while associate fellowship denoted those engaged in extra-parochial ministry.

19   Celia Parker Woolley, "Democracy and the Race Problem," *Meadville Theological School Quarterly Bulletin* 10, no. 1 (October 1915), p. 9.

20   Mark D. Morrison-Reed, *Black Pioneers in a White Denomination,* 3rd ed. (Boston: Skinner House, 1994), pp. 52–53; Arthur C. McGiffert Jr., *Pilot of a Liberal Faith: Samuel Atkins Eliot, 1862–1950* (Boston: Beacon, 1976), pp. 20–21; and Louis C. Cornish to H. Fisher Short, letter, November 23, 1920, Egbert Ethelred Brown file, UUA Inactive Ministers files 1825–1999, bMS 1446/18, Andover-Harvard Theological Library, Harvard Divinity School, Cambridge, Massachusetts [hereafter cited as Andover-Harvard Theological Library].

21   Morrison-Reed, *Black Pioneers,* pp. 72–79.

22   AUA memo, writer and recipient unknown, March 1934, Egbert Ethelred Brown file, UUA Inactive Ministers Files, 1825–1999, bMS 1446/18, Andover-Harvard Theological Library.

23   McGiffert Jr., *Pilot of a Liberal Faith,* p. 294.

24   Samuel A. Eliot Papers, subject file "Negroes," bMS 594/14 (15), Andover-Harvard Theological Library.

25   Resolution from the AUA Department of Social Relations, AUA Annual Meeting, May 24, 1934, pp. 1, 4, in archives of All Souls Unitarian Universalist Church, Kansas City, Missouri.

26 *Unitarians Face a New Age* (Boston: Commission on Appraisal, American Unitarian Association, 1936), pp. 150, 160. On pp. 152–53 the values are classified as "extrovert" ("outward-reaching," focused on action) or "introvert" ("inward-looking," focused on "the life of the spirit"). "Sense of human brotherhood" and "concern for betterment of social condition" rank first and second among the extrovert values.

27 AUA General Assembly, "Resolution on Race Relations," *Christian Register,* special issue on race, January 1943, p. 4.

28 Over the nineteen years between the 1942 resolution on race and the consolidation of the Unitarians and Universalists the AUA passed twenty-four resolutions regarding race. They are: race relations (1942, 1944), racial discrimination and exclusion (1943, 1952, 1958) social action and civic responsibilities (1944), toward an unsegregated church and an unsegregated society (1947), opposing poll taxes (1947), fair employment practices (1947), opposing segregation in the District of Columbia (1947), forbidding segregation and discrimination at Annual Meetings and General Conferences of the AUA (1948), calling for justice for Japanese Americans (1948), opposing discrimination in higher education (1948), congratulating and supporting the National Association for the Advancement of Colored People (1949), brotherhood (1948, 1954, 1956), opposing segregation in public schools (1954), against housing discrimination (1957), for civil rights (1959, 1960), for integration (1959), in support of boycotts and sit-ins (1959).

29 "Unitarians Unite!" report of the Commission on Planning and Review to the General Conference of the American Unitarian Association, October 15–17, 1947, p. 10.

30 Frederick May Eliot to Lillian Smith, letter, AUA President, Records and Correspondence, 1951–1961, bMS 11009/4, Andover-Harvard Theological Library.

31 Commission on Intergroup Relations, Interim Report of the Commission on Intergroup Relations to the American Unitarian Association, May 26, 1953, p. 1, bMS 11009/4, Andover-Harvard Theological Library.

32 "How 'Open' Is the Unitarian Door?" Report of the Commission on Intergroup Relations, *Christian Register,* April 1954, pp. 10–18.

33 There is no indication that articles on race led to the editorial confrontation that ended in Fritchman's firing by the AUA board in 1947; rather, that controversy arose in response to Fritchman's systematic and recalcitrant exclusion of any perspective that dissented from his leftist, pro-Russian worldview. In *Stephen Fritchman: The American Unitarians and Communism; A History with Documents* (Lulu.com, 2011), Charles W. Eddis offers a thorough documentation and analysis of the turmoil which centered on Fritchman and shook the AUA during the Red Scare of the 1940s and '50s.

34   "Unity and Discrimination," keynote address to the National Intercollegiate Conference, March 22, 1955, in *Frederick May Eliot: An Anthology,* ed. Alfred P. Stienmotte (Boston: Beacon Press, 1959), p. 236.

35   "Clergy Calls for a Rally against Hate," *Northern Virginia Sun,* October 20, 1958, p. 3.

36   Preface to Commissions to the Churches and Fellowships of the Unitarian Universalist Association, *The Free Church in a Changing World* (Boston: Unitarian Universalist Association, 1963).

37   Ibid., pp. 7, 9, 120, 128–29.

38   Committee to Study the Theological Education of Unitarian Universalist Ministers, "A Plan of Education for the Unitarian Universalist Ministry," report to the board of trustees of the Unitarian Universalist Association (Boston: Unitarian Universalist Association, 1962), p. 123.

39   Plenary debate transcript, 1963, UUA/AUA General Assembly Resolutions, 1926–76 file, pp. 118–20, 147–49, 143–45, 120–22, Morrison-Reed Collection.

40   Dana McLean Greeley, 1963 General Assembly newsletter, Mendelsohn/ Frediani/Morrison-Reed Selma Collection [hereafter referred to as the Selma Collection]. The core of the Selma Collection was solicited by Jack Mendelsohn and Judith Frediani in 1999 to provide stories to augment the diary of Richard D. Leonard, kept in March 1965, when it was published by Skinner House Books as *Call to Selma: Eighteen Days of Witness* in 2002. Later, Mark Morrison-Reed added to this collection the papers in the Selma file in the Morrison-Reed Collection of the Sankofa Archive of Meadville Lombard Theological School, as well as all additional sermons, articles, letters, and emails compiled during the process of writing *The Selma Awakening.* Upon completion of this project, this collection will be permanently archived at the Wiggin Memorial Library at Meadville Lombard Theological School.

41   News release, Robert Jones, executive secretary of the Commission on Religion and Race, February 12, 1964, UUA board of trustees, special commissions, Commission on Religion and Race, 1963–68, bMS 1026/1, Andover-Harvard Theological Library.

42   "Ministers March in California," *Register Leader Spotlight,* June 1964, p. 1.

43   The report "A Unitarian Universalist Presence in Mississippi: Reports and Recommendations of a Denominational Team Visit to Mississippi, January 1–9, 1965" (Mississippi Trip file, box 7, bMS 1026, Andover-Harvard Theological Library), lists the following UU students: James Adams, Jane Adams, Margaret Benes, Catherine Cade, Freeman Cocroft, Allen Cooper, Loren Cress, William Day, Leonard Edwards, Jonathan Else, Eugene Ericksen, Gail Falk, Robert Fullilove, Gene Guerrero, Joseph Harrison, Neil Hindman, Len Hyde, Alex Jack, George Kassel, Mark Levy, Cornelia Mack, Ronald Meser-

vey, Wilma Paskus, Edna Perkins, Annell Ponder, Kay Prickett, Kathryn E. Quinn, Thomas Rowe Jr., Susan Sanford, Philip W. Sharp, John Strickland, Howard Stromquist, Arthur Tenney, Jerry Von Korff, and Judith York. Gregory Kaslo was among the volunteers not on the list.

44 Jenkin Lloyd Jones, "Frederick Douglass: A Representative of the Ransomed Race; Decoration Day Sermon," All Souls Church, May 26, 1895, sermon no. 789, p. 2, Jenkin Lloyd Jones Collection, Meadville Lombard Theological School Library.

45 W. E. B. Du Bois, "John Haynes Holmes, the Community Church and World Brotherhood," in *Dedication Book: In Celebration of the New Building of the Community Church of New York, October 17, 1948* (New York, 1948), pp. 36–37.

46 John H. Dietrich, "The Myth of a Superior Race," *The Humanist Pulpit* 12, no. 11, First Unitarian Society, Minneapolis, March 24, 1929, p. 167.

47 Donald S. Harrington, "The White Problem," sermon brief, *Community News,* Community Church of New York, November 17, 1946.

48 For a detailed account of Kenneth Patton's broadcast and its consequences, see James A. Jaeger, "Declaring for Color: Kenneth Patton, Race 'Nonsense,' and the New Universalism," *Journal of Unitarian Universalist History* 35 (2011–12), UU History and Heritage Society, pp. 140–55.

49 George W. Marshall, *A. Powell Davies and His Times* (Boston: Skinner House, 1990), p. 164.

50 Robert J. Raible, "Advice to the Dallas School Board," First Unitarian Church of Dallas, September 15, 1957, in *Unitarianism in Dallas: An Outline History of the First Unitarian Church of Dallas, Texas, in Its First Seventy Years, 1899–1968,* by Wayne Gard (Dallas: First Unitarian Church, 1973), pp. 53–54.

51 Caspar Nanes, "Universalists Plan Tribute to Dr. Brooks," *Washington (D.C.) Evening Star,* January 11, 1964, p. A7.

52 Casper Nanes, "Holy, Holy, Holy, Washington's Best Preachers, the Golden Dozen of the Pulpit," *Washingtonian (D.C.),* December 1969, p. 57.

53 Laurence C. Staples, *Washington Unitarianism: A Rich Heritage* (Washington, D.C.: self-published, 1970), p. 49.

54 Dana McLean Greeley, *25 Beacon Street and Other Recollections* (Boston: Skinner House, 1971), p. 122.

55 In *Hymns of the Spirit, with Services* (Boston: Beacon, 1937), see #351 "Onward, Brothers," #402 "My Country Is the World," and #403 "Man's Comradeship."

56 Commissions to the Churches and Fellowships, *The Free Church in a Changing World,* p. 90.

57 Clarence C. Sherwood and Sylvia R. Sherwood, "Analysis of Responses to 170 Questionnaires on Unitarian Intergroup Practices and Attitudes,"

unpublished report for AUA Commission on Intergroup Relations, ca. 1953, p. 13, Meadville Lombard Theological School Library.

58   Commissions to the Churches and Fellowships, *The Free Church in a Changing World*, p. 87.

59   Arthur Vallance, "The New American Hymnal," *Inquirer*, September 9, 1964, p. 1.

60   Commissions to the Churches and Fellowships, *The Free Church in a Changing World*, p. 90.

61   Alfred W. Hobart, "Excitement (and Progress) in the South," *Christian Register*, February 1953, p. 18.

62   "American Friendship Program," Black Universalist file, p. 1, box 1, Morrison-Reed Collection.

63   Elizabeth M. Manwell and Sophia L Fahs, *Growing Bigger* (Boston: Beacon Press, 1942), pp. 109–116.

64   This discussion of the New Beacon Series is a further development of the "Beacon Series Review," a term paper submitted by Kathy Tew Rickey in March 2010 to Meadville Lombard Theological School.

65   "How 'Open' Is the Door?" p. 14.

66   Commissions to the Churches and Fellowships, *The Free Church in a Changing World*, p. 56.

67   "Report on Activities of the Commission on Religion and Race of the Unitarian Universalist Association," General Assembly, May 9–16, 1964, p. 3, Commission on Religion and Race, Records, 1963–1968 file, bMS 1026/1, Andover-Harvard Theological Library.

68   Congregations received "Curriculum in Action" programs in the UUA REACH packets. One of these was a drama written by Rev. Robert A. Storer, the minister in Winchester, Massachusetts, titled "Let My People Go," which had been performed by youth on Race Relations Sunday in February 1958, another was "On the Negro and Tensions," created while Lewis McGee was the minister of education at Throop Memorial Church in Pasadena, California. Every teacher received a copy of Louis Lomax's *The Negro Revolt*, developed a plan for each grade, and met with parents to explain it. The adult programs and the Women's Association also focused on the topic. Another curriculum, "Human Freedom and Dignity" (1966), focused on the lives of Mahatma Gandhi, George Washington Carver, and Martin Luther King Jr.

69   In the late 1940s the First Unitarian Church of Arlington, Virginia, ran an interracial summer program, as did All Souls (Washington, D.C.); in the 1960s so did North Shore Unitarian Church in Deerfield, Illinois. In 1947 and 1951 the Unitarian Service Committee ran a summer project in Harlem for college students, and in 1952 one for high school students. It also ran a work camp at the interracial Highlander Folk School. (Matilda Moore to

Frederick May Eliot, March 12, 1953, Commission on Intergroup Relations, Andover-Harvard Theological Library.) Two of the youth who attended the latter work camp, David Johnson and James Hobart, became ministers and went to Selma. In the 1950s a World Citizen Camp was held for junior high school youth at Unirondack in upstate New York, under the auspices of the Universalist Service Committee. Its objective was to provide an intercultural experience that would give young people "an emotional and educational basis for citizenship in one world." Children from South America, Europe, and Japan attended, and three of the fifteen campers were African American. ("World Citizenship Camp for Junior High Youth," *Universalist Leader*, May 1954, p. 128.) Elizabeth Strong, one of its campers, also became a UU minister. In 1965 the Unitarian Universalist Service Committee sponsored a camp, led by Richard and Joyce Gilbert, in which eight white teenagers from Chicago spent six weeks working at Jordan Neighborhood House in Suffolk, Virginia.

70   C. Conrad Wright, "American Unitarian and Universalist Historical Scholarship: A Bibliography of Items Published 1946–1995," *Journal of Unitarian Universalist History* 28, part 1 (2001).

71   In Charles H. Lyttle's *Freedom Moves West: A History of the Western Unitarian Conference, 1852–1952* (Boston: Beacon Press, 1952), Celia Woolley and her husband are designated as founders of the Frederick Douglass Center in Chicago while the African American co-founder Fannie Barrier Williams goes unmentioned (p. 204). One sentence is given to the founding of the Free Religious Fellowship by Harry I. Jones and Lewis McGee, and Kenneth Patton, who spoke there, is mistakenly identified as one of its organizers (p. 260). In "Two Centuries of Distinguished UU Women (1973)," which was published by the UU Women's Federation as a program resource in 1973, no African-American women are included among the 102 entries. Many of them one would expect to find (such as Olympia Brown, Lydia Maria Child, Susan B. Anthony, and Sophia Lyon Fahs), others are more obscure. Nonetheless, no women of color are mentioned. See Michael McCloskey, "Unitarian Universalism and Black Empowerment in the United States: A Nationwide Survey of Unitarian Universalist Attitudes toward Black Power and Participation in Militant Civil Rights Activities," (PhD diss., Loyola University of Chicago, 1974). Daniel Higgins explores this same era in "The UUA and the Color Line," (D.Min. diss., Meadville Lombard Theological School, 1977). In *A Stream of Light: A Short History of American Unitarianism* edited by Conrad Wright (Skinner House Books, 1989; originally published in 1974), Egbert Ethelred Brown is mentioned in David Parke's essay "A Wave at Crest," on pp. 99–100 and 119. The first full treatment of Unitarian involvement in the anti-slavery movement appeared in Douglas C.

Stange, *Patterns of Antislavery among American Unitarians, 1831–60*, (Rutherford, N.J.: Fairleigh Dickinson University Press, 1977). See also Mark D. Morrison-Reed, *Black Pioneers in a White Denomination*, 3rd ed. (Boston: Skinner House, 1994), for a history of the lives of Ethelred Brown and Lewis A. McGee.

72   The exception was a survey Lewis A. McGee compiled for the AUA Department of Extension and Church Maintenance while he was attending Meadville Lombard in 1947. Its purpose was to determine whether a predominantly African-American congregation could be successfully founded on Chicago's South Side.

73   Notable books published by Beacon Press in these years include
1951 Adamastor, *White Man Boss*
1954 Gordon Allport, *The Nature of Prejudice*
1955 James Baldwin, *Notes of a Native Son*
1955 Kenneth Clark, *Prejudice and Your Child*
1955 Herbert Hill and Jack Greenberg, *Citizen's Guide to Desegregation*
1956 Arnold Rose, *The Negro in America*
1957 James Baldwin, *Notes of a Native Son* (paper)
1958 Melville J. Herskovits, *The Myth of the Negro Past*
1958 Pierre Bourdieu, *The Algerians*
1959 Henrietta Buckmaster, *Let My People Go*
1961 C. Eric Lincoln, *The Black Muslims in America*
1962 C. Eric Lincoln, *The Black Muslims in America* (paper)
1962 Thomas Okuma, *Angola in Ferment: The Background and Prospects of Angolan Nationalism*
1962 Darwin J. Flakoly and Claribel Alegría, *New Voices of Hispanic America: An Anthology*
1963 Kenneth Bancroft Clark, *The Negro Protest*
1963 Kenneth Bancroft Clark, *Prejudice and Your Child* (paper)
1963 Henry Habib Ayrout, *The Egyptian Peasant*
1964 John Hope Franklin, *The Militant South* (paper)
1964 Albert Isaac Gordon, *Intermarriage*
1964 C. Eric Lincoln, *My Face Is Black*
1964 Joseph R. Washington, *Black Religion*
1964 Howard Zinn, *SNCC: The New Abolitionists*
1965 Franklin E. Frazier, *Race and Culture Contacts in the Modern World* (paper)
1965 Talcott Parsons and Kenneth B. Clark, eds., *The Negro American*

74   Lon Ray Call, "A Research on Church Extension and Maintenance since 1900: A Progress Report (1946)," pp. 2, 15, Inactive Ministers Files, 1825–1999, bMS 1446/22 Andover-Harvard Theological Library.

75 Lon Ray Call to George G. Davis, "Subject: Unitarian Brotherhood Church, Negro, Cincinnati, OH," November 14, 1938, W. H. G. Carter file, Morrison-Reed Collection.

76 Lon Ray Call, interview by Barbara Hammond, July 20, 1982, Seattle, Washington, UUA Pacific Northwest District oral history project, p. 14, personal papers, box 13, Morrison-Reed Collection.

77 Joseph Barth to George G. Davis, letter, October 18, 1942, Miami file, the Morrison-Reed Collection.

78 Frederick H. Fay, "The Unitarian Situation in Miami and Vicinity: Report on Trip to Florida, November 5–10, 1942," p. 7, personal collection of Gordon Gibson.

79 Wilbur Zelinsky, "An Approach to the Religious Geography of the United States: Patterns of Church Membership in 1952," *Annals of the Association of American Geographers* 51, no. 2 (1961), pp. 139–93.

80 Clarence C. Sherwood and Sylvia R. Sherwood, "Analysis of Responses to 170 Questionnaires on Unitarian Intergroup Practices and Attitudes," unpublished report for AUA Commission on Intergroup Relations, ca. 1953, p. 13, Meadville Lombard Theological School Library.

81 Ibid.

82 "Report of the Activities of the Commission on Religion and Race," p. 6.

83 James A. Schmid, "The Growth of Religion in the United States: Where Are We American Unitarian Universalists?" (Media, Pennsylvania: self-published, 2012), p. 39.

84 Clinton Lee Scott, *Some Things Remembered* (Boston: Church of the Larger Fellowship, 1976), p. 40.

85 David Maraniss, "Unitarians Explore Cultural Integration: Facing Racial Issues in a Liberal Religion," *Washington Post,* March 5, 1990, p. A6.

86 Laile Bartlett, *Bright Galaxy* (Boston: Beacon, 1969), pp. 183, 244.

87 May Memorial and Betts Memorial (Syracuse, New York); First Unitarian (Rochester, New York); St. John's (Cincinnati, Ohio); People's Church (Kalamazoo, Michigan); First Unitarian Church of Trenton (to Washington Crossing, New Jersey); Unitarian Church of Bloomington-Normal, Illinois; First Unitarian Church of Flint, Michigan; Unitarian Universalist Church of Akron, Ohio; Church of the Unity (Springfield, Massachusetts); First Universalist Church of Denver and First Unitarian Church of Harrisburg, Pennsylvania.

88 "How 'Open' Is the Unitarian Door?" p. 11.

89 Aron Gilmartin, "Oh Freedom," Mt. Diablo Unitarian Universalist Church, ca. February 1963, pp. 8–9, Gilmartin Papers, Starr King School for the Ministry, Berkeley, California.

90 Bartlett, *Bright Galaxy*, p. 244.

91   Holley Ulbrich, *The Fellowship Movement: A Growth Strategy and Its Legacy* (Boston: Skinner House, 2008), pp. 33, 79.

92   Rich Samuels, "Civil Rights on the North Shore: Bringing the Movement Home," WTTW-Chicago, www.wttw.com/main.taf?p=1,7,1,1,9.

93   Ulbrich, *The Fellowship Movement*, p. 97.

94   "Report of the Activities of the Commission on Religion and Race," p. 6.

95   Call, interview by Hammond, p. 14.

96   "How 'Open' Is the Unitarian Door?" p. 12.

97   "The African American Unitarian Universalist," appendix B in Morrison-Reed, *Black Pioneers*, pp. 225–28, reprinting part of "The Quality of Religious Life in Unitarian Universalist Congregations," by the Commission on Appraisal (Boston: Unitarian Universalist Association, 1989).

98   Ethelred Brown, letter to the editor, *Amsterdam News*, January 6, 1926.

99   "How 'Open' Is the Unitarian Door?" p. 12.

100   Charles Patterson, untitled and undated sermon delivered at the First Unitarian Church of San Francisco, Patterson file, Morrison-Reed Collection.

101   Ulbrich, *The Fellowship Movement*, p. 42.

102   Jeffrey W. Campbell, "Report to," [*sic*] p. 1, Campbell file, Morrison-Reed Collection.

103   "The Role of the Negro in American Unitarianism: A Growing Participation," *Christian Register*, September 1956, pp. 12–13.

104   "In Memoriam: Nathan J. Johnson," August 10, 1968, University Unitarian Church, Seattle, Wash., University Unitarian Church of Seattle Archive. Other African Americans who led UU congregations in the 1940s, '50s, and early '60s include Errold D. Collymore, president of the White Plains Community Church; Harold B. Jordan, president of All Souls in D.C.; Joseph H. Jenkins, president of the First Unitarian Church of Richmond, Virginia; and Selina L. Reed, chair of the church council at the First Unitarian Society of Chicago. Margaret Moseley, who had already served as president of the Community Church of Boston, chaired the board of the Unitarian Church of Barnstable, Massachusetts; and Isaac McNatt and Cornelius McDougald, at different times, chaired the board of the Community Church of New York.

105   The phrase "old boys' network" describes the fact that all eleven of the Universalist state superintendents and all eight Unitarian regional directors were white male ministers. It also reflects the political reality that under the AUA's bylaws, and the original bylaws of the UUA, the president was in a position to influence the nominating committee and thus the composition of the board and, according to John Buehrens (*Universalists and Unitarians in America*, Boston: Skinner House, 2011, p. 183), Dana McLean Greeley did so. Corroboratively, in *The Premise and the Promise* (Boston: Skinner House, 2001, p. 25) Warren Ross writes that Greeley "took an active part in

meetings of the Nominating Committee, as had Frederick May Eliot before him, so that he could usually count on a relatively subservient board."

106 Buehrens, *Universalists and Unitarians in America*, p. 182.

107 "Dean Atwood Reopens the Davis Case," letter to the editor, *Christian Leader*, April 4, 1942, p. 214.

108 "Report of the Activities of the Commission on Religion and Race," p. 5.

109 Charlotte A. Coté, *Olympia Brown Unitarian Universalist Church Chronicle, 1842–1992: The First 150 Years of Unitarian Universalism in Racine, Wisconsin* (n.p., 1997), p. 104.

110 Jeffrey W. Campbell, interview by Mark and Donna Morrison-Reed, Putney, Vermont, July 1979.

111 Starr King School for the Ministry commencement address, 1945, Alvin Neeley Cannon file, Starr King School for the Ministry, Berkeley, California.

112 "Basic Information on Negro Unitarian Ministers," AUA Commission on Intergroup Relations, December 1952, Andover-Harvard Theological Library.

113 "Statement by Unitarian Ministers at 'Magnolia Conference,'" AUA Commission on Intergroup Relations, December 1952, Andover-Harvard Theological Library.

114 Buehrens writes, in *Universalists and Unitarians in America* (p. 182), that in order to secure the support of the eleven Universalist state superintendents and eighteen Unitarian regional directors for consolidation of the UCA and AUA, they were invited to meet with AUA executive vice president Malcolm Sutherland. They, of course, were interested in their continued employment. By 1964, all still held a regional position, were settled in a congregation, had retired, or had died. There was one exception: in 1963, the Midwest Unitarian Universalist Conference (MUUC), in which John S. MacPhee served, reduced its staff, and Sparrow resigned as director of field and fellowship services. This allowed MacPhee to finish out the program year. At the MUUC annual meeting on April 6, 1963, Sparrow's work with fellowships was praised, and the meeting voted him a motion of appreciation. (Minutes of the MUUC annual meeting, April 6, 1963, Omaha, Nebraska, archived at Meadville Lombard Theological School Library). Ellsworth Smith continued on in the position of executive secretary of the MUUC, and in the 1964 UUA directory MacPhee appears as associate to the Unitarian Universalist Center for the Middle Atlantic States, while Sparrow was never again employed within the UUA.

115 Edward Redman to Frederick May Eliot, December 30, 1949, Sparrow file, Morrison-Reed Collection.

116 "Church Expansion Fund Voted," *Christian Register*, March 1952, p. 29.

117 Charles Mason Jr. to Frederick M. Eliot, April 8, 1952, and Frederick M.

Eliot to Charles Mason Jr., April 10, 1952, AUA President, Records and Correspondence, 1951–61, bMS 11009/4 Andover-Harvard Theological Library.

118 "Board Vote," May 28, 1952, AUA President, Records and Correspondence, 1951–61, bMS 11009/4 Andover-Harvard Theological Library.

119 Alfred McClung Lee to Grant Butler, September 24, 1952, AUA President, Records and Correspondence, 1951–61, bMS 11009/4 Andover-Harvard Theological Library.

120 "How 'Open' Is the Unitarian Door?" p. 17.

121 John H. Morgan to Mark D. Morrison-Reed, email correspondence, September 30, 2011.

122 Shelley Page, "History Happened Here," sermon, June 5, 2011, Unitarian Universalist Church of Flint, Michigan, p. 8.

123 David H. Eaton, interview by Carol Dornbrand, 1985, transcript in David Eaton file, Morrison-Reed Collection. Eaton errs in saying that the meeting with Dana Greeley took place in 1957. Greeley did not become president of the AUA until May 1958.

124 Greta W. Crosby, interview by Mark Morrison-Reed, August 3, 2013.

125 Thompson was granted fellowship by the AUA in 1906 and served the Unitarian Church of Peabody from 1906 to 1909. See John Buehrens, "Clarence Bertrand Thompson," in *Darkening the Doorways*, ed. Morrison-Reed, pp. 43–49.

126 Dan Huntington Fenn, "Des Moines, Iowa," memorandum, November 7, 1945, Cannon file, Morrison-Reed Collection.

127 Grant Butler to Dan H. Fenn, letter, June 18, 1946, Cannon file, Morrison-Reed Collection.

128 David Johnson to Mark Morrison-Reed, email correspondence, August 16, 2013.

129 "How 'Open' Is the Unitarian Door?" p. 12.

130 Gordon D. Gibson, "Unitarian Universalists and the Civil Rights Movement: What Did We Do and What Can We Learn from What We Did?" Smokey Mountain Seminar, Highlands, North Carolina, November 8–11, 1982, p. 5.

131 "To the Unitarian Churches of the United States and Canada from the Board of Directors of the American Unitarian Association," *Christian Register*, October 26, 1939, p. 626.

132 Editorial, *Christian Register*, January 5, 1939, p. 3.

133 "To the Unitarian Churches," p. 626.

134 "Report on Activities of the Commission on Religion and Race," p. 5.

135 Letter to the editor, *Christian Leader*, September 9, 1939, p. 870.

136 The early issues of *Wonder Woman* are reprinted in William Moulton Marston, *Wonder Woman,* with an introduction by Gloria Steinem (New York: Holt, Rinehart and Winston, 1972).

137 "Bring in the Candles," *Christian Register*, January 1942, p. 3.

138 Donald G. Lothrop, "Racism vs. Americanism," *Christian Register*, February 1942, pp. 46–47.

139 Malcolm S. MacLean, "A Stake in Democratic America," *Christian Register*, June 1942, pp. 193–95.

140 "From Slavery to F.E.P.C.," 1942, Samuel A. Eliot Papers, subject file "Negroes," bMS 594/14 (15), Andover-Harvard Theological Library.

141 James Luther Adams, *Not without Dust and Heat: A Memoir*, with an introduction by Max L. Stackhouse and a tribute to James Luther Adams by George H. Williams (Chicago: Exploration, 1995), p. 259. The event James Luther Adams describes is one of a sequence of events referred to on the University of Chicago Laboratory Schools website. "Amidst the racially segregated reality of Chicago and greater America in 1942, a parent arose to call for integration. Governed by the principle of equality, as demonstrated by its then long-standing history of enrolling Asian and Jewish students, the Laboratory Schools took action to become the first private school in Chicago to admit African American students." (University of Chicago Laboratory Schools, "Diversity Statement," www.ucls.uchicago.edu.) In *The History of the Laboratory Schools, 1896–1965* (Chicago: Quadrangle, 1967), long-time Lab teacher Ida DePencier writes of the letter and petition, signed by 209 families (52 families did not sign), that led the school council in 1943 to adopt a policy of integration. The University of Chicago's first black graduate was Richard A. Dawson in 1870 and by 1942 the university had a long history of matriculating African Americans, including G. Carter Woodson (AM, 1908), Ernest Everett Just (PhD, 1916), and Benjamin Mays (AM, 1925; PhD, 1935).

142 Ethel M. Gorman, "Reflections on a Turbulent Time," March 17, 1985, Birmingham Unitarian Church, Selma Collection.

143 Carl E. Ulrich to Gus and Marit Ulrich, letter on CD, March 26, 1965, Selma Collection.

144 "Minister's Path Joined with King's; Boys Prayed Together, Men Marched Together," *Maine Sunday Telegram*, January 17, 1988, pp. 1A, 33A.

145 Greeley, *25 Beacon Street*, p. 209.

146 John Haynes Holmes, *Speaking for Myself: The Autobiography of John Haynes Holmes* (New York: Harper & Brothers, 1959), p. 196.

147 *Kansas City Times*, April 13, 1922.

148 Dietrich, "The Myth of a Superior Race," p. 163.

149 "John M. Atwood Keynote," *Reading (Penn.) Eagle*, June 3, 1944, Universalist State Conventions, 1855–1961, bMS 12015, box 1, Andover-Harvard Theological Library.

150 Kenneth Patton, "A Personal Experience in Brotherhood," *Christian Register*, December 1947, pp. 468–72. See also Jaeger, "Declaring for Color."

151 Clarence Skinner, *The Social Implications of Universalism*, reprinted in *Journal of the Universalist Historical Society* 5 (1964–65), pp. 102–04.

152 Gordon McKeeman, telephone interview by Mark Morrison-Reed, December 13, 2011.

153 Charles A. Howe, ed., *Clarence R. Skinner: Prophet of a New Universalism* (Boston: Skinner House, 1999), p. 24.

154 James Luther Adams, *The Essential James Luther Adams: Selected Essays and Addresses,* ed. George Kimmich Beach (Boston: Skinner House, 1998), pp. 128, 136.

155 Hugo Leaming, "The Teaching of Social Ethics at the Meadville Theological School, 1844–1944," B.D. thesis, Meadville Lombard Theological School Library, p. 104.

156 Howard Thurman, *Jesus and the Disinherited* (Nashville: Abington Press, 1949), p. 100.

157 "Dr. Walter Fluker Extended Interview," *Religion and Ethics Newsweekly*, television series, January 18, 2002, www.pbs.org/wnet/religionandethics/2002/01/18/january-18-2002-dr-walter-fluker-extended-interview/7934.

158 Walter G. Muelder to Shuma Chakravarty, First Parish Unitarian Universalist, Dorchester, Massachusetts, January 1999, Selma Collection.

159 Homer A. Jack, *Homer's Odyssey*, p. 110.

160 Commissions to the Churches and Fellowships, *The Free Church in a Changing World*, p. 118.

161 Arvarh E. Strickland, *History of the Chicago Urban League* (Columbia: University of Missouri Press, 1966), pp. 38–39.

162 Raymond Arsenault, *Freedom Riders: 1961 and the Struggle for Racial Justice* (New York: Oxford University Press, 2006), pp. 49–50.

163 Gordon R. Carey to Ernest Sommerfield, letter, March 23, 1961, Mount Vernon Unitarian Church archives, Alexandria, Virginia.

164 Joan Singler, Jean Durning, Bettylou Valentine, and Maid Adams, *Seattle in Black and White: The Congress of Racial Equality and the Fight for Equal Opportunity*, V Ethel Willi White Books (Seattle: University of Washington Press, 2011), p. 16.

165 Charles B. Blackburn, "Looking Back: The Selma Period," sermon, February 21, 1999, First Unitarian Church of Baltimore, p. 4, Blackburn file, Selma Collection.

166 Doris B. Armstrong, *Unitarians in Ridgewood: 100 years of Freedom, Community, and Concern*, 1997, p. 46.

167 Letter to the editor, *Christian Register,* October 12, 1939, p. 593.

168 Greeley, *25 Beacon Street*, p. 104.

169 Ernest Kuebler to Walter White, letter, February 28, 1945, Council of Liberal Churches, Division of Education, Administrative Subject Files, 1922–68, bMS 10001/8, Andover-Harvard Theological Library.

170 Commissions to the Churches and Fellowships, *The Free Church in a Changing World*, p. 126.

171 Bruce Beisner, "The Revolution Goes On: Reflections on the History of Race Relations at St. John's," sermon, St John's Unitarian Universalist Church, Cincinnati, Ohio, 2009.

172 Felix Danford Lion, "A Letter to James Baldwin," sermon, January 13, 1963, Palo Alto Unitarian Church, Palo Alto, California, p. 4.

173 Duncan Howlett, *No Greater Love: The James Reeb Story* (New York: Harper & Row, 1966), p. 166.

174 Robert West, "Race in Rochester," sermon, February 7, 1965, First Unitarian Church, Rochester, New York, p. 4.

175 Clarence C. Sherwood and Sylvia R. Sherwood, "Analysis of Responses to 170 Questionnaires on Unitarian Intergroup Practices and Attitudes," unpublished report for AUA Commission on Intergroup Relations, ca. 1953, p. 13, Meadville Lombard Theological School Library.

176 "Report on the Commission on Religion and Race," pp. 6–9.

177 "Report of the Committee on Goals" (Boston: Unitarian Universalist Association, 1967), www.uua.org, table 67, p. 45.

178 Jeanette Hopkins, *Fourteen Journeys to Unitarianism* (Boston: Beacon, 1954), p. 51.

179 Dorothy Hopper to Seattle Urban League, January 15, 2007; Dorothy Hopper to Mark Morrison-Reed, email correspondence, October 17, 2012.

180 Wallace P. Rusterholz, *The First Unitarian Society of Chicago: A Brief History* (Chicago: First Unitarian Society of Chicago, 1979), p. 17.

181 Armstrong, *Unitarians in Ridgewood*, p. 168.

182 Greeley, *25 Beacon Street*, p. 104.

183 Charles B. Blackburn, "Arlington Awakening," *Washington (D.C.) Post and Times Herald*, October 20, 1958, p. A16.

184 Blackburn, "Looking Back," pp. 6–7.

185 "A Unitarian Universalist Presence in Mississippi: Reports and Recommendations of a Denominational Team Visit to Mississippi," January 1–9, 1965, p. 12.

186 Gordon D. Gibson to Jack Mendelsohn, letter, March 2, 1999, follow-up to a letter of February 22, 1999, G. Gibson folder, Selma Collection.

187 Gordon D. Gibson to Jack Mendelsohn, letter, February 22, 1999, G. Gibson folder, Selma Collection, p. 1.

188 Ibid.

189 Coretta Scott King, *My Life With Martin Luther King, Jr.* (New York: Holt, Rinehart and Winston, 1969), p. 256.

190 Gordon Gibson, "Selma, Alabama, U.S.A.," sermon, February 21, 1965, Theodore Parker Unitarian Church, West Roxbury, Massachusetts, Gordon Gibson folder, p. 1, Selma Collection.

191 Donald S. Harrington, "Sounding the South: A Report on a Journey through Mississippi, Alabama, and Georgia," sermon, March 7, 1965, Community Church of New York, p. 14.

192 Homer A. Jack, *Homer's Odyssey: My Quest for Peace and Justice,* ed. Alex Jack (Becket, Massachusetts: One Peaceful World, 1996), p. 318; and Charles Blackburn to Mark Morrison-Reed, email correspondence, September 5, 2010.

193 Charles B. Blackburn, "Looking Back: The Selma Period," p. 8.

194 King to Greeley, telegram.

195 Gene Reeves to Mark Morrison-Reed, email correspondence, August 1, 2010.

196 Richard D. Leonard, *Call to Selma: Eighteen Days of Witness* (Boston: Skinner House, 2002), p. 7.

197 David A. Johnson, "Selma," sermon, March 14, 1965, Unitarian Universalist Church of Bloomington, Indiana, p. 1, Selma Collection.

198 "U-U Ministers, Laymen Bear Witness in Selma, Alabama, Endure Harassment, Beatings, Martyrdom," *Unitarian Universalist Register-Leader,* April 1965, p. 23.

199 Johnson, "Selma," p. 2.

200 Ford Lewis, "What I Learned in Selma," sermon, March 21, 1965, First Unitarian Church, Sacramento, California, p. 2, Selma Collection.

201 Blackburn, "Looking Back," p. 11.

202 Francis C. Anderson Jr., "The Selma Segment . . . and Still the Dream," Martin Luther King Day address, January 19, 1998, Hilton Head Community Memorial Celebration, p. 3, Selma Collection.

203 Arthur B. Jellis to Jack Mendelsohn, letter, February 21, 1999.

204 Gordon D. Gibson to Jack Mendelsohn, letter, March 29, 1999, follow-up to a letter of February 22, 1999.

205 "Rev. Reeb's Change in Plans Fatal?" *Boston Traveler,* March 12, 1965, Gerry Krick folder, Selma Collection.

206 John M. Wells, "Report on Selma," sermon, March 14, 1965, Mt. Vernon Unitarian Church, Virginia, p. 5.

207 "Rev. Reeb's Change in Plans Fatal?" Selma Collection.

208 Mario Savio, speaking on Sproul Plaza, University of California, Berkeley, December 2, 1964.

209 Fred Cappuccino, "Unitarians in Selma," unpublished and undated memoir, Maxville, Ontario, p. 2, Cappuccino folder, Selma Collection.

210 Orloff W. Miller, "Orloff—What Took *You* to Selma?," address to the Unitarian Universalist Fellowship of Paris, January 26, 2003, www.uufp.info; and Miller's personal diary kept during the trip to Selma, March 1965.

211 Ibid.

212 Rollene Sumner Wells, interviews by Barbara Wells ten Hove, February 8, 2013, and by Mark Morrison-Reed, August 3, 2013.

213 Blackburn, "Looking Back," p. 12.

214 Ibid.

215 Ralph W. Stutzman, unpublished memoir sent to Jack Mendelson in 1999 (having been written "a few years" earlier), p. 1, Selma Collection.

216 Hunter S. Leggitt, "In Selma, Alabama," sermon, March 21, 1965, Beverly Unitarian Church of Chicago, p. 3, Selma Collection.

217 Ibid.

218 Ibid., p. 4.

219 Clark Dewey Wells to Jack Mendelsohn, letter, February 23, 1999, Selma Collection.

220 Lawrence E. McGinty, "Lawrence McGinty," *the liberal context,* no. 14 (spring 1965), p. 19.

221 Leonard, *Call to Selma,* p. 27.

222 Stutzman, memoir, p. 1, Selma Collection.

223 David A. Johnson to Jack Mendelsohn, email correspondence, compiled December 2, 1999; *Wilderness Journey: The Struggle for Black Empowerment and Racial Justice within the UUA,* documentary film by Ron Cordes (DVD, uufilms.com); and an informal presentation by David Johnson at Collegium, Chicago, November 16, 2012.

224 Ernie Pipes, "Martin Luther King Sunday," chalice lighting reading, Unitarian Universalist Community Church of Santa Monica, date unknown, Selma Collection.

225 John B. Wolf to Mark Morrison-Reed, letter, January 4, 2012, Selma Collection.

226 Hope Holway, *Hope Holway's History of All Souls-Unitarian Church of Tulsa 1921–1971* (Tulsa, Okla.: All Souls Unitarian Church, 1971), p. 54.

227 Eugene Navias, untitled and undated note, Selma file, Morrison-Reed Collection.

228 "Both King, Killers Blamed in Death," *Memphis Commercial Appeal,* March 15, 1965, morning edition, James Madison Barr, Ministry file, Andover-Harvard Theological Library.

229 Henry Nelson Wieman, "Memorial for James Reeb," Unitarian Fellowship, Carbondale, Ill., March 14, 1965, Carbondale file, Morrison-Reed Collection.

230 Roger Greeley, "The Age of Analysis," sermon, March 14, 1965, People's Unitarian Church, Kalamazoo.

231 Robert L. Schaibly to Mark Morrison-Reed, email correspondence, September 25, 2012.

232 Robert West, "Murder of Jim Reeb," sermon, March 14, 1965, First Unitarian Church of Rochester, New York.

233 Robert M. Hemstreet to Jack Mendelsohn, letter, April 22, 1999, Selma Collection.

234 Lawrence E. McGinty, "Lawrence E. McGinty," quoted in A. Phillip Hewett, "What Unitarians Did at Selma," sermon, June 6, 1965, Unitarian Church of Vancouver, p. 6.

235 "To Bear Witness: Unitarian Universalists, Selma to Montgomery" (Boston: Unitarian Universalist Association, 1965), unpaginated.

236 Joseph N. Ulman Jr., "Two Days in Alabama, 1965," *Unitarian Universalist Register-Leader,* May 1965, p. 6.

237 Minutes of the UUA Board of Trustees meeting, March 12–13, 1965, p. 16, UUA Board of Trustees, 1961–1981 file, bMS 1032/2, Andover-Harvard Theological Library.

238 Leonard, *Call to Selma,* p. 56.

239 Christopher G. Raible, "The Selma Wall," sermon, March 21, 1965, Unitarian Universalist Church West, Brookfield, Wisconsin, Selma Collection.

240 Peter Weller, reminiscence, Selma Collection.

241 www.ptsem.edu/Publications/inspire2/6.2/feature_4/feature4_index.htm

242 Ibid.

243 Lewis McGee, "Martin Luther King Jr.," April 7, 1968, McGee Collection, Sankofa Archive, Meadville Lombard Theological School, Chicago.

244 Judith Frediani to Mark Morrison-Reed, email correspondence, May 29, 2012.

245 Gerry Bailey, "Transformation of Faith at Selma," term paper, March 21, 1980, and March 3, 1999, Landaff, New Hampshire, p. 3, Selma Collection.

246 James Hobart to Mark Morrison-Reed, email correspondence, July 29, 2012.

247 Bailey, "Transformation of Faith at Selma," pp. 3–4.

248 David H. Cole, "The Selma Experience," unpublished memoir, Brunswick, Maine, 1999, p. 1, Selma Collection.

249 James Hobart to Mark Morrison-Reed, email correspondence, July 29, 2012.

250 Jane Boyajian to Jack Mendelsohn, letter, March 6, 1999; and Jane Boyajian, telephone interview by Mark Morrison-Reed, December 27, 2012.

251 Ibid.

252 Newsletter, March 21, 1965, folder 3, box 37, Unitarian Universalist Church of Atlanta records.

253 Liz McMaster to Judith Frediani, email correspondence, April 21, 1999, Selma Collection.

254 Diary of Joseph F. Nerad, Sr., entry for March 30, 1965.

255 Leonard, *Call to Selma*, p. 80.

256 Ibid.

257 Steve Graves to Mark Morrison-Reed, email correspondence, December 2 and 5, 2013.

258 Diary of Joseph F. Nerad Sr., March 30, 1965.

259 Pipes, "Martin Luther King Sunday."

260 David Johnson to Jack Mendelsohn, December 2, 1999.

261 These words of Greg Street, spoken at Judy Street's memorial, were sent by Linda Olsen Peebles to Jack Mendelsohn, June 1, 1999, Selma Collection.

262 History Book Committee, *Cedar Lane Unitarian Universalist Church: The First Fifty Years* (Bethesda, Maryland: The Church, 2001), p. 83.

263 Dick Henry to Mark Morrison-Reed, email correspondence, November 17, 2012, Selma Collection.

264 Lawrence E. McGinty, "16 Days of Crisis in Birmingham Recalled," *UU World,* March 15, 1985, pp. 1, 11.

265 Charles Gaines to Gordon Gibson, letter, August 27, 2011, Selma Collection.

266 Leon M. Despres, "Awesome View of Southern Hospitality," *Hyde Park Herald,* March 31, 1965.

267 Jane Boyajian to Jack Mendelsohn, March 6, 1999; and Jane Boyajian, telephone interview by Mark Morrison-Reed, December 27, 2012.

268 "The High Cost of Participation in the Civil-Rights Movement," *Unitarian Universalist Register-Leader,* June 1965, p. 19. This article quoted the initial reporting of the *Daily Olympian.*

269 Homer Jack to board of trustees, Mt. Diablo Unitarian Universalist Church, March 31, 1965, Gilmartin file, Starr King School for the Ministry, Berkeley, California. The annual report of the Commission on Religion and Race differs from Jack's report of the march—the commission estimated that a hundred ministers and several hundred laity marched.

270 Howard G. Matson, "Report on Montgomery," sermon, April 4, 1965, First Unitarian Church of San Francisco, pp. 2–3, Selma Collection.

271 Raymond Manker, "Pilgrimage to Montgomery, Phoenix, Arizona," sermon, April 4, 1965, p. 9, Selma Collection.

272 Leonard, *Call to Selma*, pp. 112–13.

273 Martin Luther King Jr., "Address at the Conclusion of the Selma to Montgomery March," March 25, 1965, http://mlk-kpp01.stanford.edu/index.php/encyclopedia/documentsentry/doc_address_at_the_conclusion_of_selma_march.

274 Arthur Hughes, "Selma, 1965: A Reminiscence," sermon, March 6, 2005, Unitarian Church of Vancouver, pp. 7–9, Selma Collection.

275 "Freedom Fund Soars," *Register/Leader Spotlight*, May 1965.

276 "Aftermath of a Demonstration," *Register/Leader Spotlight*, June 1965.

277 "At Assembly Meeting in Swansea," *Inquirer*, May 1, 1965.

278 Greeley, *25 Beacon Street*, p. 110.

279 "The Colour Problem," Resolution 12, 1955. The British General Assembly of Unitarians and Free Christian Churches passed "Native Peoples of S.W. Africa (Resolution 4, 1952) and "The Colour Problem" (Resolution 12, 1955).

280 "Report of the Activities of the Commission on Religion and Race," p. 5.

281 Greeley, *25 Beacon Street*, p. 103.

282 David Pohl to Mark Morrison-Reed, email correspondence, December 12, 2012.

283 John Morgan to Homer Jack, letter, March 29, 1965, UUA Commission on Religion and Race, 1963–68, bMS 1026/9–10, Selma Presence folders 1–3, Andover-Harvard Theological Library.

284 Charles E. Fager, *Selma, 1965: The March That Changed the South*, 2nd ed. (Boston: Beacon Press, 1985), p. 177.

285 Arnold Thaw to Homer Jack, letter, June 2, 1965, bMS 1026/9–10, Selma Presence folders 1–3, Andover-Harvard Theological Library.

286 Phillip A. Hewett to Mark Morrison-Reed, email correspondence, March 1, 2012.

287 Angus Cameron, "Don't Hammer on the Bulge," First Unitarian Church of Philadelphia, March 14, 1965, p. 21, Cameron Papers, archives of the Unitarian Church of Montreal.

288 William P. Jenkins, "Memorial to James Reeb," sermon, March 14, 1965, Unitarian Church of Winnipeg, p. 4.

289 A. Phillip Hewett, "What Unitarians Did at Selma," sermon, June 6, 1965, Unitarian Church of Vancouver.

290 The women listed in the 1964–65 UUA Directory as holding full or associate fellowship are Hazel R. Gredler (1921), Helene R. Ulrich (1922), Dorothy Spoerl (1929), Edna Bruner (1930), Vilma S. Harrington (1939), Ida Mabel Folsom (1952), Janet Hartzell Bowering (1955), Greta W. Crosby (1959), Sophia Lyon Fahs (1959), Patricia Bateman Cope (1961), Berjounie Andeassian Bergler (1962), Violet A. Kochendoerfer (1962), Nancy Wynkoop (1963), and Serene Esther McGuire (1963).

291 Committee to Study the Theological Education of Unitarian Universalist Ministers, "A Plan of Education," pp. 119–20.

292 Commissions to the Churches and Fellowships, *The Free Church in a Changing World*, pp. 19, 128–30.

293 Fred Cappuccino, "A Vision Unbearably Wonderful," p. 64. This passage comes from an interim revision of the memoir referred to in note 209, received by the author August 16, 2013, Cappuccino folder, Selma Collection.

294 Charles Johnson, "Praying and Dancing," in *Been in the Storm So Long*, ed. Jacqui James and Mark Morrison-Reed (Boston: Skinner House, 1991), p. 23.

295 Dan McKanan, *Prophetic Encounters: Religion and the American Radical Tradition* (Boston: Beacon Press, 2011), p. 204. Also see http://en.wikipedia. org/wiki/Mary_King_(political_scientist)

296 Leonard, *Call to Selma*, pp. 4–5.

297 Duncan Howlett, *No Greater Love: The James Reeb Story* (New York: Harper & Row, 1966), pp. 197–98.

298 Rollene Sumner Wells, interview by Barbara Wells ten Hove, February 8, 2013, McMaster folder, Selma Collection.

299 Nancy Doughty to Mark Morrison-Reed, email correspondence, June 3, 2012.

300 Elizabeth McMaster to Judith Frediani, email correspondence, April 21, 1999.

301 Orloff Miller to Tom Stites, email correspondence, March 15, 2000.

302 Rudi Gelsey to Judith Frediani, email correspondence, April 20, 1999, Gelsey folder, Selma Collection.

303 Jack Mendelsohn, *The Martyrs: Sixteen Who Gave Their Lives for Racial Justice* (New York: Harper & Row, 1966), p. 176.

304 Constance Burgess, "After Selma—What Can Women Do?" *The Bridge*, Unitarian Universalist Women's Federation, June 1965.

305 John Wolf to Mark Morrison-Reed, email correspondence, January 4, 2012.

306 Greeley, *25 Beacon Street*, p. 11.

307 "Report of the Committee on Goals," table 8, page 26; and Commission on Appraisal, "The Quality of Religious Life in Unitarian Universalist Congregations" (Boston: Unitarian Universalist Association, 1989), p. 46.

308 Greeley, *25 Beacon Street*, p. 108.

309 Commissions to the Churches and Fellowships, *The Free Church in a Changing World*, p. 90.

310 Clarke Dewey Wells to Jack Mendlesohn, letter, February 23, 1999, Clarke Dewey Wells folder, Selma Collection.

311 Edwin A. Lane to Jack Mendelsohn, undated (ca. 1999), Lane folder, Selma Collection.

312 Manker, "Pilgrimage to Montgomery," p. 12.

313 Sister Mary Paul, O.S.M., "Letters from Selma: A Portfolio," *Prairie Schooner*, March 1965, pp. 208, 211.

314 Sister Joseph Gertrude, ACSW, "Witness at Selma," *Golden Gate Chapter News*, April 1965, p. 7, Gilmartin file, Starr King School for the Ministry, Berkeley, California.

315 Fager, *Selma, 1965*, p. 124.

316 Annette S. Marquis to Mark Morrison-Reed, email correspondence recounting conversations with Dick Gregory, Jesse Jackson, and Amelia Boynton, November 12, 2011.

317 Frederick Lipp to Mark Morrison-Reed, email correspondence, December 22, 2012, and January 29, 2013.

318 Harry Hoehler to Mark Morrison-Reed, email correspondence, November 17, 2012.

319 Juliet Haines Mofford, *The History of North Parish Church of North Andover, 1645–1974: And Firm Thine Ancient Vow* (North Andover, Massachusetts: Mofford, 1975), p. 270.

320 David Pettee to Mark Morrison-Reed, email correspondence, December 5, 2012.

321 "Report of the Activities of the Commission on Religion and Race," p. 5.

322 Charles Gaines to Gordon Gibson, email correspondence, August 27, 2011.

323 A. C. Pease to Department of Social Responsibility, May 9, 1965, UUA, Board of Trustees, Special Commissions, Commission on Religion and Race, Records, 1963–68, bMS 1025, box 9, Selma Survey, Andover-Harvard Theological Library.

324 This seems to have been part of an ongoing battle. A. C. (Helen) Pease was a member of a group in the church called the Servetus Society. When the society invited Alfonse J. Jackson Jr., who in 1972 would be elected to the Louisiana House of Representatives, to speak at the church, it met resistance from some longtime members. The Shreveport police made their displeasure known by sending squad cars up and down the street during the service. However, in the early 1970s the Peases returned to be active and honored members of the congregation. (Russ Pease to Susan Caldwell, August 13, 2013.)

325 Virginia B. Wheelwright and Farley W. Wheelwright, "Rowing toward God: An Odyssey," Northeast Conference of the UU Retired Ministers and Partners Association, Attleboro, Minnesota, October 8, 2005, pp. 15, 16, Wheelwright folder, Selma Collection.

326 The History of the Unitarian Universalist Church of Central Nassau, September 1962 to June 30, 1966, p. 7, Central Nassau, Morrison-Reed Collection.

327 Robert T. Dick and Helen H. Dick to Jack Mendelsohn, letter, February 26, 1999, Dick folder, Selma Collection.

328 Congressional Record H6113–14 (March 30, 1965).

329 "How 'Open' Is the Unitarian Door?" *Christian Register*, p. 18.

330 Jack, *Homer's Odyssey*, p. 154.

331 "Both King, Killers Blamed in Death," James Madison Barr, Ministry file, Andover-Harvard Theological Library.

332 Television review, *Memphis Press-Scimitar*, March 22, 1965, James Madison Barr, Ministry file, Andover-Harvard Theological Library.

333 George D. Davis, president of the Unitarian Universalist Fellowship of Memphis, and Lois Freeman, secretary, with the approval of the membership, to the editor of the *Memphis Commercial Appeal*, March 16, 1965, James Madison Barr, Ministry file, Andover-Harvard Theological Library.

334 James Madison Barr to Judith Quinn, April 23, 1964, James Madison Barr ministry file, Andover-Harvard Theological Library.

335 "Both King, Killers Blamed in Death."

336 Ronald E. Roberts (member of the Unitarian Fellowship), letter to the editor of unknown publication, March 16, 1965, James Madison Barr ministry file, bMS 1446, Andover-Harvard Theological Library.

337 "A New Direction for the Denomination?" *Unitarian Universalist Register-Leader*, May 1965, p. 22.

338 Leonard, *Call to Selma*, pp. 72–73.

339 Manker, "Pilgrimage to Montgomery," pp. 12–13.

340 Margaret Moseley, *Moving Mountains One Stone at a Time: Memoirs of Margaret Mosley*, as told to Berry Shea, ed Judith Barnet (Barnstable, Massachusetts: Unitarian Church of Barnstable, 1993), pp. 21–27.

341 Carl Lindquist's condolences were included in a letter from Grace Lindquist to Jack Mendelsohn, March 15, 1999, Lindquist folder, Selma Collection.

342 Unitarian Universalist Commission on Religion and Race, *Second Annual Report for 1964–65*, May 12, 1965, p. 2.

343 Una Joyce Williams, "Selma Reflections," undated manuscript sent to Jack Mendelsohn, Williams folder, Selma Collection.

344 Homer Jack, "Re: Next Steps after Selma/Montgomery," memo to Commission on Religion and Race, March 30, 1965, UUA, President, Dana McLean Greeley, Records, 1958–69, bMS 1014, box 10, Andover-Harvard Theological Library.

345 The participants in the Unitarian Universalist Presence in Selma were Rev. Robert Lawson (March 26–April 2), Rev. Eugene Luening (April 1–20), Rev. Harold Shelley (April 19–May 4), Rev. Fred Rutledge (May 3–18), Thomas Boulaine (May 17–June 3), Mr. and Mrs. Jerry Lewis (June 2–15), Rev. Ben Kjelshus (June 14–29), Rev. Theodore Webb (June 28–July 13), Rev. Donald L. Wassman (June 28–July 13), Rev. C. Leon Hopper Jr. (July 12–27), Robert E. Senghas (July 26–August 10), Rev. John Ruskin Clark Jr. (August 9–24), Rev. Steward E. Hild (August 23–September 7), and Rev. John A. Farma-

kis (September 6–16). The death of James Hobart's daughter forced Hobart, who was paired with Hopper, to cancel. See UUA Commission on Religion and Race, 1963–68, bMS 1026/9–10, Selma Presence folders 1–3, Andover-Harvard Theological Library.

346 Joanne Giannino, biography of Viola Liuzzo, in the *Dictionary of Unitarian and Universalist Biography,* an online resource of the Unitarian Universalist History and Heritage Society, www25.uua.org/uuhs/duub.

347 Leon Hopper to Homer Jack, August 16, 1965, Hopper folder, Selma Collection.

348 Theodore A. Webb to Jack Mendelsohn, letter, undated, 1999, Selma Collection.

349 John Ruskin Clark to Homer Jack, "Re: Unitarian Universalist Presence in Selma," memo, August 8–24 and August 28, 1965, UUA Commission on Religion and Race, 1963–68, bMS 1026/9–10, Selma Presence folders 1–3, Andover-Harvard Theological Library.

350 Richard Boeke, "Three Little Known Affirmative Actions," 2008, Lewis McGee file, Morrison-Reed Collection.

351 Dana McLean Greeley to Hopkins, Mendelsohn, Barth, Trueblood, Cloyd, and Ulman, letter, April 6, 1965, Unitarian Universalist Association, Board of Trustees, Special Commissions, Commission on Race and Religion, Records, 1963–1968, bMs 1026/1, Andover-Harvard Theological School Library.

352 Board of Trustees, Special Commissions, "After Selma Committee," April 14, 1965, pp. 1–3, Records of the Board (and Executive Board) of Trustees, 1961–81, bMS 1032/2 (8), Andover-Harvard Theological Library.

353 John W. Brigham, "Negroes in the Unitarian Universalist Ministry," May 6, 1965, Commission on Religion and Race, Integrated Ministry 1965–66, bMS 1026/4, Andover-Harvard Theological Library. In its brief existence, this committee was first called the Intra-denominational Committee on the Integrated Ministry and later the Ad Hoc Committee for an Integrated Ministry.

354 "Toward Integrating the UU Ministry" was issued by the Ad Hoc Committee for an Integrated Ministry, which comprised John W. Brigham, Leon C. Fay, Raymond C. Hopkins, Homer A. Jack, Orloff W. Miller, Virgil Murdock, Leslie T. Pennington, and George J. Spencer. Commission on Religion and Race, Integrated Ministry, 1965–66, bMS 1026/4, Andover-Harvard Theological Library.

355 Homer A. Jack, "A Flaw Within: Toward Integrating Our Liberal Ministry," *Unitarian Universalist Register-Leader*, May 1967, pp. 9–11.

356 Mark Morrison-Reed, "African-American Unitarian Universalist Ministries, 1988," in *Darkening the Doorways,* ed. Morrison-Reed, pp. 264–67.

357 Homer A. Jack, "Like It Was," address, August 4, 1969, International Affairs Workshop, Star Island, New Hampshire, p. 1, personal papers of Mark D. Morrison-Reed.

358 Richard Gilbert to Mark Morrison-Reed, email correspondence.

359 Howlett, *No Greater Love,* p. 197.

360 Neal W. Ferris to Mark Morrison-Reed, email correspondence and interview, November 20–21, 2013.

361 John Wolf to Mark Morrison-Reed, email correspondence, January 4, 2012.

362 Clark Olsen to Mark Morrison-Reed, email correspondence, December 30, 2013.

363 Miller, "Orloff—What Took *You* to Selma?" When Miller hitchhiked down to Cousins's wedding in Winston-Salem, North Carolina, he found himself the only white person there. Cousins went on to become a bishop in the AME tradition and to serve as president of the National Council of Churches from 1983 to 1987.

364 Fred Lipp to Mark Morrison-Reed, email correspondence, January 29, 2013.

365 Steve Graves to Mark Morrison-Reed, email correspondence, January 26, 2013.

366 Cathy Cade, *How My Being in the Civil Rights Movement Affected My White Family,* 2002, www.crmvet.org.

367 Miller, "Orloff—What Took *You* to Selma?"

368 John A. Taylor, "The March from Selma," in *How Open the Door? Afro-Americans' Experience in Unitarian Universalism: A Multimedia Program for Adults,* by Mark D. Morrison-Reed (Boston: Unitarian Universalist Association, 1989), p. 41.

369 Farley W. Wheelwright to the members and friends of the Unitarian Universalist Church of Central Nassau, New York, March 12, 1965, UUA, Board of Trustees, Special Commissions, Commission on Religion and Race, Records, 1963–68, bMS 1025/3, Andover-Harvard Theological Library.

370 John Collins to Mark Morrison-Reed, email correspondence, February 6, 2013.

371 Carl E. Ulrich to Gus and Marit Ulrich, letter on CD, March 26, 1965.

372 Helen Dick to Bob Cook, letter, August 8, 1965, Dick folder, Selma Collection.

373 "Mrs. Liuzzo 'Felt She Had to Help': Husband Failed to Deter Her from Fated Rights Trip," *New York Times,* March 27, 1965, p. 10.

374 George Collins, "Why Go to Selma? Hub Cleric Explains," *Boston Globe,* March 15, 1965.

375 William James, "The Moral Equivalent of War," 1906, Wikisource, en.wikisource.org/.

376 William R. Jones, "The Negro's Image of White America," First Unitarian Church of Providence, Rhode Island, 1964, William R. Jones file, Morrison-Reed Collection.

377 "Report of the Committee on Goals," tables 68–70, pp. 45–46.

378 American Religious Identity Surveys, Unitarian Universalists in the United States 1990–2008: Socio-demographic Trends and Religious Patterns, Barry A. Kosmin & Ariela Keysar, Hartford, CT: Institute for the Study of Secularism in Society & Culture, 2012: http://commons.trincoll.edu/aris/publications/2008-2/unitarian-universalists-in-the-united-states-1990-2008-socio-demographic-trends-and-religious-patterns.

379 Minutes of the board of trustees, March 12–13, 1965, UUA, Board (and Executive Board) of Trustees, Records, 1961–81, bMS 1032/2 (8), Andover-Harvard Theological Library.

380 "Report of the Committee on Goals," tables 15, 48, 18, pp. 28, 39, 29.

381 Commission on Religion and Race, Integrated Ministry, 1965–1966, bMS 1026/4, Andover-Harvard Theological Library. See note 354.

382 Special Report: Emergency Conference on the Unitarian Universalist Response to the Black Rebellion: Proceedings (Boston: Unitarian Universalist Association, 1967), p. 2.

383 Commission on Appraisal, Empowerment: One Denomination's Quest for Racial Justice, 1967–1982 (Boston: Unitarian Universalist Association, 1983), p. 100.

384 This estimate is based on the findings of the 1989 UUA Commission of Appraisal survey that found 1.2 percent of its sample self-identified as black and found no comparable earlier figures. "The Quality of Religious Life in Unitarian Universalist Congregations" (Boston: Unitarian Universalist Association, 1989), p. 56.

385 John Lewis with Michael D'Orso, Walking with the Wind: A Memoir of the Movement (New York: Simon & Schuster, 1998), p. 365.

386 Benjamin Scott, The Coming of the Black Man (Boston: Beacon Press, 1967), p. 12.

387 Taylor, "The March from Selma," p. 43.

388 Minutes of the UUA board of trustees meeting, June 18–19, 1965, pp. 4–5, bMS 1032/2 (9), Andover-Harvard Theological Library.

389 Greeley, 25 Beacon Street, pp. 105–06.

390 "Lexington, Massachusetts Population: Census 2010 and 2000 Interactive Map, Demographics, Statistics, Quick Facts," CensusViewer, http://census-viewer.com/city/MA/Lexington.

391 Dana McLean Greeley, 25 Beacon Street, p. 104.

392 Dana McLean Greeley, "Christianity and the Brotherhood of Man," February 14, 1943, p. 3, Dana McLean Greeley Papers, 1925–86, bMS 130/12, Andover-Harvard Theological Library.

393 Dana McLean Greeley, *Toward Larger Living: Sermons on Personal Religion* (Boston: Beacon Press, 1944), p. 47.

394 Greeley, *25 Beacon Street*, pp. 35, 69, 104. Dana McLean Greeley, "What Boston Needs," sermon, October 26, 1946, Dana McLean Greeley Papers, 1925–86, bMS 130/16, Andover-Harvard Theological Library.

395 Stephen H. Fritchman, *Heretic: A Partisan Autobiography* (Boston: Skinner House Books, 1977), pp. 295–96.

396 Dana McLean Greeley, "I Have a Dream," in *Forward through the Ages: Writings of the Reverend Dana McLean Greeley, 1970 through 1986* (Concord, Massachusetts: First Parish in Concord, 1986), p. 166.

397 Ibid., p. 157.

398 Leon Hopper, "One [*sic*] a Thousand," sermon, June 13, 1965, Jefferson Unitarian Church, Boulder, Colorado, pp. 8–10, Hopper folder, Selma Collection.

399 Victor H. Carpenter, *Long Challenge: The Empowerment Controversy, 1967–1977* (Chicago: Meadville Lombard Theological School Press, 2003), p. 90.

400 John Ruskin Clark to Homer Jack, "Re: Unitarian Universalist Presence in Selma," August 8–24 and August 28, 1965, Selma Presence folders 1–3, boxes 9–10, bMS 1026, Andover-Harvard Theological Library.

401 Gordon Gibson and James Hobart, who were in Selma (at different times) and were later supporters of the Black Affairs Council, have reviewed the list of UU ministers who participated in Selma and Montgomery. Gibson has also written extensively about the civil rights movement in the UUA.

402 Harry A. Thor to Jack Mendelsohn, letter, September 15, 1999, p. 2, Harry Thor folder, Selma Collection.

403 Harry Hoehler to Mark Morrison-Reed, email correspondence, November 17, 2012.

404 Howard G. Matson, "Report on a Visit to Selma, Alabama," sermon, March 21, 1965, First Unitarian Church of San Francisco, p. 4.

405 William C. Rau, "Following Moses in the Land of Pharaohs: My Days in the Southern Civil Rights Movement," sermon, June 12, 2005, Unitarian Universalist Church of Bloomington-Normal, Illinois, p. 6., Rau folder, Selma Collection.

406 Irene K. Murdock, "The Selma Experience—A Personal Account," sermon, July 16, 1995, Unitarian Universalist Church of Sarasota, Florida, pp. 7–10, Selma Collection.

407 Jack, *Homer's Odyssey*, p. 114.

408 "Report of the Committee on Goals," table 6, p. 25.
409 Robert A. Kilgore, "Trip to Selma," *Journal of the Liberal Ministry*, Spring 1965, Selma Collection.
410 Leggitt, "In Selma, Alabama," p. 4.
411 Diary of Joseph F. Nerad Sr., entry for March 30, 1965.
412 G. Robert Hohler, "It Can't Stop Here," *The Lamplighter*, April 1965, p. 5.
413 Stutzman, memoir, p. 2.
414 Leggitt, "In Selma, Alabama," p. 5.

INDEX